ON THE ROLE OF PARADIGMS IN FINANCE

I dedicate this work to my family

On the Role of Paradigms
in Finance

KAVOUS ARDALAN
School of Management, Marist College, USA

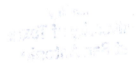

ASHGATE

Published by
Ashgate Publishing Limited
Gower House
Croft Road
Aldershot
Hampshire GU11 3HR
England

Ashgate Publishing Company
Suite 420
101 Cherry Street
Burlington, VT 05401-4405
USA

www.ashgate.com

British Library Cataloguing in Publication Data
Ardalan, Kavous
On the role of paradigms in finance. - (Alternative voices in contemporary economics)
1. Finance - Study and teaching (Higher) 2. Paradigms (Social sciences)
I. Title
332'.0711

Library of Congress Cataloging-in-Publication Data
Ardalan, Kavous.
On the role of paradigms in finance / by Kavous Ardalan.
p. cm. -- (Alternative voices in contemporary economics)
Includes bibliographical references and index.
ISBN 978-0-7546-4524-5
1. Finance--Study and teaching (Higher) 2. Paradigms (Social sciences) I. Title.

HG152.A73 2008
332.071'1--dc22

2008002372

ISBN 978 0 7546 4524 5

Mixed Sources
Product group from well-managed forests and other controlled sources
www.fsc.org Cert no. SA-COC-1565
© 1996 Forest Stewardship Council
FSC

Printed and bound in Great Britain by
MPG Books Ltd, Bodmin, Cornwall.

Contents

List of Figures

Preface

This book reflects the change in the way that I think about the world and in writing it I hope that it will do the same for others. It began a few years after I received my Ph.D. in Finance from York University in Toronto. But, the origin of it goes back to the time I was a doctoral candidate and took a course in Philosophy and Method with Professor Gareth Morgan. At that time, I was exposed to ideas which were totally new to me. They occupied my mind and every day I found them more helpful than the day before in explaining what I experienced in my daily, practical, and intellectual life.

When in high school, I grew up overseas and I was raised to appreciate mathematics and science at the expense of other fields of study. Then in college, I was exposed only to Economics to receive my bachelor of arts. Afterwards, in order to obtain my masters and doctoral degrees in Economics, I attended University of California, Santa Barbara and I received my specialized training in Economics. My further specialized studies in Finance ended in another doctoral degree. As is clear, throughout the years of my education, I was trained to see the world in a special narrow way.

Among all courses which I took during all these years of training one course stood out as being different and, in the final analysis, as being most influential. It was the Philosophy and Method course which I took with Professor Gareth Morgan. It was most influential because none of the other courses gave me the vision which this one did. Whereas all the other courses trained me to see the world in one special narrow way, this course provided me with the idea that the world may be seen from different vantage points, where each one would be insightful in its own way. Over the years, constant applications of this idea in my daily, practical, and intellectual life were quite an eye-opener for me such that I naturally converted to this new way of thinking about the world. This happened in spite of the fact that my entire education, almost exclusively, trained me to see the world in a narrow and limited way. Since then I have been writing articles in this area and the current book represents what has been accumulated up to the time of its publication.

This book crosses two existing lines of literature; philosophy of social science and the academic field of finance. More specifically, its frame of reference is Burrell and Morgan (1979) and Morgan (1984) and applies their ideas and insights to finance. Clearly, a thorough treatment of all the relevant issues referred to in this work is well beyond just one book. Within such limits, this book aims at only providing an overview, a review, a taxonomy, or a map of the topics and leaving further discussions of all the relevant issues to the references cited herein. In other words, the aim of this work is not so much to create a new piece of puzzle as it is to fit the existing pieces of puzzle together in order to make sense of it. To implement this aim, and given the unfamiliarity of the majority of finance academicians with the philosophy of social science, the book discusses Burrell and Morgan (1979) and in this context brings relevant finance literature into focus. The choice of what to be included in the book and what to be excluded has been a hard one. In numerous occasions, it is decided to refer to some massive topics very briefly. At others, some long quotations from the finance literature are decided upon to make the point of the application to finance clear. In any case, this book is only an overview, but provides a comprehensive set of references to avoid some of its shortcomings. That is, there are too many references to too many topics with too little explanation.

The main theme of the book is as follows. Social theory can usefully be conceived in terms of four key paradigms: functionalist, interpretive, radical humanist, and radical structuralist. The four paradigms are founded upon different assumptions about the nature of social science and the nature of society. Each generates theories, concepts, and analytical tools which are different from those of other paradigms.

The mainstream academic finance is based upon the functionalist paradigm; and, for the most part, finance theorists are not always entirely aware of the traditions to which they belong. An understanding of different paradigms leads to a better understanding of the multifaceted nature of finance. Although a researcher may decide to conduct research from the point of view of a certain paradigm, an understanding of the nature of other paradigms leads to a better understanding of what one is doing.

Knowledge of finance is ultimately a product of the researcher's paradigmatic approach to this multifaceted phenomenon. Viewed from this angle, the pursuit of financial knowledge is seen as much an ethical, moral, ideological, and political activity, as a technical one. Mainstream academic finance can gain much from the contributions of the other paradigms.

The ancient parable of six blind scholars and their experience with the elephant illustrates the benefits of paradigm diversity. There were six blind scholars who did not know what the elephant looked like and had never even heard its name. They decided to obtain a mental picture—that is, knowledge—by touching the animal. The first blind scholar felt the elephant's trunk and argued that the elephant was like a lively snake. The second bind scholar rubbed along one of the elephant's enormous legs and likened the animal to a rough column of massive proportions. The third blind scholar took hold of the elephant's tail and insisted that the elephant resembled a large, flexible brush. The fourth blind scholar felt the elephant's sharp tusk and declared it to be like a great spear. The fifth blind scholar examined the elephant's waving ear and was convinced that the animal was some sort of a fan. The sixth blind scholar, who occupied the space between the elephant's front and hid legs, could not touch any parts of the elephant and consequently asserted that there were no such beasts as elephant at all and accused his colleagues of making up fantastic stories about non-existing things. Each of the six blind scholars held firmly to their understanding of an elephant and they argued and fought about which story contained the correct understanding of the elephant. As a result, their entire community was torn apart, and suspicion and distrust became the order of the day.

This parable contains many valuable lessons. First, probably reality is too complex to be fully grasped by imperfect human beings. Second, although each person might correctly identify one aspect of reality, each may incorrectly attempt to reduce the entire phenomenon to their own partial and narrow experience. Third, the maintenance of communal peace and harmony might be worth much more than stubbornly clinging to one's understanding of the world. Fourth, it might be wise for each person to return to reality and exchange positions with others to better appreciate the whole of the reality.[1]

In the chapters that follow, first the four paradigms are reviewed. Then the organization and structure of academic finance paradigm are discussed. This is where it is shown that academic finance operates only within the functionalist paradigm and, therefore, the book recommends paradigm diversity and discusses its benefits. The remaining chapters show opportunities arising from paradigm diversity by discussing the following topics from four different paradigmatic view points: development of academic finance, mathematical language of academic finance, mathematics of academic finance, money, corporate governance, markets, technology, and education. The final chapter concludes the discussion in the book by recommending paradigm diversity.

Kavous Ardalan, Ph.D.
Poughkeepsie, New York

---

1 This parable is taken from Steger (2002).

Acknowledgements

The writing of the chapters of this book involved extensive work over several years. It required peace of mind and extended uninterrupted research time. My deepest expressions of gratitude go to my wife Haleh, my son Arash, and my daughter Camellia for their prolonged patience, unlimited understanding, sustained support, constant cooperation, and personal independence during all these long years. I hold much respect for my late parents (Javad and Afagholmolouk) who instilled in their children (Ghobad, Golnar, Alireza, and Kavous) the grand Ardalan family's values of tolerance, openness, and love of learning, among others.

The ideas expressed in this work are based on the teachings, writings, and insights of Professor Gareth Morgan, to whom the nucleus of this work is owed. Needless to say, I stand responsible for all the errors and omissions. I would like to thank Professor Gareth Morgan who taught me how to diversely view the world and accordingly inspired my work.

I am thankful of the Marist College library staff for their timely provision of the requested printed literature from various sources. Certainly, I would like to thank Ashgate Publishing for recognizing the significance of this project and immediately offering me a publishing contract.

I also wish to thank the following journal publishers for permission to reproduce in this book my articles which were originally published in their journals: *Academy of Accounting and Financial Studies Journal, Academy of Educational Leadership Journal, American Review of Political Economy, International Journal of Social Economics, Journal of Global Business, Southern Business Review, and Southwestern Economic Review.* The complete reference information for these articles is provided in the bibliography of the book under my name.

Kavous Ardalan, Ph.D.
Poughkeepsie, New York

Chapter 1

Paradigms

Social theory can usefully be conceived in terms of four key paradigms: functionalist, interpretive, radical humanist, and radical structuralist. The four paradigms are founded upon different assumptions about the nature of social science and the nature of society. Each generates theories, concepts, and analytical tools which are different from those of other paradigms.

All theories of academic finance are based on a philosophy of science and a theory of society. Many theorists appear to be unaware of, or ignore, the assumptions underlying these philosophies. They emphasize only some aspects of the phenomenon and ignore others. Unless they bring out the basic philosophical assumptions of the theories, their analysis can be misleading; since by emphasizing differences between theories, they imply diversity in approach. While there appear to be different kinds of theory in mainstream academic finance, they are founded on a certain philosophy, worldview, or paradigm.[1] This becomes evident when these theories are related to the wider background of social theory.

The functionalist paradigm has provided the framework for current mainstream academic finance, and accounts for the largest proportion of theory and research in its academic field.

In order to understand a new paradigm, theorists should be fully aware of assumptions upon which their own paradigm is based. Moreover, to understand a new paradigm one has to explore it from within, since the concepts in one paradigm cannot easily be interpreted in terms of those of another. No attempt should be made to criticize or evaluate a paradigm from the outside. This is self-defeating since it is based on a separate paradigm. All four paradigms can be easily criticized and ruined in this way.

These four paradigms are of paramount importance to any scientist, because the process of learning about a favored paradigm is also the process of learning what that paradigm is not. The knowledge of paradigms makes scientists aware of the boundaries within which they approach their subject. Each of the four paradigms implies a different way of social theorizing in general, and finance, in particular.

Before discussing each paradigm, it is useful to look at the notion of "paradigm." Burrell and Morgan (1979)[2] regard the:

---

1 McGoun (1992a) is probably the first paper to examine the ontology and epistemology of finance, and their implications for research.

2 This work borrows heavily from the ideas and insights of Burrell and Morgan (1979) and Morgan (1983) and applies them to finance. Burrell and Morgan (1979) state: "The scope for applying the analytical scheme to other field of study is enormous ... readers interested in

... four paradigms as being defined by very basic meta-theoretical assumptions which underwrite the frame of reference, mode of theorizing and modus operandi of the social theorists who operate within them. It is a term which is intended to emphasize the commonality of perspective which binds the work of a group of theorists together in such a way that they can be usefully regarded as approaching social theory within the bounds of the same problematic.

The paradigm does ... have an underlying unity in terms of its basic and often "taken for granted" assumptions, which separate a group of theorists in a very fundamental way from theorists located in other paradigms. The "unity" of the paradigm thus derives from reference to alternative views of reality which lie outside its boundaries and which may not necessarily even be recognized as existing. (pp. 23–24)

Each theory can be related to one of the four broad worldviews. These adhere to different sets of fundamental assumptions about; the nature of science—that is, the subjective-objective dimension—and the nature of society—that is, the dimension of regulation-radical change—as in Figure 1.1.[3]

Assumptions related to the nature of science are assumptions with respect to ontology, epistemology, human nature, and methodology.

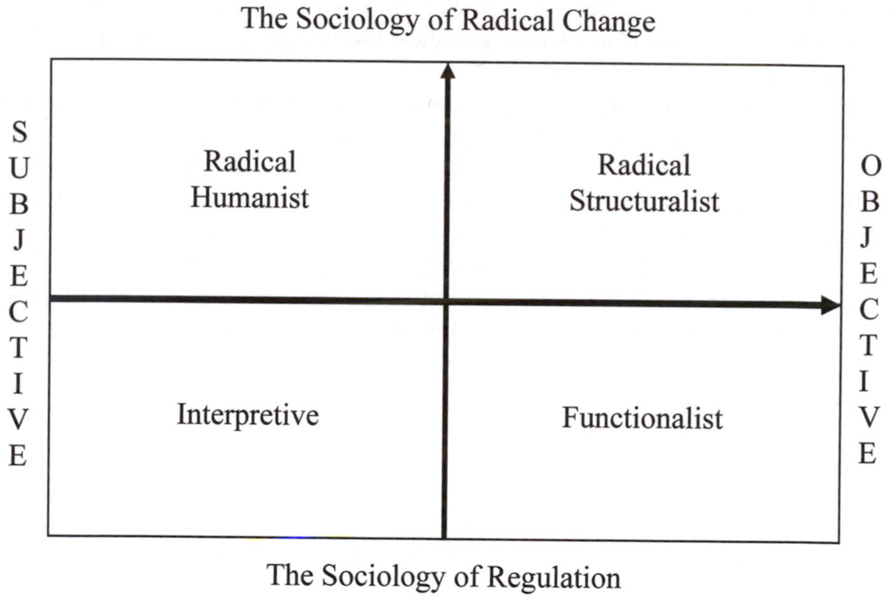

The Sociology of Radical Change

| S U B J E C T I V E | Radical Humanist | Radical Structuralist | O B J E C T I V E |
| | Interpretive | Functionalist | |

The Sociology of Regulation

Figure 1.1   The Four Paradigms

---

applying the scheme in this way should find little difficulty in proceeding from the sociological analyses ... to an analysis of the literature in their own sphere of specialised interest." (p. 35).

3 This can be used as both a classifactory device, or more importantly, as an analytical tool. Bettner, Robinson, and McGoun (1994) and Frankfurter, Carleton, Gordon, Horrigan, McGoun, Philippatos, and Robinson (1994) have also referred to the scheme shown in Figure 1.1.

The assumptions about ontology are assumptions regarding the very essence of the phenomenon under investigation. That is, to what extent the phenomenon is objective and external to the individual or it is subjective and the product of individual's mind.

The assumptions about epistemology are assumptions about the nature of knowledge. That is, they are assumptions about how one might go about understanding the world, and communicate such knowledge to others. That is, what constitutes knowledge and to what extent it is something which can be acquired or it is something which has to be personally experienced.

The assumptions about human nature are concerned with human nature and, in particular, the relationship between individuals and their environment, which is the object and subject of social sciences. That is, to what extent human beings and their experiences are the products of their environment or human beings are creators of their environment.

The assumptions about methodology are related to the way in which one attempts to investigate and obtain knowledge about the social world. That is, to what extent the methodology treats the social world as being real hard and external to the individual or it is as being of a much softer, personal and more subjective quality. In the former, the focus is on the universal relationship among elements of the phenomenon, whereas in the latter, the focus is on the understanding of the way in which the individual creates, modifies, and interprets the situation which is experienced.

The assumptions related to the nature of society are concerned with the extent of regulation of the society or radical change in the society.

Sociology of regulation provides explanation of society based on the assumption of its unity and cohesiveness. It focuses on the need to understand and explain why society tends to hold together rather than fall apart.

Sociology of radical change provides explanation of society based on the assumption of its deep-seated structural conflict, modes of domination, and structural contradiction. It focuses on the deprivation of human beings, both material and psychic, and it looks towards alternatives rather than the acceptance of *status quo*.

The subjective-objective dimension and the regulation-radical change dimension together define four paradigms, each of which share common fundamental assumptions about the nature of social science and the nature of society. Each paradigm has a fundamentally unique perspective for the analysis of social phenomena.

Functionalist Paradigm

The functionalist paradigm assumes that society has a concrete existence and follows certain order. These assumptions lead to the existence of an objective and value-free social science which can produce true explanatory and predictive knowledge of the reality "out there." It assumes scientific theories can be assessed objectively by reference to empirical evidence. Scientists do not see any roles for themselves, within the phenomenon which they analyze, through the rigor and technique of the scientific method. It attributes independence to the observer from the observed. That is, an ability to observe "what is" without affecting it. It assumes there are universal standards of science, which determine what constitutes an adequate explanation of what is observed. It assumes there are external rules and regulations governing the external world. The goal of scientists is to find the orders that prevail within that phenomenon.

The functionalist paradigm seeks to provide rational explanations of social affairs and generate regulative sociology. It assumes a continuing order, pattern, and coherence and tries to explain what is. It emphasizes the importance of understanding order, equilibrium and stability in society and the way in which these can be maintained. It is concerned with the regulation and control of social affairs. It believes in social engineering as a basis for social reform.

The rationality which underlies functionalist science is used to explain the rationality of society. Science provides the basis for structuring and ordering the social world, similar to the structure and order in the natural world. The methods of natural science are used to generate explanations of the social world. The use of mechanical and biological analogies for modeling and understanding the social phenomena are particularly favored.

Functionalists are individualists. That is, the properties of the aggregate are determined by the properties of its units.

Their approach to social science is rooted in the tradition of positivism. It assumes that the social world is concrete, meaning it can be identified, studied and measured through approaches derived from the natural sciences.

Functionalists believe that the positivist methods which have triumphed in natural sciences should prevail in social sciences, as well. In addition, the functionalist paradigm has become dominant in academic sociology and mainstream academic finance. The world of finance is treated as a place of concrete reality, characterized by uniformities and regularities which can be understood and explained in terms of causes and effects. Given these assumptions, the individuals are regarded as taking on a passive role; their behavior is being determined by the economic environment.

Functionalists are pragmatic in orientation and are concerned to understand society so that the knowledge thus generated can be used in society. It is problem orientated in approach as it is concerned to provide practical solutions to practical problems.

In Figure 1.1, the functionalist paradigm occupies the south-east quadrant. Schools of thought within this paradigm can be located on the objective-subjective continuum. From right to left they are: Objectivism, Social System Theory, Integrative Theory, Interactionism, and Social Action Theory.

Interpretive Paradigm

The interpretive paradigm assumes that social reality is the result of the subjective interpretations of individuals. It sees the social world as a process which is created by individuals. Social reality, insofar as it exists outside the consciousness of any individual, is regarded as being a network of assumptions and intersubjectively shared meanings. This assumption leads to the belief there are shared multiple realities which are sustained and changed. Researchers recognize their role within the phenomenon under investigation. Their frame of reference is one of participant, as opposed to observer. The goal of the interpretive researchers is to find the orders that prevail within the phenomenon under consideration; however, they are not objective.

The interpretive paradigm is concerned with understanding the world as it is, at the level of subjective experience. It seeks explanations within the realm of individual consciousness and subjectivity. Its analysis of the social world produces sociology of regulation. Its views are underwritten by the assumptions that the social world is cohesive, ordered, and integrated.

Interpretive sociologists seek to understand the source of social reality. They often delve into the depth of human consciousness and subjectivity in their quest for the meanings in social life. They reject the use of mathematics and biological analogies in learning about the society and their approach places emphasis on understanding the social world from the vantage point of the individuals who are actually engaged in social activities.

The interpretive paradigm views the functionalist position as unsatisfactory for two reasons. First, human values affect the process of scientific enquiry. That is, scientific method is not value-free, since the frame of reference of the scientific observer determines the way in which scientific knowledge is obtained. Second, in cultural sciences the subject matter is spiritual in nature. That is, human beings cannot be studied by the methods of the natural sciences, which aim to establish general laws. In the cultural sphere human beings are perceived as free. An understanding of their lives and actions can be obtained by the intuition of the total wholes, which is bound to break down by atomistic analysis of functionalist paradigm.

Cultural phenomena are seen as the external manifestations of inner experience. The cultural sciences, therefore, need to apply analytical methods based on "understanding;" through which the scientist can seek to understand human beings, their minds, and their feelings, and the way these are expressed in their outward actions. The notion of "understanding" is a defining characteristic of all theories located within this paradigm.

The interpretive paradigm believes that science is based on "taken for granted" assumptions; and, like any other social practice, must be understood within a specific context. Therefore, it cannot generate objective and value-free knowledge. Scientific knowledge is socially constructed and socially sustained; its significance and meaning can only be understood within its immediate social context.

The interpretive paradigm regards mainstream academic finance theorists as belonging to a small and self-sustaining community, which believes that corporations and financial markets exist in a concrete world. They theorize about concepts which have little significance to people outside the community, which practices financial theory, and the limited community which financial theorists may attempt to serve.

Mainstream academic finance theorists tend to treat their subject of study as a hard, concrete and tangible empirical phenomenon which exists "out there" in the "real world." Interpretive researchers are opposed to such structural absolution. They emphasize that the social world is no more than the subjective construction of individual human beings who create and sustain a social world of intersubjectively shared meaning, which is in a continuous process of reaffirmation or change. Therefore, there are no universally valid rules of finance and financial management. Interpretive finance research enables scientists to examine aggregate market behavior together with ethical, cultural, political, and social issues.

In Figure 1.1, the interpretive paradigm occupies the south-west quadrant. Schools of thought within this paradigm can be located on the objective-subjective continuum. From left to right they are: Solipsism, Phenomenology, Phenomenological Sociology, and Hermeneutics.

Radical Humanist Paradigm

The radical humanist paradigm provides critiques of the status quo and is concerned to articulate, from a subjective standpoint, the sociology of radical change, modes of domination, emancipation, deprivation, and potentiality. Based on its subjectivist approach, it places great emphasis on human consciousness. It tends to view society as anti-human. It views the process of reality creation as feeding back on itself; such that individuals and society are prevented from reaching their highest possible potential. That is, the consciousness of human beings is dominated by the ideological superstructures of the social system, which results in their alienation or false consciousness. This, in turn, prevents true human fulfillment. The social theorist regards the orders that prevail in the society as instruments of ideological domination.

The major concern for theorists is with the way this occurs and finding ways in which human beings can release themselves from constraints which existing social arrangements place upon realization of their full potential. They seek to change the social world through a change in consciousness.

Radical humanists believe that everything must be grasped as a whole, because the whole dominates the parts in an all-embracing sense. Moreover, truth is historically specific, relative to a given set of circumstances, so that one should not search for generalizations for the laws of motion of societies.

The radical humanists believe the functionalist paradigm accepts purposive rationality, logic of science, positive functions of technology, and neutrality of language, and uses them in the construction of "value-free" social theories. The radical humanist theorists intend to demolish this structure, emphasizing the political and repressive nature of it. They aim to show the role that science, ideology, technology, language, and other aspects of the superstructure play in sustaining and developing the system of power and domination, within the totality of the social formation. Their function is to influence the consciousness of human beings for eventual emancipation and formation of alternative social formations.

The radical humanists note that functionalist sociologists create and sustain a view of social reality which maintains the *status quo* and which forms one aspect of the network of ideological domination of the society.

The focus of the radical humanists upon the "superstructural" aspects of society reflects their attempt to move away from the economism of orthodox Marxism and emphasize the Hegelian dialectics. It is through the dialectic that the objective and subjective aspects of social life interact. The superstructure of society is believed to be the medium through which the consciousness of human beings is controlled and molded to fit the requirements of the social formation as a whole. The concepts of structural conflict, contradiction, and crisis do not play a major role in this paradigm, because these are more objectivist view of social reality, that is, the ones which fall in the radical structuralist paradigm. In the radical humanist paradigm, the concepts of consciousness, alienation, and critique form their concerns.

In Figure 1.1, the radical humanist paradigm occupies the north-west quadrant. Schools of thought within this paradigm can be located on the objective-subjective continuum. From left to right they are: Solipsism, French Existentialism, Anarchistic Individualism, and Critical Theory.

Radical Structuralist Paradigm

The radical structuralist paradigm assumes that reality is objective and concrete, as it is rooted in the materialist view of natural and social world. The social world, similar to the natural world, has an independent existence, that is, it exists outside the minds of human beings. Sociologists aim at discovering and understanding the patterns and regularities which characterize the social world. Scientists do not see any roles for themselves in the phenomenon under investigation. They use scientific methods to find the order that prevails in the phenomenon. This paradigm views society as a potentially dominating force. Sociologists working within this paradigm have an objectivist standpoint and are committed to radical change, emancipation, and potentiality. In their analysis they emphasize structural conflict, modes of domination, contradiction, and deprivation. They analyze the basic interrelationships within the total social formation and emphasize the fact that radical change is inherent in the structure of society and the radical change takes place though political and economic crises. This radical change necessarily disrupts the *status quo* and replaces it by a radically different social formation. It is through this radical change that the emancipation of human beings from the social structure is materialized.

For radical structuralists, an understanding of classes in society is essential for understanding the nature of knowledge. They argue that all knowledge is class specific. That is, it is determined by the place one occupies in the productive process. Knowledge is more than a reflection of the material world in thought. It is determined by one's relation to that reality. Since different classes occupy different positions in the process of material transformation, there are different kinds of knowledge. Hence class knowledge is produced by and for classes, and exists in a struggle for domination. Knowledge is thus ideological. That is, it formulates views of reality and solves problems from class points of view.

Radical structuralists reject the idea that it is possible to verify knowledge in an absolute sense through comparison with socially neutral theories or data. But, emphasize that there is the possibility of producing a "correct" knowledge from a class standpoint. They argue that the dominated class is uniquely positioned to obtain an objectively "correct" knowledge of social reality and its contradictions. It is the class with the most direct and widest access to the process of material transformation that ultimately produces and reproduces that reality.

Radical structuralists' analysis indicates that the social scientist, as a producer of class-based knowledge, is a part of the class struggle.

Radical structuralists believe truth is the whole, and emphasize the need to understand the social order as a totality rather than as a collection of small truths about various parts and aspects of society. The financial empiricists are seen as relying almost exclusively upon a number of seemingly disparate, data-packed, problem-centered studies. Such studies, therefore, are irrelevant exercises in mathematical methods.

This paradigm is based on four central notions. First, there is the notion of totality. All theories address the total social formation. This notion emphasizes that the parts reflect the totality, not the totality the parts.

Second, there is the notion of structure. The focus is upon the configurations of social relationships, called structures, which are treated as persistent and enduring concrete facilities.

The third notion is that of contradiction. Structures, or social formations, contain contradictory and antagonistic relationships within them which act as seeds of their own decay.

The fourth notion is that of crisis. Contradictions within a given totality reach a point at which they can no longer be contained. The resulting political, economic crises indicate the point of transformation from one totality to another, in which one set of structures is replaced by another of a fundamentally different kind.

In Figure 1.1, the radical structuralist paradigm occupies the north-east quadrant. Schools of thought within this paradigm can be located on the objective-subjective continuum. From right to left they are: Russian Social Theory, Conflict Theory, and Contemporary Mediterranean Marxism.

Conclusion

This chapter briefly discussed social theory, its complexity, and diversity. It indicated that finance theorists are not always entirely aware of the traditions to which they belong.

The diversity of theories presented in this section is vast. While each paradigm advocates a research strategy that is logically coherent, in terms of underlying assumptions, these vary from paradigm to paradigm. The phenomenon to be researched is conceptualized and studied in many different ways, each generating distinctive kinds of insight and understanding. There are many different ways of studying the same social phenomenon, and given that the insights generated by any one approach are at best partial and incomplete, the social researcher can gain much by reflecting on the nature and merits of different approaches before engaging in a particular mode of research practice.

Knowledge of finance is ultimately a product of the researcher's paradigmatic approach to this multifaceted phenomenon. Viewed from this angle, the pursuit of financial knowledge is seen as much an ethical, moral, ideological, and political activity, as a technical one. Academic finance can gain much by exploiting the new insights coming from other paradigms.

Chapter 2

Organization of Academic Finance Paradigm

This chapter shows that mainstream academic finance is founded on the functionalist paradigm. The chapter is based on the notion that worldviews underlie academic fields, in general, and finance, in particular. It refers to the idea that any worldview can be positioned on a continuum formed by four basic worldviews or paradigms: functionalist, interpretive, radical humanist, and radical structuralist. Then, the chapter examines theories, Ph.D. programs, journals, and conferences in mainstream academic finance. It notes that they adhere, almost exclusively, to the functionalist paradigm. Finally, the chapter discusses the principles of paradigm diversity, its implications, and requirements. It notes instances of paradigm diversity in theories, Ph.D. programs, journals, and conferences in finance. It concludes that without some fundamental changes, there will be less opportunity for mainstream academic finance to benefit from contributions of the other three paradigms.

Any adequate analysis of the role of paradigms, in academic fields, must recognize the assumptions that underwrite that paradigm or worldview. Academic fields can be conceived in terms of four key paradigms: functionalist, Interpretive, radical humanist, and radical structuralist. The four paradigms are founded upon mutually exclusive views of the social world. Each generates theories, Ph.D. programs, journals, and conferences which are different from those of other paradigms.

Academic Finance

This section is intended to show how worldviews underlie academic fields in general, and finance, in particular. It relates paradigms and the academic field of finance by examining its theories, Ph.D. programs, journals, and conferences. It notes that, within this broader universe, the academic field of finance is founded only on the functionalist paradigm. This section adds to a better understanding of the underlying assumptions of the academic field of finance.

The remainder of this section is, therefore, organized as follows. First it considers academic finance theories, then it examines academic finance Ph.D. programs, afterwards it investigates academic finance journals, and finally it discusses academic finance conferences.

Theories

As in Jensen and Smith (1984) and Smith (1990),[1] the following lists current theories and policies in mainstream academic finance. Additionally, it emphasizes that they are based on the functionalist paradigm.

Since 1950, a number of major theories and policies in finance have developed; namely:

1. *Efficient market theory:* Fama (1970, 1976, 1991) reviews theory and evidence. Jensen (1978) provides a review of some anomalies, Schwert (1983) surveys the size-related anomalies, and Moy and Lee (1991) compile a bibliography of different stock market anomalies. Ball (1996) updates the review of literature.[2]
2. *Portfolio theory:* Markowitz (1952, 1959) emphasizes the benefit of portfolio diversification and lays down the foundation for the Capital Asset Pricing Theory.
3. *Capital asset pricing theory:* Jensen (1972) surveys the literature, and Roll (1977) criticizes tests of the model.[3]
4. *Option pricing theory:* For a review of theory, and its applications, see Cox and Ross (1976) and Smith (1976, 1979).
5. *Agency theory:* Jensen and Ruback (1983) and Jensen and Smith (1985) provide reviews of this literature. Garvey and Swan (1994) review the literature on corporate governance.
6. *Arbitrage pricing theory:* Ross (1976) proves the K-factor determination of asset prices.
7. *Capital budgeting policy:* Aggarwal (1993) provides an overview of capital budgeting under uncertainty.
8. *Capital structure policy:* Fama (1978) reviews the literature.[4] And,
9. *Dividend policy:* Black (1976) provides a summary of the issues. For a review see Allen and Michaely (1994).[5]

Bettner, Robinson and McGoun (1994) note that the common threads among theories and policies in mainstream academic finance are:

---

1 For overviews of the finance literature, see also Brennan (1995) and Weston (1994). See also Borokhovich, Bricker, and Simkins (1994), Cooley and Heck (1981), Faulhaber and Baumol (1988), Friend (1973), Jensen and Smith (1984), Merton (1995), Miller (1986), Naslund (1986), Roll (1994), Smith (1990), and Weston (1966, 1967, 1974, 1981).

2 Haugen (1995) discusses the subject from a different perspective. For a controversy on the capital market efficiency, see Haugen (1996) and Shanken and Smith (1996), who provide two alternative views.

3 For critical reviews see Frankfurter (1995) and McGoun (1992a). For a controversy on the capital asset pricing theory, see Haugen (1996) and Shanken and Smith (1996), who provide two alternative views.

4 Frankfurter and Philippatos (1992) critically evaluate its evolution.

5 For critical reviews, see Frankfurter and Lane (1992) and Frankfurter and Wood (1995).

1. There is a cause and effect mechanism underlying all nature and human activity (ontology);
2. It is known through the set of nomological connections between initial conditions and final outcomes (epistemology);
3. Human beings interact with each other and their society in accordance with this mechanism (human nature); and
4. Information regarding all natural and human activity can be acquired through observations and measurements unaffected by individual perceptual differences (methodology), (p. 3)

which lead to the conclusion that the current theories in finance are clearly based on the functionalist paradigm.[6]

McGoun (1992) in his reflection "On the Knowledge of Finance" states:

The behavior of most scientists implies their having made certain tacit assumptions regarding scientific activity:

1. There is a real external environment out there independent of science;
2. It is possible, at least in principle, to determine the truth of a scientific statement regarding the external environment;
3. Scientists will never state all truths regarding the external environment; and
4. Over time, scientists state more precise truths regarding the external environment. (p. 161)

Weston (1994) in providing "A (Relatively) Brief History of Finance Ideas" applies the above principles and provides a general explanation[7] by stating:

Review and analysis of financial history suggest five generalizations. One, the developments of each historical period and the creators of these developments were responding to the pressing economic, financial, and socio-political problems of the period. Two, financial thought has also responded to the maturation of financial markets, internationalization, and increased competition. Three, the development and/or uses of new tools, new mathematical models, and new methodologies have facilitated the creation of theories to explain financial behavior. Four, practice has reflected the new learning with varying time lags but has also stimulated the development of theory to understand, explain, and predict financial behavior. Five, new ideas have built on the ideas provided by previous knowledge. (p. 7)

---

6 See McGoun (1992b) and Bettner, Robinson and McGoun (1994) for more complete treatments. The same conclusion may be inferred from: Bicksler (1972), Findlay and Williams (1980), Frankfurter, Carleton, Gordon, Horrigan, McGoun, Philippatos, and Robinson (1994), Friedman (1953), Kavesh (1970), McGoun (1992b), Merton (1995), Sauvain (1967), Weston (1966, 1967, 1974), and Whitley (1986). McGoun (1992) is probably the first paper to have examined the ontology and epistemology of finance and their implications for research. For an extensive analysis of how the business finance has been transformed into financial economics see Whitley (1986).

7 For a more detailed and specific explanation, see Weston (1966).

Ph.D. Programs

The design of a finance Ph.D. program is often reflected in its business school catalogue. This contains information on courses offered. These consist of core and specialized finance area courses. In writing this paper, a survey of Ph.D. programs was conducted.

A letter of request, for the provision of information regarding Ph.D. program design, requirements, core and finance area courses, was sent to the attention of the Ph.D. Program Director of each institution. The letter stated that the information is for a study of Ph.D. programs in Business, with concentration in Finance. Appendix 1 provides the text of the letter which was sent to the institutions. Appendix 2 lists the universities with Ph.D. programs in Business. The list is obtained from "The Official Guide to MBA Programs," as it also indicates which universities offer Ph.D. programs in business. In appendix 2, universities that either did not reply, did not provide sufficient information, or did not offer a Ph.D. program in finance, are marked with an asterisk. Among the 105 universities surveyed, 78 replied, a response rate of about 74 per cent.

The information received was carefully analyzed with respect to the research methodologies taught and required. With no exception, all programs taught and required economics and quantitative methods. That is, they all advocate the functionalist paradigm. Only one university offered other methodologies, as well; the George Washington University. They offer a course entitled, The Philosophical Foundations of Administrative Research, which deals with the nature of the knowledge encompassed by their School of Business and Public Management and with the problems of inquiry posed by such knowledge.[8]

The results of the study were consistent with previous results obtained by Shin and Hubbard (1988). That is:

1. The majority of the doctoral programs require algebra, calculus, statistics, and computer courses for entry into the Ph.D. program. (p. 67)
2. Most doctoral programs require students to study a series of core business courses such as accounting, marketing, management, economics, finance, information systems, and quantitative methods. In general, these schools require 3-credit hours of each of these foundation courses except quantitative methods of which they require 6-credit hours. (pp. 67–68)
3. Most schools require 6–12 credit hours each in economic theory, quantitative methods, and electives beyond the master's level. ... There is a strong desire by the schools to enhance the student's knowledge in the areas of economic theory and quantitative methods. (p. 68)
4. Almost all the responding schools offer the traditional finance courses. ... Strong emphasis in courses in financial theory is seen in the offerings by these schools. (pp. 68–69)
5. The most widely used data files among the responding schools are Compustat Industrial and CRSP tapes. (p. 74)

---

8 One might suspect that this course is more directed to the other areas of management, rather than finance.

6. Ranked schools tended to require more economic theory and quantitative method courses in their program. (p. 76)
7. Ranked schools tended to own more data tapes than unranked schools. (p. 77)

Klemkosky and Tuttle (1977a) noticed that there is a significant relationship between the academic institutions' research productivity and the quality of the institutions' finance doctoral degree programs as rated by peers. Moreover, research productivity is concentrated in a small number of institutions which consistently dominate the number of pages and articles published.

Schweser (1977), in search of the doctoral origins of contributors to the *Journal of Finance*, finds that 46.2 per cent of all *Journal of Finance* authors received their doctorate from 10 universities and 20 schools produced 72.3 per cent of all who published in the *Journal of Finance*.

The phenomena that a small number of institutions that is most research productive is also providing the highest rated finance doctoral programs is of notable interest here. It shows how the Ph.D. graduates from these institutions will in turn become prominent researchers and train new Ph.D. graduates who are rated highly. They, therefore, help to promote, perpetuate, and refine what they have learned during their own years of doctoral education, that is, the functionalist finance.

Journals

Zivney and Reichenstein (1994) categorized academic finance journals as "core" and "non-core." Based on their definition, they find that there are sixteen "core," and two "non-core" finance journals. Journals, in their "aims and scope," specify the type of research they are interested in publishing. Among the sixteen "core" finance journals, thirteen advocate traditional functionalist research. They are: *Journal of Finance, Journal of Financial and Quantitative Analysis, Journal of Business, Financial Analysts Journal, Financial Management, Journal of Portfolio Management, Journal of Banking and Finance, Journal of Business Finance and Accounting, Journal of Financial Research, Review of Financial Studies, Journal of Financial Services Research, Journal of Financial Education,* and *Review of Futures Markets*.

One of the "core" finance journals, *Financial Review*, admits the acceptance of methodological articles; and two, *Journal of Financial Economics* and *Journal of Futures Markets*, admit the acceptance of clinical contributions, case studies, and descriptive analyses.

It is interesting to expand the above analysis to include the more recent "core" finance journals. In their search for "core" finance journals, Zivney and Reichenstein (1994) started with the eighteen journals covered by Heck's (1989) Finance Literature Index and came up with sixteen as the "core" finance journals, as were listed above. Unfortunately, there is no current study which parallels Zivney and Reichenstein (1994). However, given the close proximity of Heck's (1989) Finance Literature Index to the "core" finance journals, as defined by Zivney and Reichenstein (1994), one might use Heck's (1999) Finance Literature Index to approximately define the current "core" finance journals, then analyze the aims and scope of the more recent "core" journals.

There are twenty-three new finance journals in Heck's (1999) Finance Literature Index. Among them, twenty-one advocate traditional functionalist research. They are: *Applied Financial Economics, Financial Services Review, Global Finance Journal, International Journal of Finance, International Review of Economics and Finance, Journal of Applied Corporate Finance, Journal of Corporate Finance, Journal of Economics and Finance, Journal of Empirical Finance, Journal of Financial Engineering, Journal of Financial Intermediation, Journal of Fixed Income, Journal of International Financial Markets, Institutions, and Money, Journal of Investing, Journal of Multinational Financial Management, Journal of Small Business Finance, Mathematical Finance, Pacific-Basin Finance Journal, Quarterly Journal of Economics and Finance, Review of Financial Economics,* and *Review of Quantitative Finance and Accounting.*

Among the twenty-three new journals, only two allow alternative research: (1) *Financial Practice and Education* encourages clinical studies, and (2) *International Review of Financial Analysis* advocates open inquiry.

The state of the art of finance is reflected, to a large extent, in its journal literature. This literature plays a crucial role in determining the direction and nature of research.[9] The functionalist journal editorial policy performs a quality control function, designed to regulate the direction of developments in the field.

Borokhovich, Bricker, Brunarski, and Simkins (1995) note that the distribution of publications among institutions is highly skewed, with 20 per cent of the institutions publishing over 66 per cent of the articles. Moreover, the distribution of influential research is at least as skewed as total publications, with 20 per cent of the institutions accounting for over 76 per cent of total influence. Furthermore, prestigious business schools tend to have high research productivity and influence.

Dyl (1991) notes that "… decisions about hiring, promoting, and rewarding faculty members are based largely on evaluations of scholarly research. Moreover, the more prestigious the academic institution, the greater the weight placed on research." (p. 11). In the academic community the promotion to the rank of editor or editorial board of journals, especially the prestigious ones, is subject to the same scrutiny in terms of high quality research. In academic finance, the members of the editorial boards of journals have passed such hurdles and by evaluating submitted manuscripts by the criteria of the functionalist finance help to perpetuate, enhance, and refine the functionalist finance.

---

9 Journal publication is the single most important performance evaluation criterion in academic finance, whether it is used for: (1) desirability of Ph.D. graduates as job applicants, (2) salary determination, tenure, promotion, evaluation, mobility, recognition of faculty members, (3) prestige, recognition, ranking of doctoral programs and academic finance departments, or (4) research funding. See Bertin and Zivney (1991, 1992), Borokhovich, Bricker, Brunarski, Simkins (1995), Bures and Tong (1993), Ehrenberg and Hurst (1996), Frankfurter and McGoun (1996), Heck, Cooley, and Hubbard (1986), Klemkosky and Tuttle (1977a, 1977b), Niemi (1987), Tripathy and Ganesh (1996), and Zivney and Bertin (1992).

Crane (1967), for example, found that in the selection of articles for publication in social science journals authors' institutional affiliations tended to correspond to those of the editors of the journals that published their work. Crane concluded that, as a result of academic training, editors respond to certain aspects of methodology, theoretical orientation, and mode of expression in the writings of those who received similar training; moreover, personal ties also seemed to influence the evaluation of manuscripts. Yoels (1974) found that editorial appointments were influenced by similarity in institutional affiliation between outgoing editors and their appointees.

Conferences

In their "Call for Papers," academic finance conferences often indicate the type of research they consider for presentation. This paper examined the "Call for Papers" for finance conference meetings which are usually announced in Financial Management. The latest full-year in which Financial Management has been published is 1998. There are ten finance conferences announced in all 1998 issues. Generally, all of them state that they consider papers in all traditional areas of finance, but there is no reference to alternative approaches and methodologies. For instance, when they list the areas of their interest, only three conferences explicitly indicate "methodology/ statistical methods" s a desirable area, though it is not quite clear how they define it. These conferences are: Eastern Finance Association, Financial Management Association International, and Midwest Finance Association. Three other conferences indicate "miscellaneous finance topics," which might be interpreted to include "methodological issues," in which case they down-play such research efforts. These conferences are: Academy of Economics and Finance, Southern Finance Association, and Southwestern Finance Association. The other four conferences that do not fit in within these two categories are: Academy of Financial Services, American Finance Association, Midwest Academy of Finance and Insurance, and Western Finance Association.

It can be concluded that the academic finance conferences' openness to alternative paradigms is limited. To confirm this point, see Sweetser and Petry (1981) for a history of the seven academic finance associations and their contributions to the development of the mainstream academic finance. They state: "Today the discipline is widely understood and accepted, well balanced internally, and an effective force in academic and management circles; credit for much of this development may be attributed to academic professional associations." (p. 46)

Academic associations publish journals and are the major players in organizing annual conferences. On the academic side, in these conferences, researchers present papers which are in their developmental stage. Papers, for presentation, come under scrutiny by conference organizers applying almost the same evaluative criteria as papers submitted to journals for publication.

Pettijohn, Udell, and Parker (1991) mention that "... finance faculty at all levels are pressured to publish if they are to be promoted or retained, with few exceptions." (p. 52). In the academic community the promotion to the rank of administrators of associations and conferences, especially the prestigious ones, is subject to the same scrutiny in terms of high quality research. In academic finance, the administrators of the associations and conferences have passed such hurdles and by evaluating submitted manuscripts by the criteria of the functionalist finance help to perpetuate, enhance, and refine the functionalist finance.

In summary, this section related paradigms and the academic field of finance, by examining its theories, Ph.D. programs, journals, and conferences. It noted that, within this broader universe, the academic field of finance has been founded almost exclusively on the functionalist paradigm.

Academic finance, in the process of its development, has narrowed its scope of professional concerns within the functionalist paradigm, which has limited its understanding of others. This concentration of research in a narrow area has defined the academic field of finance. The frame of reference in academic financial research is based on taken-for-granted underlying assumptions. Since these assumptions are continually affirmed and reinforced in financial research, they may have remained not only unquestioned, but also beyond conscious awareness. In this way the current view may come to assume a status as real, right, and self-evident.

Financial research aims for affirmation rather than for refutation of its theories and research method. The role of doubt is overlooked in favor of achieving "significant" results. The role of doubt or refutation is often reduced to statistical tests of significance. Financial research very seriously ensures that it accurately meets the requirements of scientific method. However, the underlying assumptions on which the research is based are commonly overlooked.

Paradigm Diversity

This section discusses the principles of paradigm diversity, its implications, and requirements. It discusses points of view advocated by the other three paradigms. It notes instances of paradigm diversity in theories, Ph.D. programs, journals, and conferences in finance. It emphasizes that they are almost exclusively underwritten by the other three paradigms, and are considered non-mainstream by academic finance. This chapter emphasizes that academic finance could benefit from contributions by the other paradigms. This would entail fundamental changes in current perspective held by academic finance.[10]

Paradigm diversity is based on the idea that more than one theoretical construction can be placed upon a given collection of data. In other words, any single theory, research method, or particular empirical study is incapable of explaining the nature of reality in all of its complexities.

It is possible to establish exact solutions to problems, if one defines the boundary and domain of reality. Functionalist research, through its research approach, defines an area in which objectivity and truth can be found. Any change in the research approach, or any change in the area of applicability, would tend to result in the break down of such objectivity and truth.

---

10 For an extensive analysis of an array of alternative philosophical views, their research implications, and their contributions see Morgan (1984).

The knowledge generated through functionalist research relates to certain aspects of the phenomenon under consideration. Recognition of the existence of the phenomenon beyond that dictated by the research approach, results in the recognition of the limitations of the knowledge generated within the confines of that approach.

It is almost impossible to find foundational solution to the problem of creating specific kind of knowledge. Researchers are encouraged to explore what is possible by identifying untapped possibilities. By comparing a favored research approach in relation to others, the nature, strengths, and limitations of the favored approach become evident. By understanding what others do, researchers are able to understand what they are not doing. This leads to the development and refinement of the favored research approach. The concern is not about deciding which research approach is best, or with substituting one for another. The concern is about the merits of diversity, which seeks to enrich research rather than constrain it, through a search for an optimum way of doing diverse research.

There is no unique evaluative perspective for assessing knowledge generated by different research approaches. Therefore, it becomes necessary to get beyond the idea that knowledge is foundational and can be evaluated in an absolute way.

Different research approaches provide different interpretations of a phenomenon, and understand the phenomenon in a particular way. Some may be supporting a traditional view, others saying something new. In this way, knowledge is treated as being tentative rather than absolute.

All research approaches have something to contribute. The interaction among them may lead to synthesis, compromise, consensus, transformation, polarization, or simply clarification and improved understanding of differences. Such interaction, which is based on differences of viewpoints, is not concerned with reaching consensus or an end point that establishes a foundational truth. On the contrary, it is concerned with learning from the process itself, and to encourage the interaction to continue so long as disagreement lasts. Likewise, it is not concerned with producing uniformity, but promoting improved diversity.

Paradigm diversity is based on the idea that research is a creative process and that there are many ways of doing research. This approach leads to the development of knowledge in many different, and sometimes contradictory, directions such that new ways of knowing will emerge. There can be no objective criteria for choosing between alternative perspectives. The number of ways of generating new knowledge is bounded only by the ingenuity of researchers in inventing new approaches.[11]

The functionalist paradigm regards research as a technical activity and depersonalizes the research process. It removes responsibility from researchers and reduces them to agents engaged in what the institutionalized research demands.

Paradigm diversity reorients the role of researchers and places responsibility for the conduct and consequences of research directly with them. Researchers examine the nature of their activity to choose an appropriate approach and develop the capacity

---

11 For example, Dalton was not a chemist, but he was a meteorologist. Partly because his training was in a different specialty, he approached problems with a paradigm different from that of contemporary chemists. For instance, Galileo was not trained as an Aristotelian, but in the tradition of scholastics.

to observe and question what they are doing, and take responsibility for making intelligent choices that are open to realize the many potential types of knowledge.

To implement paradigm diversity, some fundamental changes need to be directed to the way research is presently managed in academic finance. In other words, paradigm diversity implies and requires changes. The most fundamental change is to understand the multifaceted nature of finance as a phenomenon. This, in turn, will diversify theories, Ph.D. programs, journals, and conferences.

An understanding of paradigms provides a valuable means for exploring the nature of the phenomenon being investigated. Furthermore, an understanding of other paradigms provides an invaluable basis for recognizing what one is doing.

Contemporary finance Ph.D. programs are dominated by the requirements of methodology or technique. In comparison, the need to understand the multifaceted nature of finance is given close to no attention.

The editorial policy followed by academic finance journals and academic finance conferences hinder the development of new styles of research. To facilitate the innovation and risk-taking necessary to undertake other research perspectives, such restrictive policies need to be relaxed.

The rest of this section, therefore, considers theories, examines Ph.D. programs, investigates journals, and discusses conferences, all in the light of paradigm diversity, its implications, and requirements.

Theories

All theories of finance are based on a philosophy of science and a theory of society. Many theorists appear to be unaware of, or ignore, the paradigmatic assumptions underlying finance theories. They emphasize only some aspects of the phenomenon, and ignore others. Unless they bring out the paradigmatic assumptions which underlie the theories, their analysis can be misleading; since by emphasizing differences between theories, they imply diversity in approach.

A prime example is Frankfurter who stated: "... I came across Karl Popper's book, ... Thomas Kuhn and some other philosophers of science. ... Having read these materials, I realized that, for twenty or so years, after quantitative publications, I actually did not know what I was doing except imitating other people." (Frankfurter, Carleton, Gordon, Horrigan, McGoun, Philippatos, and Robinson 1994, pp. 190–191). The point of this example becomes more prominent when one notes that George M. Frankfurter at the time was the Lloyd F. Collette professor of financial services at the College of Business Administration at Louisiana State University in Baton Rouge. He has been a member of the editorial board an editor of several finance journals.

While there appear to be different kinds of theories in mainstream academic finance, they are founded only on the functionalist paradigm. This becomes evident when these theories are related to the wider context of social theory. Despite the apparent diversity in theories, the issues which separate them are of minor significance. The larger issues are rarely discussed, lying hidden beneath the commonality of perspectives and assumptions.

With the above in mind, the rest of this subsection looks at the other three paradigms and a sample of their research.

Interpretive paradigm   The interpretive paradigm regards mainstream academic finance theorists as belonging to a small and self-sustaining community which believes that corporations and financial markets exist in a concrete world. They theorize about concepts which have little significance to people outside the community, which practices financial theory, and the limited community which financial theorists may attempt to serve.

Mainstream academic finance theorists tend to treat their subject of study as a hard, concrete and tangible empirical phenomenon which exists "out there" in the "real world." Interpretive researchers do not believe in such a structural absolutism. They emphasize that the social world is no more than the subjective construction of individual human beings who create and sustain a social world of intersubjectivity shared meaning, which is in a continuous process of reaffirmation or change. Therefore, there are no universally valid rules of finance and financial management. Interpretive finance research enables scientists to examine aggregate market behavior together with ethical, cultural, political, and social issues. Scientific knowledge is socially constructed and socially sustained; its significance and meaning can only be understood within its immediate social context.

An example is provided by McGoun:

> When we ask whether the CAPM is right or wrong we are assuming that there is some underlying reality there and that we can find out something about it. I would argue that reality, in this case, is really what we think it is—that if we all believe in the CAPM, it works; if we do not, it does not work. I feel the same thing about option pricing. If you look at the coincidence of the publication of the option-pricing formula, that sale of computers that actually have it programmed in, and the start of organized options exchanges, we really have to question whether we have explained something or whether we have created something. (Frankfurter, Carleton, Gordon, Horrigan, McGoun, Philippatos, and Robinson 1994, p. 201)

Interpretive research in finance is negligible compared to the functionalist research. The following lists examples of interpretive research, which are provided by Bettner, Robinson, and McGoun (1994): Baker (1992), Baker and Wruck (1989), Cray and Haines (1992), Frankfurter and Lane (1992), Kryzanowski and Roberts (1993a, 1993b), Lintner (1956), O'Barr and Conley (1992), and Rosen (1990).[12]

Radical humanist paradigm   The radical humanist paradigm in finance would seek to demonstrate the sources of alienation inherent within a totality, which converge in corporations and financial markets. It would provide a systematic critique by identifying the factors which impinge upon, and dominate, human consciousness in the form of seemingly objective social forces, over which man appears to have no

---

12 For description and further examples of interpretive research in finance, see Bettner, Robinson, and McGoun (1994) and the references cited therein.

form of direct control. Among the factors worthy of critique, the following would be accorded considerable importance:[13]

1. The concept of purposive rationality as the dominant and most valued mode of cognition within corporations and financial markets.
2. Rules and control systems which monitor the exercise of rational action.
3. Roles which constrain and confine human activities within narrowly defined limits.
4. The language used in corporations and financial markets.
5. The ideological mechanisms through which human beings are habituated to accept the roles, rules, and language used.
6. The worship of technology as a liberating force.
7. Reification, such as the concepts of: work, leisure, scarcity, and profitability, which serve to mystify the relationship between workers and the world in which they live.

The radical humanist paradigm assumes that reality is socially created and sustained. An example is provided by Tinker, Merino, and Neimark (1982):

> There are many examples that show scientific knowledge to be artifact rather than merely the outcome of a search for absolute truth. Breakthroughs in scientific theory frequently occur in times of crisis for a discipline or its underlying social system. For example, Edmund Burke's ideas came in response to the challenge of forces for democratization; Adam Smith's thought served as an important theoretical justification of laissez faire; Marxism was an attempt to provide an explanation of the more disturbing consequences of capitalism; marginal analysis was a counterblast to Marxism; Weber's bureaucratic theory can be viewed as a rationalization and, therefore, a theoretical justification of the contradictions of large-scale German monopolies operating within an environment of laissez-faire ideology; Keynesian economics was an intellectual and pragmatic response to the crisis of mass unemployment and the inability of neoclassical economics to locate the cause ... In a similar vein, the philosopher Wittgenstein has argued that even mathematical theory is better understood when viewed as an invention rather than just a discovery ... (pp. 172–173)

Radical humanist research in academic finance is non-existent. Examples of radical humanist research outside academic finance, although not even mentioned in academic finance, are: Biewener (1999, 2000), Cullenberg (1994, 1997, 2000), Perelman (1987, 1993, 1999), and Tinker, Merino, and Neimark (1982).

Radical structuralist paradigm The radical structuralist paradigm believes truth is the whole, and emphasizes the need to understand the social order as a totality rather than as a collection of small truths about various parts and aspects of society. The financial empiricists are seen as relying almost exclusively upon a number of

---

13 This part is taken from Burrell and Morgan (1979), pp. 316–325, and slightly changed to suit the field of finance.

seemingly disparate, data-packed, problem-centered studies. Such studies, therefore, are exercises in mathematical methods.

This paradigm is based on four central notions: totality, structure, contradiction, and crisis. Applied to the study of finance, these notions assume significance in the following ways.

Totality implies that corporations and financial markets can only be understood within the wider social formation in which they exist, and which they reflect.

Structure implies that corporations and financial markets are structural elements of a wider structure which they reflect and from which they derive their existence and true significance.

The notion of contradiction implies that it is in the corporations that the contradictions between the relations and the means of production, capital, and labor, are seen as working themselves out.

The notion of crisis implies that corporations and financial markets monitor and reflect the movement of totality from one crisis to another. Crisis of ownership and control and Wall Street crashes yield considerable insights into the nature of the social formation concerned.

These notions thus provide core concepts for radical finance theory in the tradition of the radical structuralist paradigm.

Radical structuralist research in academic finance is non-existent. The literature in this area but outside academic finance has been, historically, quite extensive, although there has been no mention of their existence in academic finance. Some examples of radical structuralist research are: Gill (1999), Magdoff and Sweezy (1987), Sweezy (1942, 1994, 1997), and Sweezy and Magdoff (1972).

Ph.D. Programs

Ph.D.s learn concepts, theories, and their applications, through education. These applications and others accompany the theory into the textbooks from which future students learn.

Students proceed from the early courses in the undergraduate program to the doctoral dissertation, and finally to their independent research careers. The problems assigned to them during years of education become more complex, and the problems encountered by them during years of independent research become less completely precedented. However, they are all modeled on theories learned earlier.

> The reality of academic work is that we make progress very slowly. Each decade, if we are lucky, there are one or two major innovations in the development of thought followed by a prodigious amount of secondary and tertiary effort to test and consolidate the implications of these ideas. Most academicians are like surfers who, with their shiny new doctoral surfboards tucked under them, paddle out in search of an intellectual wave created by a force outside themselves and who, with a host of others, will proceed to mount and ride the crest until the wave loses its energy and breaks as a gentle ripple on the shore of established thought. It is a sobering question to ask: How many of us ride more than one major wave in our academic lifetime? The wave of the past decade or more has, of course, been efficient market theory. (Gordon Donaldson 1978, pp. 9–10)

Through extensive education, most students obtain a vision similar to those of the educators, such that they see what the educators see and respond as they do.[14]

Students are expected to use textbooks during their years of extensive training in the Ph.D. program. Some educators, who assign supplementary reading of research papers, restrict such assignments to the most advanced courses, and to materials that take up, more or less, where the textbooks leave off. Until the very last stage in the education of a Ph.D., textbooks are systematically substituted for the creative scientific literature that made them possible.

Of course, it is a narrow education. This is because students are not made aware of the variety of problems that their predecessors attempted to solve. More importantly, they are not made aware of competing paradigms and theories and the solutions they provide to problems; solutions that these Ph.D. students must ultimately evaluate for themselves.

Researchers use theoretical models, acquired through education and exposure to literature, often without knowing what characteristics have given them their paradigmatic status. Researchers are usually well-versed in particular hypothesis that underlie their research. However, they are mostly incapable of characterizing the paradigmatic basis of their field.

Currently, Ph.D. programs in finance place their educational emphasis only on quantitative methods and economics. This takes place partially at the expense of any formal education in philosophy (although the doctorate is in philosophy), and partially at the expense of any formal education in alternative theories and research methods.

It is very rare to find a Ph.D. program in finance which deviates from the mainstream and shows interest in paradigm diversity. Exceptionally, York University in Toronto, Ontario, Canada, offers a very unique and multi-faceted Ph.D. program in finance, whose core courses, according to their Ph.D. Program calendar, not only include economics and quantitative methods, but also the following courses:[15]

Philosophy and Methods in Social Sciences: This course examines the major philosophical debates in the social sciences and explores the rationale of different approaches to social research. Students learn how to select and develop appropriate research strategies and how to critically examine the use of various research strategies.

Qualitative Methodology: This course provides students with detailed exposure to the qualitative research methodologies that have begun to exert a major influence on management research over the last ten years.

---

14 A physicist and a chemist were asked if a single particle of helium was a molecule. Their answers were different. The chemist viewed the atom of helium as a molecule because it behaved as per the kinetic theory of gases. The physicist regarded the helium atom not as a molecule, because it displayed no molecular spectrum. Both of them talked about the same particle, but they were viewing it through their own research training and practice.

15 Chris Robinson of York University stated: "By the way, my Ph.D. program does have courses in philosophy and qualitative research." Frankfurter, Carleton, Gordon, Horrigan, McGoun, Philippatos, and Robinson (1994), p. 186.

Practicum in Research Writing Skills: This is designed to equip students with improved skills in converting their research into formal publications. The emphasis is on examining good practice in different kinds of research (e.g. quantitative and qualitative) and on helping students to acquire key skills. The practicum is offered on a non-credit basis.

Practicum in Teaching Skills: This optional Practicum is available to Ph.D. students who wish to improve their teaching skills. The Practicum introduces students to the University Teaching Practicum offered by the Faculty of Graduate Studies' Center for the Support of Teaching. This Practicum gives students intensive hands-on training in the practice and analysis of university teaching.

Journals

The state of the art of finance is reflected, to a large extent, in its journal literature. Since this literature plays a crucial role in determining the direction and nature of research, it becomes important to examine the consequences of journal editorial policy with respect to the evaluation of research.

Journal publication, is used as a measure of research productivity, and is the single most important performance evaluation criterion in academic finance, whether it is used for: (1) desirability of Ph.D. graduates as job applicants, (2) salary determination, tenure, promotion, evaluation, mobility, recognition of faculty members, (3) prestige, recognition, ranking of doctoral programs and academic finance departments, or (4) research funding. In other words, journal publication is the hallmark of academic success, which creates visibility and is rewarded within the discipline.[16]

Finance journal editorial policy starts with the view that defines knowledge as the outcome of functionalist research. Therefore, there is a tendency for the criteria, traditionally used to evaluate functionalist research, to be used in the evaluation of other research. Non-functionalist research is often viewed with skepticism because the approaches and methods adopted are deemed unscientific. This foundational view hampers the development of other research approaches, which seek to produce other kinds of knowledge. Different research approaches may be different in nature and require different criteria for their evaluation. These conflicts may be rooted in different views about the nature of scientific inquiry and scientific knowledge.

More specifically, functionalists in search of generalizable, objective knowledge, require research to be systematic, comparative, replicative observation and measurement. This approach to evaluation of research takes the rules for conducting it as the rules of the evaluation of knowledge. Therefore, research designs that do

---

16 See Bertin and Zivney (1991, 1992), Borokhovich, Bricker, Brunarski, Simkins (1995), Bures and Tong (1993), Cheng and Davidson III (1995), Cooley and Heck (1981), Ederington (1979), Ehrenberg and Hurst (1996), Frankfurter and McGoun (1996b), Heck and Cooley (1988), Heck, Cooley, and Hubbard (1986), Klemkosky and Tuttle (1977a, 1977b), Niemi (1987), Petry and Fuller (1978), Pettijohn, Udell, and Parker (1991), Schweser (1977), Sweetser and Petry (1981), Tripathy and Ganesh (1996), Tompkins, Hermanson, and Hermanson (1996), Tompkins, Nathan, Hermanson, and Hermanson (1997), and Zivney and Bertin (1992).

not adhere to the functionalist standards of the detached, neutral observer may not be fairly judged. This is because they seek different kinds of insights, adopt different methodologies, and require different criteria for evaluation of their research.

Different paradigms use different research designs and generate different kinds of knowledge. They deserve to be evaluated by their respective appropriate criteria. This requires a change in the process of evaluation such that it supplements the purely technical considerations of functionalists, with considerations that recognize that the significance of knowledge is not merely technical, but ideological, political, ethical, and moral as well.

The foregoing suggests that it may be necessary to modify the journal editorial policy with respect to the evaluative process of research. Journals have two basic choices with respect to their primary function. The first choice is to perform a quality control function, designed to regulate the direction of developments in their field. The second choice is to contribute to the promotion of open inquiry, dialogue, and debate. If they choose the former, they publish specialist journals with a defined domain, for which technical evaluative criteria may be applied. If they choose the latter, they open themselves to paradigm diversity, and commit to preserve variety in the field. A rare example is The International Review of Financial Analysis, which uniquely defines its "aims and scope" as follows:

> The International Review of Financial Analysis is dedicated to the highest professional standards whose primary goal is the advancement of the field of finance. This is accomplished by giving the opportunity to researchers in the field to communicate with others. We are independent, both economically and ideologically, of school, geography, methodology, or any other categorization that may create a selection bias of the material we publish. The only yardstick of acceptance of articles for publication is academic quality. We advocate dialogue, criticism and inquiry, especially in issues of controversy. Our reviewing process is careful, constructive, and accountable. We regard the contributor-researcher as the fundamental, sine qua non building block of the scholastic discourse we mean to serve.

"To move ahead, we must all adopt a more flexible attitude with less emphasis on argument and more on open-minded analysis." Findlay and Williams (1980), p.16.

Conferences

Academic associations publish journals and are the major players in organizing annual conferences. On the academic side, in these conferences, researchers present papers which are in their developmental stage. Papers, for presentation, come under scrutiny by conference organizers applying almost the same evaluative criteria as papers submitted to journals for publication. Therefore, the discussion in the previous subsection, with respect to journals, is to a large extent applicable here as well.

In contrast to the other academic finance conferences, which adhere to the functionalist paradigm, there is a unique, "non-mainstream" conference, which advocates paradigm diversity. It is organized under the title "Alternative Perspective on Finance." It encourages research based on alternative paradigms. The call for papers for their conferences contains the following opening paragraph:

We invite papers on finance that use alternative views and modes of investigation—behavioral, social, critical, legal, historical, and philosophical. The prevailing academic discourse rejects ideas that do not conform to a rigid set of rationalist assumptions. We hope to broaden the dialogue in finance by encouraging research that is interdisciplinary or that challenges the prevailing views. Paradigms from other disciplines and fresh evidence from non-traditional sources can lead to greater understanding of old problems.

In summary, this section discussed the principles of paradigm diversity, its implications, and requirements. It discussed points of view advocated by the other three paradigms. It noted instances of paradigm diversity in theories, Ph.D. programs, journals, and conferences in finance. It pointed out that they are exclusively underwritten by the other three paradigms, and are considered non-mainstream by academic finance. The paper emphasized that academic finance could benefit from contributions by other paradigms. This would entail some fundamental changes in current perspective held by mainstream academic finance.

Conclusion

This chapter examined theories, Ph.D. programs, journals, and conferences in mainstream academic finance. It noted that they adhere, almost exclusively, to the functionalist paradigm. Moreover, the chapter discussed the principles of paradigm diversity, its implications, and requirements. It noted instances of paradigm diversity in theories, Ph.D. programs, journals, and conferences in finance. It concluded that without some fundamental changes, there would be less opportunity for mainstream academic finance to benefit from contributions of the other three paradigms.

Knowledge of finance is ultimately a product of the researcher's paradigmatic approach to this multifaceted phenomenon. Viewed from this angle, the pursuit of financial knowledge is seen as much an ethical, moral, ideological, and political activity, as a technical one. Academic finance can gain much by exploiting the new insights coming from other paradigms.

Appendix 1

This appendix shows the text of the letter sent to the Ph.D. Program Directors of all the US universities that offered Ph.D. programs in business. The list was derived from "The Official Guide to MBA Programs," as the guide also indicated which universities offer Ph.D. programs in business.

Ph.D. Program Director

Dear Senior Colleague:

As part of my research, I am doing a study of Ph.D. programs in business with concentration in finance. The information that I need is the Ph.D. program design and requirements, core courses, finance area courses, and the description of courses. For most universities this information is provided in the Ph.D. Program Calendar.

I very much appreciate if you arrange for the provision of the necessary information.

Sincerely yours,
Kavous Ardalan

Appendix 2

This appendix lists the universities with Ph.D. programs in business. This list is obtained from "The Official Guide to MBA Programs." A letter of request, for the provision of information regarding their Ph.D. program design and requirements, core courses, and finance area courses, was sent to the attention of the Ph.D. Program Director of each institution. The letter stated that the information is for a study of the Ph.D. programs in business, with concentration in finance. Universities which neither replied to the request, nor provided sufficient information, nor offered a Ph.D. program in finance, are marked with an asterisk.

Alabama.
1.   Auburn University *
2.   University of Alabama
Arizona.
3.   Arizona State University
4.   University of Arizona *
Arkansas:
5.   University of Arkansas *
California:
6.   Claremont Graduate School *
7.   Stanford University
8.   United States International University *
9.   University of California, Berkeley *
10.   University of California, Irvine
11.   University of California, Los Angeles *
12.   University of Southern California
Colorado:
13.   University of Colorado *
Connecticut:
14.   University of Connecticut
15.   Yale University
District of Columbia:
16.   The George Washington University
Florida:
17.   Florida Atlantic University *
18.   Florida International University

19.   Florida State University
20.   Nova Southeastern University
21.   University of Central Florida *
22.   University of Florida
23.   University of Miami *
24.   University of South Florida
Georgia:
25.   Georgia Institute of Technology
26.   Georgia State University
27.   University of Georgia
Illinois:
28.   Illinois Institute of Technology *
29.   Northwestern University
30.   Southern Illinois University at Carbondale *
31.   University of Chicago *
32.   University of Illinois at Chicago *
33.   University of Illinois at Urbana-Champaign
Indiana:
34.   Indiana University *
35.   Purdue University *
Iowa:
36.   Maharishi International University *
37.   University of Iowa
Kansas:
38.   The University of Kansas
Kentucky:
39.   University of Kentucky
Louisiana:
40.   Louisiana State University
41.   Tulane University
42.   University of New Orleans
Maryland:
43.   Loyola College in Maryland *
44.   University of Maryland
Massachusetts:
45.   American International College *
46.   Massachusetts Institute of Technology
Michigan:
47.   Michigan State University *
48.   The University of Michigan *
Minnesota:
49.   University of Minnesota
Mississippi:
50.   Mississippi State University
51.   University of Mississippi

Missouri:
52.   Saint Louis University *
53.   University of Missouri-Columbia
54.   Washington University
Nebraska:
55.   University of Nebraska-Lincoln
New Jersey:
56.   Rutgers, The State University of New Jersey
57.   Stevens Institute of Technology *
New Mexico:
58.   New Mexico State University *
New York:
59.   Columbia University
60.   Cornell University
61.   Pace University *
62.   Rensselar Polytechnic Institute
63.   Syracuse University
64.   Union College *
65.   University at Albany (SUNY) *
66.   University at Buffalo (SUNY)
67.   University of Rochester
North Carolina:
68.   Duke University
69.   University of North Carolina at Chapel Hill *
Ohio:
70.   Case Western Reserve University *
71.   Cleveland State University
72.   Kent State University
73.   Ohio State University
74.   University of Cincinnati *
Oklahoma:
75.   Oklahoma State University
76.   University of Oklahoma
Oregon:
77.   Portland State University
78.   University of Oregon
Pennsylvania:
79.   Carnegie Mellon University
80.   Drexel University *
81.   Lehigh University *
82.   Penn State University Park Campus
83.   Temple University
84.   University of Pittsburgh
85.   University of Pennsylvania
Rhode Island:
86.   University of Rhode Island *

South Carolina:
87.   University of South Carolina
Tennessee:
88.   Memphis State University *
89.   University of Tennessee, Knoxville
90.   Vanderbilt University
Texas:
91.   Texas A&M University
92.   Texas Tech University *
93.   University of Houston
94.   University of North Texas
95.   University of Texas at Arlington
96.   University of Texas at Austin
97.   University of Texas at Dallas
Utah:
98.   University of Utah
Virginia:
99.   George Mason University *
100.   Old Dominion University
101.   University of Virginia
Washington:
102.   University of Washington
103.   Washington State University
Wisconsin:
104.   University of Wisconsin-Madison
105.   University of Wisconsin-Milwaukee

Chapter 3

Structure of Academic Finance Paradigm

This chapter focuses on one paradigm, discusses its structure, and relates it to the controversies within the paradigm. It builds on the previous chapter which examined paradigms, emphasized their diversity, and showed that the functionalist paradigm forms the context of the mainstream academic finance.

The hierarchical structure of paradigms consists of three consecutive levels: paradigm, metaphor, and puzzle solving. Theories and controversies in mainstream academic finance, despite their apparent diversity, are founded on the functionalist paradigm and are associated with its metaphor level.

Structure of a Paradigm

The hierarchical structure of a paradigm consists of three consecutive levels: paradigm; metaphor; and puzzle solving. (See Figure 3.1).[1]

Paradigm can be regarded the same as worldview, or way of seeing reality. It refers to both implicit and explicit views of reality. Paradigms are defined and characterized by a set of fundamental assumptions, which, in turn, translate into certain rules and standards for scientific practice. These are common among the theorists and researchers who share the same paradigm, although their work may appear different and sometimes at odds with each other.

Paradigms provide researchers not only with a map but also with directions essential for map-making. Since, in learning a paradigm the researcher acquires theories, methods, and standards together, in a cohesive manner.

Paradigms or worldviews consist of different schools of thought. These are different ways of studying a shared reality. Schools of thought accept and use special metaphors in their studies. The network of commitments—conceptual, theoretical, and methodological—is the principal source of the metaphor[2] that relates paradigm to puzzle solving. Because it provides rules that tell the researchers what both the world and their science are like, they can concentrate with assurance upon the problems that these rules and existing knowledge define for them.

---

1 See Morgan (1980) for a discussion of paradigms, metaphors, and puzzle solving.

2 For discussions and examples of metaphors in finance, such as: "abnormal return," "market for corporate control," and "signaling," see Bettner, Robinson, and McGoun (1994) and Frankfurter and McGoun (1993, 1995). For discussions and examples of other metaphors, such as "efficiency," "system," "asset pricing," "equilibrium," "structure," "hierarchy," "work," "leisure," "scarcity," and "profitability," see Burrell and Morgan (1979) and Morgan (1980).

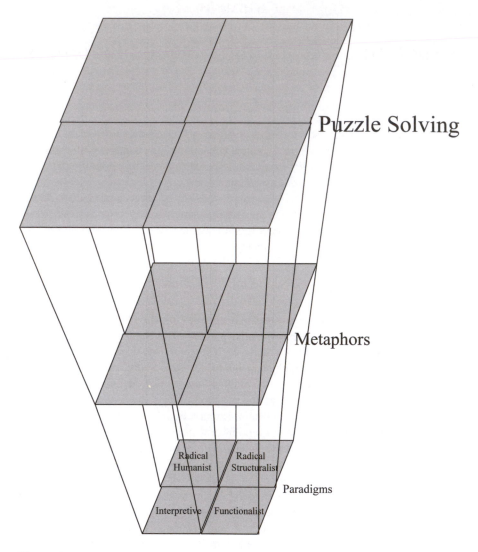

Figure 3.1   The Structure of a Paradigm

A metaphor creatively produces a crossing of images. It plays an important role in the way human beings conceive conceptions about their reality and, therefore, in the development of the social and natural sciences. In the process of scientific inquiry, scientists view the world metaphorically. This is accomplished through the choice of metaphors. Schools of thought are based on the insights associated with different metaphors as the logic of metaphor has important implications for the process of theory construction.

A metaphor serves to generate an image for studying a subject. This image provides the basis for detailed scientific research that attempts to discover the extent to which features of the metaphor are found in the subject of inquiry. Much of the puzzle-solving activity of scientists is of this kind. They attempt to examine, operationalize, and measure detailed implications of the metaphorical insight upon which their research is implicitly or explicitly based. Different metaphors capture the nature of the subject of study in different ways. Each generates distinctive, but essentially partial insight. New metaphors create new ways of viewing the subject of study that overcome the weaknesses of traditional metaphors. They offer supplementary or even contradictory approaches to the analysis of the subject of study.

At the puzzle-solving level of analysis, research activities seek to operationalize the detailed implications of the metaphor defining a particular school of thought. Schools of thought, at their puzzle-solving level, get involved with detailed analysis of specific phenomena or problems, and use specific models and tools. Resolution of a research problem requires the solution of all sorts of complex puzzles. The rules and standards defined by the paradigm limit both the nature of acceptable solutions and the steps by which they are to be obtained. The current theoretical and empirical researches in academic finance, and most of their consequent debates and controversies, are at this level.

Controversies in Finance

Theories and controversies in mainstream academic finance, despite their apparent diversity, are founded on the functionalist paradigm and are associated with its metaphor level.

This section considers two metaphors and brings out current controversies about them. These controversies are about two of the assumptions in mainstream academic finance. The first controversy is related to a relatively new idea, proposed by behavioral finance, which has challenged the assumption of rationality. The second controversy is related to another assumption of the mainstream finance which has been brought into question, namely the goal of share-value maximization.

Rationality

Behavioral finance is perhaps the most controversial area in mainstream finance. Current finance theories are based on the assumption that economic agents are expected utility maximizers. The agents have rational expectations, and non-economic factors do not enter their utility functions. Behavioral finance states that not all economic decisions can be explained by such a model.

Thaler (1993) is a collection of 21 articles, selected from the existing work in behavioral finance. In the introduction he writes:

> There is an interesting contrast between the academic discipline of financial economics and the coverage the field receives on the nightly newscast. ... The image one gets from the news is that financial markets are dominated by people. In contrast, a reading of a standard textbook ... can create the impression that financial markets are merely computing important numbers such as present values and rates of return, an analysis of risk and how it is priced, much discussion of how much a firm should borrow and how

much it should pay out in dividends ... and even a primer on how to price options. But virtually no people. (Thaler 1993, p. xv)

In response to the question: "What is behavioral finance?" Thaler states:

> I think of behavioral finance as simply "open-minded finance." Sometimes, in order to find the solution to an empirical puzzle, it is necessary to entertain the possibility that some of the agents in the economy behave less than fully rationally some of the time. Any financial economist willing to consider this possibility seriously is ready to take a try at behavioral finance. (Thaler 1993, p. xvii)

Thaler closes the introduction by:

> What are the main conclusions to be drawn from this collection? I would suggest two. First, it is possible to do good economic research even if the assumption of universal rationality is relaxed. Second, we can understand much more about the behavior of markets, even financial markets, if we learn more about the behavior of the people who operate in these markets. (Thaler 1993, p. xxi)

Shiller raises one of the most controversial issues in Thaler (1993). In financial economics, there exists a heated debate around the empirical findings of, and theoretical proposal made, by Shiller. Following the empirical works of LeRoy and Porter (1981), Shiller (1981, 1984) finds further confirmation that; observed stock price movements greatly exceed those consistent with rationally forecasted future cash flows, and concludes that; mass psychology may well be the dominant cause of movements in the price of the aggregate stock market. In this way, the well-established stock valuation model, and its underpinnings, that is rationality and efficient market hypotheses, are challenged.

Shiller (1984) proposes a radical change in the behavioral assumptions underlying economic models of stock price:

> Investing in speculative assets is a social activity. Investors spend a substantial part of their leisure time discussing investments, reading about investments, or gossiping about others' successes or failures in investing. It is thus plausible that investor's behavior (and hence prices of speculative assets) would be influenced by social movements. Attitudes or fashions seem to fluctuate in many other popular topics of conversation, such as food, clothing, health, or politics. These fluctuations in attitude often occur widely in the population and often appear without any apparent logical reason. It is plausible that attitudes of fashions regarding investments would also change spontaneously or in arbitrary social reaction to some widely noted events. (Shiller 1984, p. 457)

The matter is still in debate. The empirical finding of Shiller (1984) has been under careful review, and has been criticized by the proponents of the established view. Moreover, it has been claimed that Shiller's proposal is not capable of competing with the existing theory on the grounds that it cannot explain what the existing theory already explains.

Share Value Maximization

In August 1992, *Capital Choices*, a report published by Professor Michael Porter and 25 other academics, stated that US firms are too shortsighted in their investment decisions. It considers over-emphasis on stock prices and shareholder returns as the flaw in the American corporate governance system. Theoretically, the assumption of share value maximization, as the goal of the financial manager, is questioned. In this section, representative views in this debate are presented. Merton Miller supports the existing assumption, and C.K. Prahalad opposes it.

Merton Miller believes:

... in a US-style stock market, focusing on current *stock* prices is no short-termism ... stock prices, which reflect not just today's earnings, but the earnings the market expects in all future years as well. (Miller 1994, p. 33)

... the complaint ... is ... that ... ownership of American corporations is so widely dispersed ..., US managers ... are left free to pursue objectives that may, but need not, conform to those of the stockholders. (Miller 1994, p. 35)

Shareholders, however, are not powerless ... shareholders do have the right to elect the company's Board of Directors. And the Board, in turn, by its power to unseat management, and ... to design the program for executive compensation, has command ... for aligning management's objectives with those of the shareholders. (Miller 1994, p. 36)

... market forces are constantly at work to remove control over corporate assets from managers who lack the competence or the vision to deploy them efficiently. (Miller 1994, p. 39)

C.K. Prahalad, on the other hand, believes:

The finance literature assumes that the *primary market discipline* on top managers comes from the capital market. (Prahalad 1994, p. 45)

But the world has changed, ... the services of stakeholder groups such as consumers, employees, and suppliers now each deserve to be regarded as trading in a separate "market" in its own right, ... key stakeholders, like capital markets, also impose a unique set of internal disciplines on firms. (Prahald 1994, p. 45)

Creating wealth for investors through efficient use of capital depends critically on management's ability to manage the disciplines of the product market (imposed by sophisticated customers around the world), the labor market (specialized talent), and the technology market (specialist suppliers). (Prahalad 1994, p. 46)

The above two subsections provided two examples of the current prominent controversies in mainstream academic finance. Other examples, such as controversies on the efficient market and the capital asset pricing theories, are Haugen (1995) and Shanken and Smith (1996), who provide two alternate views. These and other controversies in main stream academic finance are the natural outcome of the progress within a paradigm. They are all based on the same basic and fundamental assumptions which define the paradigm.

Brav and Heaton (2000) show that both the "rational finance" and the "behavioral finance" despite their differing theoretical foundations, they share remarkable mathematical and predictive similarities and differ mainly in the labels they attach to similar modeling techniques and in the interpretations they give to resulting predictions. Furthermore, they use similar metaphors which are the products of the same paradigm. Even when these different schools of thought tend to debate each other's metaphors, they do not debate the fundamental assumptions of their common paradigm. This paradigm, as discussed in previous chapter by reference to Bettner, Robinson, and McGoun (1994), is the functionalist paradigm. In other words, theories and controversies in mainstream academic finance, despite their apparent diversity, are founded on the functionalist paradigm.

Conclusion

Any adequate analysis of the role of paradigms, in social theory, must recognize the assumptions that underwrite that paradigm or worldview. Social theory can usefully be conceived in terms of four key paradigms: functionalist, interpretive, radical humanist, and radical structuralist. The four paradigms are founded upon different views of the social world. Each generates theories, concepts, analytical tools, and controversies which are different from those of the other paradigms.

Most mainstream academic finance theories are located within the bounds of the functionalist paradigm. They leave the other paradigms unexplored. Despite the apparent diversity in theories, the issues, which separate them, are of minor significance. The larger issues are rarely discussed, lying hidden beneath the commonality of perspectives and assumptions.

Knowledge of finance is ultimately a product of the researcher's paradigmatic approach to this multifaceted phenomenon. Viewed from this angle, the pursuit of financial knowledge is seen as much an ethical, moral, ideological, and political activity, as a technical one. Academic finance can gain much by exploiting the new insights coming from other paradigms.

Chapter 4

Methodology of Academic Finance Paradigm

Any adequate analysis of the relationship between paradigms and research methodologies must recognize the assumptions that underwrite that paradigm or worldview. Social theory can usefully be conceived in terms of four key paradigms: functionalist, interpretive, radical humanist, and radical structuralist. The four paradigms are founded upon mutually exclusive views of the social world. Each generates theories, methodologies, concepts, and analytical tools which are different from those of other paradigms.[1]

This chapter shows that the adherence of the academic finance to the functionalist paradigm and the use of scientific methodology would most likely produce the divergence between research and practice, whereas the other three paradigms use other methodologies which tend to more closely relate research and practice. To do this, the chapter takes the interpretive paradigm, as an example, and compares its research methodology (that is, clinical methodology) with that of the functionalist paradigm (that is, scientific methodology).

This chapter also notes that academic finance has begun to utilize clinical approach in its research. The extent of its appropriate use is a serious point for consideration. This chapter examines how mainstream functionalist finance intends to use the interpretive clinical approach in its research. While this step toward a more balanced approach to research in finance is appreciated, the chapter points out that clinical approach can be more appropriately used when certain fundamental, contextual, paradigmatic assumptions are met.

Research-versus-Practice Controversy

The research-versus-practice debate in mainstream academic finance has been a topic for discussion, both in the past and present. However, there has been no fundamental account of the underpinnings of such a debate.

More specifically, there was a heated debate in the not too distant past. This has been captured by Kavesh (1970) in his address to the American Finance Association, which was made with reference to exchanges between Sauvain, Durand, and Weston. Kavesh (1970) stated:

---

1 This chapter borrows heavily from the ideas and insights of Burrell and Morgan (1979) and Morgan (1983, 1985) and applies them to finance. The main purpose of this paper is not so much to generate a new piece of puzzle as it is to put the existing pieces of puzzle together in order to make sense of them.

But disciplines change, new thinking evolves, controversies flair. In finance ... The early years were filled with descriptive articles ... Slowly, the mathematical and model-building revolution was revealed ... And feelings (pro and con) ran high. Balance and perspective were sought then—and are sought now—but to many it was the battle between the "new" vs. "old" finance. (p. 5)

Sauvain (1967) encouraged balance and cooperation between the "new" and "old" finance. Durand (1968) believed that the "new" finance is more interested in demonstrating its mathematical power than solving genuine practical problems. Weston (1967), based on the development of finance since the end of the World War II, predicted an increasing ratio of analytical-theoretical materials with quantitative testing of models to studies dealing with institutions and instruments.

More recent debates continue along the same line. Some scholars are not totally satisfied with the "new" finance. Findlay and Williams (1985) are critical of the real-world decision making implications of the "new" finance and note that finance practitioners are ever more inclined to employ "theoretical" as antonym for "practical" or "useful." Gordon (1996) and Frankfurter and Lane (1992) are critical of the explanatory power of finance theories and believe that the "new" finance theories do not explain anything, but they just say that there are imperfections. Frankfurter and Wood (1995) advise that the "new" finance should consider finance as a cultural phenomenon rather than to expend efforts in mathematical model building.

Merton (1995), in support of the "new" finance, states that the mathematical models of finance have had a direct and significant influence on the practice of finance.

The debate still continues.[2] A fair examination of this debate necessarily should uncover their underlying worldviews and their fundamental assumptions.

In order to understand the role of paradigms in research methodology, it is necessary to understand the relationship between specific modes of research and the worldviews that they reflect. Research methodologies in finance, as in other social sciences, are linked directly to assumptions that characterize and define their underlying worldviews.

A research methodology,[3] whether scientific or clinical,[4] cannot be considered in the abstract. Any methodology embodies assumptions regarding; the nature of the phenomenon to be investigated, the nature of knowledge, and the methods through which that knowledge can be obtained. Therefore, it is necessary to examine methodology within this wider and deeper context in order to develop a framework within which the consequences of the adoption of different methodologies might be inferred.

---

2 See, for example, Aggarwal (1993), Frankfurter, Carleton, Gordon, Horrigan, McGoun, Philippatos, and Robinson (1994), Gitman (1992), Heaton (1992), Molbey and Kuniasky (1992a, 1992b), and Weaver (1993).

3 Since the focus of this section is on the methodologies of functionalist and interpretive paradigms, it will restrict attention to the interpretive and functionalist paradigms. A full discussion of research practices should also consider perspectives characteristic of the radical humanist and radical structuralist paradigms.

4 Of course, this is an oversimplified dichotomization.

Different worldviews provide different basis for knowledge. As assumptions change, along the subjective-objective continuum of the scheme presented earlier, the nature of what constitutes knowledge changes.[5] For instance, the extreme objectivist view of the social world, as a concrete structure, encourages an emphasis on studying the nature of relationships among the elements constituting the structure. Knowledge of the social world implies a need to understand the social structure, which gives rise to scientific methodology, which emphasizes the empirical analysis of concrete relationships in an external social world. It encourages an objective form of knowledge, which specifies the precise nature of laws, regularities, and relationships among phenomena measured in terms of social facts.

At the other extreme, the highly subjectivist view of reality emphasizes the processes through which human beings concretize their relationship to their world. This perspective challenges the idea that there can be any form of objective knowledge, which can be specified and transmitted in a tangible form. This is because the knowledge, thus created, is often no more than an expression of the manner in which the scientist, as a human being, has arbitrarily imposed a personal frame of reference on the world, which is mistakenly perceived as lying in an external and separate world.

The bases for what constitutes knowledge in each of these perspectives are totally different, because of the fundamentally different social reality to which they adhere.

The scientific methodology, which is also used in natural sciences, is appropriate when the social world is viewed as a concrete structure. By analyzing large sets of data through sophisticated quantitative approaches, social scientists are, in effect, viewing the social world as a concrete structure, and human beings' character formed by a deterministic set of forces. They believe the social world can be objectively measured, and they can reveal the nature of that world by examining lawful relations between elements which, for the sake of accurate definition and measurement, have to be abstracted from their context.

The clinical methodology[6] relaxes the assumption that the social world is a concrete structure, and believes that human beings, not only respond to the social world, but also actively contribute to its creation. It views the social world as an open-ended process, and, therefore, any method that focuses its approach on a laboratory, or narrow empirical snapshots of isolated phenomena at fixed points in time, limits its view of the nature of the subject. A different methodology is required for studying these phenomena, and most often they focus on qualitative, rather than quantitative, aspects of the subject of study. Quantitative techniques may have an important, but partial, role to play in social science; and their appropriateness comes under closer scrutiny in the more subjectivist positions on the subjective-objective continuum. In these situations, scientists can no longer remain an external observer, measuring what they see; they must investigate the subject from within, and apply a research methodology appropriate to the situation.

---

5 The transition from one perspective to another is a gradual one, and often the advocates of a certain position incorporate insights from others.

6 For classic works, see Berg and Smith (1985) and Taylor and Bogdan (1984).

Clinical methodology is based on the idea that knowledge and understanding are context bound. It approaches research problems from within the social phenomena, by making explicit essential dimensions of a social process. On the other side, the scientific methodology studies phenomena from without. Consequently, it imposes a definition on the subject of study and postulates hypothetical relationships. In this way, it defines the problem of study such that the researcher is in control. It suggests that obtaining knowledge depends on the adequacy of theory and methodology, rather than the nature of the phenomenon being studied.

Clinical research states that such techniques are distanced from the reality they study. That is, the methodologies or theories have priority over how members create social reality in practice. Such methodologies are defended on the grounds that they are scientific and verifiable. But, theories and research methodologies have their own internal logic, which is imposed on the situation and constitutes what is scientific. Thus, the understanding, or knowledge achieved, may be more an artifact of the theory or methodology than the reality observed. This problem is part of all research, including that based on clinical methodology. However, clinical methodology, in using the "meaning structure of individuals" as the research base, does less harm to the reality observed. The social world is not viewed as a concrete structure against which theory can be examined. Observations of social reality are not neutral to fit some *a priori* theory, because they carry as much knowledge-related weight as the observer's construction.

Clinical methodology regards theories as being exploratory instruments that have no priority over the social phenomenon observed. The researcher formally reconstructs the social phenomenon that captures the themes of the situation and the way they are created by members. Often this involves a deep understanding of the logic in use, which requires a methodology that avoids damaging the member's explanation. The analysis should accommodate the clinical scheme used by those studied, while recognizing the researcher's own influence on the situation. The researcher's involvement in a situation, as interviewer or participant, for example, influences the definition of the situation. This is because; the researcher brings theories and interpretive schemes both as a scientist and a member of the situation. Over time, the concepts used by social scientists become a part of the concepts used by members of the situation. Thus, in the same way actor's logic forms a part of the analysis, so do the standards and concepts used by the researcher, both as a participant and a scientist.

Clinical methodology regards science as a process of interaction. Scientists interact with the subject of study through their paradigm, its protocol, and technique. What they observe in, and understand from the object, is as much a product of such interaction as it is of the object itself. Moreover, since it is possible to engage an object of study in different ways, the same object is capable of yielding different kinds of knowledge.

The selection of an actual methodology implies some view of the situation being studied. This is because; any decision on how to study a phenomenon embodies certain assumptions about what is being studied.

The methodology traditionally favored in the study of social sciences is called scientific. It is based on its paradigmatic assumptions, and therefore is committed to the method of observation.

The scientific methodology consists of the following five principal stages:[7]

1. Observation,
2. Theory building,
3. Hypothesis: systematic doubt,
4. Experimental framework/design, and
5. Test: rejection, reformulation, or confirmation of the theory.

The scientific methodology begins with the observation of phenomenon. It is based on the idea that the researcher observes what is "out there." Reality is the source of ideas, which is the basis for the development of theory. This is the process which is called theory building. The scientist makes sense of what is observed "out there" in the "real world."

The theory often starts as a very broad idea, which is rather imprecise. In the next stage, the scientist comes up with a hypothesis, or a set of hypotheses, which translates the theory into a testable form.

A hypothesis should have the crucial property of being refutable, that is, the possibility that it is untrue. In other words, the development of a hypothesis is based on "systematic doubt," which is crucial for the scientific process. Without bringing doubt on research, it is not scientific. Scientists should try to refute, or disprove, their favored theory, perhaps not to reject it altogether, but to proceed in terms of a methodological process of rejection, reformulation, or confirmation of the theory.

The test of a hypothesis is based on the specification of the hypothesis in a testable form, so that it can be refuted. The testing, based on systematic doubt, leads to the rejection or confirmation of the hypothesis. But, to be scientific, confirmation should not be sought, but should come through the process of attempting to reject. This process is an open one: when the hypothesis is not confirmed, it is reformulated, which, in turn, may lead to the reformulation of the theory. In other words, the results of the experiments may lead to the recommencement of the process.

The scientific methodology is an iterative process. It begins with stage 1, goes through the various steps to stage 5, and then goes back to stages 2 or 1. This is to obtain an improved understanding of the subject of study.

The model presented above represents a scientific methodology. Its aim is to generate ever better descriptions and explanations of reality.

The clinical methodology consists of the following five stages:[8]

---

7 See Morgan (1983), chapters 3–6, and Morgan (1985).
8 See Morgan (1983), chapters 9–11, and Morgan (1985).

1. Get inside: get deeply involved in the situation,
2. Adopt the role of a learner,
3. Map the system of symbols and their meanings,
4. Identify key themes and explanations, and
5. Test against opinion in the situation: reject, reformulate, or confirm themes and explanations.

The clinical methodology starts with the idea that, instead of observing reality from the outside, one should attempt to understand it from within. Whereas the scientist applying the scientific methodology observes the phenomenon from a distance, the clinical scientist makes direct and unstructured contact with it, with no preconception in terms of what is to be discovered. The clinical scientist becomes a participant[9] in the situation to be investigated. The main goal is to understand how people construct their world.

The clinical scientist gets inside the situation to understand how it is put together from within. This is done without taking on the role of an expert, with a theory about how that phenomenon works, as a scientist applying scientific methodology does. Rather, the researcher takes on the role of a learner, who attempts to understand the situation being researched.

The next stage of research is mapping the rich fabric of the phenomenon:[10] the symbols, the meanings, the rituals, the routines, the folklore, and the history, which the researcher documents.

Clinical methodology relies heavily on keeping rigorous documentation of the scientist's observations and actions within the phenomenon. The clinical scientists keep journals of their visits about: observation of events and situations; who interacts and talks with whom, conversations, and interviews. Such journals sensitively document from within, what people are seeing, and saying from their standpoint. Once the clinical scientists are well advanced with this mapping stage, they will have built a large file of documents containing explanations and descriptions of the pattern of symbols and meanings that seem relevant to the phenomenon.

The next stage of the research process is identifying the key themes and interpretations of the situation. This is similar to the theory building, stage 2, of the scientific methodology. In clinical methodology, it is delayed until stage 4. This is because it believes that the theory should not be brought in from the outside, but should make sense from the inside. The clinical scientist attempts to explain how reality is constructed. Therefore, the methodology used should be compatible with the internal mechanisms of this reality construction process.

The process of interpreting what happens in the situation, and of theory building, is totally different from that of the scientific methodology. The scientists applying the scientific methodology often bring their explanation into the situation. The clinical scientists take their explanation out of the situation. The latter focuses on themes and interpretations, in the situation being studied, to generate a detailed theory. The

---

9 In fact, one of the techniques in clinical research is called "participant observation," which is very flexible.

10 Actually, this process starts at the beginning of research, and continues throughout.

clinical scientist looks at the data collected and makes sense of the main patterns or, looks for what makes the situation sensible from the standpoint of an actor within the situation.

The next stage of research is to test the validity of the theory, by bringing systematic doubt into the explanations and themes. In other words, the clinical scientist tests whether the explanations produced from the situation make sense to the people in it. This is diametrically different from the scientific methodology, since the scientist applying the scientific methodology leaves the situation with the data. Often, the statistics collected are tested through mathematical statistical techniques to bring systematic doubt.

In contrast, the clinical scientist goes back into the researched situation to test the theory. The basis of the test is; if the theory is correct, then it must make sense to the people in the situation. This might be conducted by asking members of the situation to comment on the explanation, and to refine or correct it wherever it has a deficiency, or is wrong. It is only after the process of giving the members in the situation an opportunity to reject the theory, view, or explanation, that the clinical scientist can claim it as knowledge.

It is not necessary for the clinical scientist's explanations to be consistent with the common sense understanding of members in the situation. The clinical scientist might bring out an explanation which participants never considered before, but recognize its truth. Clinical research is not limited to making common sense knowledge explicit. Often, it involves a process of interpreting the common sense knowledge with a wider view.

Clinical research is not the replication of what is obvious. It might be a new, novel insight, but one which makes sense to the members in the situation. The clinical research must employ a process of systematic doubt if it is to constitute a scientific one. An unfavorable test result leads to the reformulation of the initial insight, explanation, and theory. There is a feedback loop that goes from stage 5 to stage 4 in an iterative manner. The final outcome is an explanation which is consistent with the process of reality construction within the situation. This case study is the knowledge product of clinical research.

Scientific methodology does not consider the case study of one situation as an adequate contribution to knowledge. It views knowledge as being about laws and regularities in an external world. It is concerned with the generalization of facts. The aim is to discover facts in one situation that can explain all others. This translates into the study of many situations.

The clinical methodology does not search for facts, laws, or relationships which apply everywhere. The idea of finding facts that apply everywhere, assumes the standpoint of an observer who presumes the world is "out there" operating in accordance with generalizable laws. Clinical methodology believes that since reality is constructed and reconstructed everywhere, seemingly similar facts are not constructed in the same way and do not have the same significance universally.

Scientific and clinical methodologies are totally different, because they view knowledge in totally different ways. The clinical methodology is interested in the insight that explains the process of reality construction, rather than generalizable facts. It searches for intriguing explanations for the way processes work in reality. This is why one single study is legitimate in clinical research.

A case study may produce an insight which can be generalized to other situations. The scientific methodology is concerned with generalizability of facts, laws, and relationships. The clinical methodology looks for the generalizability of insights. A case study of a phenomenon makes sense in explanation of another. This process does not depend upon whether the phenomena are factually the same, or they belong to the same population. One phenomenon may be in a given context, another phenomenon might be in another context. The case study in one context helps to explain processes that are at work in the other.

From the standpoint of clinical methodology, a single case study may contain rich insight. Although situation-specific, it may transform one's understanding of other situations, which may be understood in similar terms. The insight obtained from a single case study may be far superior to the abstract sets of relations obtained from the systematic study of a large number of similar phenomena through scientific methodology.

The scientific methodology is concerned with laws and relationships between variables, generalizable across the whole population. The clinical methodology looks for that spark of insight which may resonate with other researchers. The basis of science is: generalizability based on systematic doubt. Generalizability should be there, but it should not necessarily be the generalizability of facts.

In short, functionalists have atomistic view with deductive logic; are in search of generalizable, objective knowledge of rules and regularities of elements of the subject of study; require research to be systematic, comparative, replicative observation and measurement; and, therefore, abstract from the situation being analyzed. This most likely leads to the divergence between research and practice.

Interpretive research has a holistic view which recognizes that knowledge is not merely technical, but ideological, political, ethical, and moral as well. With its inductive logic, the interpretive researcher gains generalizable insights by analyzing the subject of study in its own right, from within, in its entirety and within the given context. This most likely leads to combining research and practice. The other two paradigms, that is, the radical humanist and radical structuralist paradigms, also most likely combine research and practice, especially in view of their emphasis on wholeness and totality.[11]

Academic Finance and Clinical Research

The *Journal of Financial Economics* (*JFE*), starting with its 1989 (vol. 24) issue, has allocated a section to clinical papers. The following consists of excerpts from the editorial section of that issue:

---

11 Mobley and Kuniansky's (1992a) survey of practitioners in Finance supports their previous surveys in Marketing and Management Information Systems, that is, divergence of research and practice. Note that, business schools, in general, do research within the functionalist paradigm.

The objective of the clinical papers section is to provide a high-quality professional outlet for scholarly studies of specific cases, events, practices, and specialized applications.

Clinical work can guide theorists and empiricists to empirically relevant (imperfect market) theories by providing in-depth analysis of the important dimensions of a phenomenon.

The advantages of specialization imply that different groups of researchers will tend to concentrate on theory, empirical tests, and clinical studies. These three groups complement each other. Theory provides discipline and precise hypotheses for both empirical and clinical researcher. Empirical tests direct theorists by identifying irrelevant models and suggest where clinical research might find counter examples. Clinical studies help set the agenda for both theory and empirical work. Because of this complementarity and the importance of communication between these groups, the journal of financial economics is committed to publishing all three types of research.

That is, the clinical research, although essentially an interpretive methodology, is intended, by mainstream functionalist finance, to be used within the functionalist methodology. The *JFE* is interpreting the clinical methodology as a clinical method which is to be used as an explanatory stage within the scientific methodology.

The *JFE* regards clinical method as an explanatory stage in the hypothesis generation of the scientific methodology. That is, the *JFE* recommends going through the first four stages of clinical methodology as a way of beginning scientific methodology, then, generating hypothesis, setting up a rigorous experimental framework, testing the hypothesis, either rejecting or reformulating until it is verified. This, of course, reduces the significance of clinical methodology drastically and treats it only as a research method, that is, clinical method.

This becomes much clearer if a close look is taken at the papers presented and discussions performed at the Harvard Business School Conference which was jointly sponsored by the *JFE* and the *Harvard Business School* (*HBS*) during July 7–9, 1999 and posted on the internet (http://www.hbs.edu/hbsjfe). The conference papers appeared in the May 2001 issue of the *JFE*.

The telling title of conference is: "Complementary Research Methodologies: The Interplay of Theoretical, Empirical and Field-Based Research in Finance," where, "field-based research" is interpreted as "clinical research." The Conference Purpose is described as:

There is a growing interest in field-based research in Finance, in which a careful investigation of firms or industries can complement large-scale empirical research and theory. Field-based research can perform a variety of roles: firms' experiences can suggest interesting problems and questions, they can suggest hypotheses which can be more formally tested, and they can be used to "test" theory under certain circumstances.

This conference will focus on the interplay between field-based research and more "traditional" types of research in Finance. We seek to showcase a mix of clinical papers, empirical studies, and theoretical pieces in which (1) field-based research poses questions and exposes issues that can fruitfully be studied using other techniques, or (2) "traditional" research can be enhanced through a careful investigation of a company or market. The clinical or field-based papers would tend to focus on the behavior of managers, firms, or specific markets; use field interviews and primary source materials as an important source of data; and would tend to generate, rather than test, hypothesis. The empirical and theoretical papers, while fully grounded in their own methodologies, would be ones where clinical research could help researchers determine whether the models and tests proposed are reasonable representations of the actual business settings. The spirit of the conference is the recognition that there are many complementary means of conducting research, ...

This provides clear support for the understanding that HBS-JFE conference is centered on the idea that clinical research is treated as a complementary component of the "traditional" functionalist research.

The above theme is further elaborated by Peter Tufano's (the conference reviewer) introductory talk entitled "Our Research Methodologies, the Scientific Method and Roles for Clinical/Field Research." The following consists of excerpts from his speech:

What roles can clinical observation play? In ... scientific method where you have theory, hypotheses, and tests what role can observation play? ... In what ways can direct observation of the world which might be resident in pieces of clinical type research ... might enlighten us? In the theory ... world, they might suggest theory. We observe something in the world then we step back and we say here is a theory that would explain those observations. ... I observe a set of phenomena and then step back and say "what I think is happening is this" and "here is my theory and my set of hypotheses."

What can we use the clinical data for? Well, we can use clinical data to verify the theory. What does verify mean? It is that phrase that I kept underlining when I read most of the papers: the data is consistent with the theory.

There is another thing we can do with clinical observation; which is to document the applicability of the theory. ... which is to say here is the theory, I believe there is enough data to support it, so I now believe it. Now, we want to apply it in a prescriptive fashion. What decisions do I make based on that theory? So, let us take that theory and document how it works. To understand how that works, it is sometimes useful to do that in the context of a real decision.

And then finally, every once in a while we can use clinical observation to actually falsify the theory. ... Unfortunately, most of the scientific theories that we work with are not ... that sharp and therefore one observation is not typically enough to reject. On the other hand, there are some other circumstances where that is possible. So, may be this is a particularly powerful use of clinical data if we have particularly sharp theories.

We can do field work ... but we still do not have to give up any of our statistical tests or training. We can still use the same comfortable methodology we are used to doing but yet we can actually ... find things out that we could not otherwise have found out by sitting in our offices.

This theme is followed in all fifteen papers presented and discussed in the five sessions of the conference. For instance, the authors (John Graham and Campbell Harvey) of the second paper, entitled "The Theory and Practice of Corporate Finance: Evidence from the Field," in the session on Financing provide a specific example of the interplay of scientific methodology and the clinical method, when the managers of corporations tell them that:

> The number one, most important, factor affecting equity policy decisions is earnings per share dilution. Now, this is, I think, pretty interesting. Because if you read Brealey and Myers, they call this a fallacy. Earnings per share should not be diluted if it hits the required return on equity when you get your new funds. And yet management tells us this is the most important reason. So, we have one of two things going on here. We either have … management are putting too much weight on earnings per share here and that is wrong and we have got to teach them not to do that … or may be management is telling us that … our models are missing something, or our models are too simple. This turns out to be more important than we realize. … May be we need to go back and do a clinical study, re-evaluate the theory, do another type of large sample study that can … dig into some of these issues a little deeper.

The discussion leader (Karen Wruck) of the second session on "Restructuring" regarding methodology commented as follows:

> Really the choice of method is driven by the research questions that we are asking. … Empirical research obviously addresses the aggregate associations overall trends and outcomes and benchmark performance. And that is really important if we want to understand a phenomenon in the world in the aggregate. However, if we are interested in understanding a little bit more about underlying structural models or organizational management mechanisms that underlie aggregate associations, chains of cause and effect, more process oriented things then detailed analysis of small numbers of firms can be very informative. … So, there is an interplay there between those two things and there is certainly an interplay between all of them and the development of theory.

That is, the discussion leader takes the functionalist paradigm as her point of departure and states that the choice of method, whether empirical or clinical, is dependent on the type of question we ask. Whereas if the point of departure is taken to be the universe of worldviews or paradigms, then the choice of method and methodology would be dependent on the worldview or paradigm which that one believes to be applicable to the situation under consideration.

Finally, the authors (Upinder Dhillon and Gabriel Ramirez) of the last paper, entitled "Bond Calls, Credible Commitments, and Equity Dilution: A Theoretical and Clinical Analysis of Simultaneous Tender and Call (STACS) Offers," based on their game theoretic paper provide another specific example of the interplay of scientific methodology and the clinical method in the session on Security/Market Design:

> In general, what I think I am doing when I am doing theory work is that there is a … reality out there, it is very messy and very complicated, and I do not really understand it too well. … I try to … map one thing that happens in reality into something else that happens in reality. … One then tries to figure out … models of reality, some model, some set of incentives, which can be converted to something neat and stylized, like a game, may be not necessarily a game, … Then you apply some kind of solution concepts, you get a prediction, and that prediction yields the result in reality or the thing that I am trying to map that actually occurs. …

> But, the problem with this is that in most situations one is really uncomfortable about picking the right model. … Frequently, there is a huge number of possible models which could be plausibly associated with what is going on, and from moving from solution concept to model the empirical work … makes sure that you connect these two points together correctly.

> Experimental research is very good to make sure this connection is right. That is, you picked the right solution concept. Because if I perform an experiment I can actually control and make sure exactly which model is being played. Perhaps I cannot do it perfectly even in an experiment because I have the problem controlling the subject's preferences. … But, you can do a lot, you can get a good idea … But, … what is exactly the right model?

In other words, experimental research (that is, clinical or field research) can be used to get further information to perfect a theory.

To summarize, the *HBS* and *JFE* regard the clinical research as a complement to or a stage in the scientific method, rather than considering clinical research as an independent research methodology on its own terms by relating it to its underlying paradigm.

While there can be little doubt that a more balanced approach to research in finance is required, there are many problems involved in the choice of a methodology. In particular, there is a need to examine the important relationship between paradigms and methodologies.

Depending on the paradigmatic context in which clinical research is set, it may be used in at least the following two ways: (1) as a self-contained cohesive methodology of research that generates insight and generalizable insight, and (2) as the first stage in the scientific methodology. Each is legitimate and makes a valid contribution to knowledge, according to its underlying paradigm.

Clinical methodology stands for an approach, rather than a set of techniques. The extent of its appropriate use, like that of scientific methodology, depends on the nature of the phenomenon under investigation. Clinical methodology aims at research from within the situation. The functionalists' reducing the significance of the clinical methodology to clinical method and using it as the introductory phase of research might be quite beneficial. It might lead to changing the underlying assumptions of the research, the reformulation of problems in a very different way, or to revise some of the explanations given for phenomena observed at a distance. That is, even if a researcher is interested in applying the scientific methodology, there is a benefit from getting into the situation, rather than observing it at a distance all the time.

Essentially, *JFE* and *HBS* seem to recommend that research may begin with the clinical method to set-up a hypothesis, and continue with the scientific methodology to test the hypothesis. This recommendation is not problematic only if, at the end of the clinical research stage, the researcher is confident enough to adopt the view of the world, and the related set of assumptions, to enable the scientific methodology to be used with validity. If such a standpoint cannot be taken, then automatically adopting a scientific methodology in the second stage of the research may not be appropriate.

In other words, the scientific methodology is appropriate only in situations where it is possible to adequately deduce reality through the use of independent and dependent variables, and the statistical relationships among them. Deductive logic, however, is based on the assumption that variables do not carry any context-related meanings. Such interpretations of variables are often made in the natural sciences, but the same stance cannot be taken in social research. Many aspects of the social world cannot be reliably captured in the form of variables with literal properties.

Of course, it should not be implied that scientific methodology should not be used in studying the social world. Whenever meanings of variables are stable, the scientific methodology is quite appropriate. However, it might first be necessary to use the clinical method to establish if meanings are stable and situation-independent. If they are not, understanding these phenomena might better be implemented through the clinical methodology.

Conclusion

In order to foundationally address the research-versus-practice controversy, this chapter started with the premise that any paradigm or worldview can be positioned on a continuum formed by four basic paradigms: functionalist, interpretive, radical humanist, and radical structuralist. It showed how worldviews underlie theories and methodologies in general, and those of finance, in particular. Then, the chapter took the interpretive paradigm, as an example, and compared its research methodology with that of the functionalist paradigm. These methodologies are called clinical and scientific, respectively. The chapter showed how fundamental, paradigmatic assumptions translate into the methodology of research. It concluded that the functionalist paradigm would most likely produce the divergence between research and practice, whereas the other three paradigms tend to more closely relate research and practice.

This chapter also noted that academic finance has begun to utilize clinical approach in its research. The chapter pointed out that clinical approach can be more appropriately used when certain fundamental, contextual, paradigmatic assumptions are met.

Chapter 5

Theory and Practice of Academic Finance Paradigm

The purpose of this chapter is to provide an explanation for the way the reality in the world of finance comes to be formed, among other things, by the theory of finance. It shows that financial behavior is not independent of the theory of finance. The chapter, therefore, starts with reference to Chapter 2, in which certain aspects of the academic field of finance, that is, theories, Ph.D. programs, journals, and conferences, were discussed and it was concluded that they adhere, almost exclusively, to the functionalist paradigm. Then, the chapter discusses the role of finance graduates as employees of universities, corporations, and financial institutions in forming the practice of finance. In this way, the chapter provides an explanation for the social construction of the world of finance.

The finance literature prior to the early 1950s was in large part descriptive and contained institutional detail. In the 1950s, fundamental changes began to take place and modern finance became prominent.

Modern finance proceeds as if there is financial behavior out there and empirically tests theoretical statements regarding financial behavior to determine their truths. Notwithstanding, this chapter intends to provide an explanation for the idea that financial behavior is not independent of the theory of finance. The chapter, therefore, aims to provide an explanation for the way the reality in the world of finance comes to be formed, among other things, by the theory of finance.

The difference between the natural and social sciences is rooted in their respective relationships to the phenomena they study. In the social sciences, research changes the phenomena under investigation more than does research in the natural sciences. Social behavior is shaped by culturally shared frameworks of conceptual understanding, which is the chief product of social science. Therefore, as the concepts and theories are communicated and filtered into daily life, they reconstitute the very reality they seek to investigate. This is especially true in sciences of business administration, including finance, where theories function as instruments of managerial control. These practically oriented sciences provide advice regarding potential interventions in daily affairs of businesses. The relationship between finance theory and managerial practice is a dialectical one, whereby theory not only reflects but also structures its own subject matter. This is why the natural scientific yardstick for theoretical appraisal, namely objectivity, or truth value, is not germane for the social sciences. The yardstick of objectivity presupposes stability in the phenomena under investigation, and application of this criterion to the constant flux of the interaction between researcher and the object studied is not possible.

The remainder of this chapter first recalls the discussion of theories, Ph.D. programs, journals, and conferences in academic finance and their, almost exclusive, adherence to the functionalist paradigm. Then it notes that the growing number of technologically trained sophisticated finance graduates who become employees of universities, corporations, and financial institutions, which are carrying an ever-increasing weight in financial markets. In addition, it notes that the education of the graduates affect the formation of their perception, attitude, belief, behavior, and, therefor, the practice of finance. These play their roles in the social construction of the reality of finance.

Academic Finance

Chapter 2 examined theories, Ph.D. programs, journals, and conferences of the academic field of finance. It noted that the academic field of finance is founded almost exclusively on the functionalist paradigm. It also noted that, within the existing world of academic finance, how researchers, professors, Ph.D. graduates, journal editors, associations, and conference organizers help to refine, enhance, and perpetuate the functionalist finance.

Practice of Finance

Finance students who graduate from academia receive special training. This training helps to shape graduates' perception, attitude, beliefs, and behavior in a special way. Students will carry these traits with them to their professional careers. These careers are mostly in universities, corporations, and financial institutions. This section shows how the increasing number of finance graduates who work for universities, corporations, and financial institutions, which play an increasing role in financial markets, will help to create a reality which the finance theory intends to explain.

Role of Education in Formation of Perception, Attitude, Belief, and Behavior

Financial education helps to shape financial reality by influencing the perception, attitude, belief, and behavior of graduates.

Through education, most students obtain a vision similar to those of the educators, such that they see what the educators see and respond as they do. For instance, researchers use theoretical models, acquired through education and exposure to literature. It is a narrow education because students are not made aware of competing paradigms and theories and the solutions these provide to problems; solutions that the students must ultimately evaluate for themselves.

In general, education helps to shape students' perception, attitude, belief, and behavior in a special way. Frank, Gilovich, and Regan (1993) did several behavioral studies on economics students. In one, first-year graduate students, economics and non-economics, were given some money to be divided into two accounts called "private" and "public." Money in the private account would be given to the student at the end of the experiment. Money in the public account would be pooled, multiplied by a factor of more than one, and then divided equally among all the students. For society as a whole the best decision for the students is to put all their money into the public account. That creates the biggest pie, which is then shared equally. But for each individual student, the best decision is to put all the money into the private account. In this way, the student would get back all the money invested plus a full share of the pool provided by everyone. The study found that economics students contributed, on average, 20 per cent of their stakes to the public account. Students of other subjects contributed 50 per cent.

Another study involved a game played by an "allocator" and a "receiver." The allocator was given $10.00 to be divided between the allocator and the receiver. The receiver could either accept the division (in which case, both parties kept the sums proposed by the allocator) or refuse it (in which case, both got nothing). "Fairness" calls for an equal split. But what does economics "self-interest" tell the allocator to do? The answer is: keep $9.99 and give the receiver one cent. The receiver will not refuse because one cent is better than nothing. Note also that the game was played just once for each pair, so there was no reason for the receiver to refuse in the hope of promoting a better offer next time. As before, the study found that economics students performed significantly more in accord with the self-interest model than non-economists.

Still another study considered the prisoners' dilemma (a game in which two players have to decide whether to co-operate with each other or cheat) which has long been of great interest to economists. The key feature is that for each player, "defecting" secures the best outcome regardless of what the other does. But if both players accept this logic and defect, they end up worse off than if they had "co-operated." The research conducted an experiment involving 267 prisoners' dilemma games. Economics students defected 60 per cent of the time; non-economists defected 39 per cent of the time.

A further study experimented to see whether students became more or less "honest" in a hypothetical situation, after studying some economics. The experiment compared three sets of students: the first took a course in mainstream microeconomics, taught by an instructor with an interest in industrial organization and game theory; the second took a similar course, but taught by a specialist on development in Maoist China; the third took a placebo (astronomy). Across a range of questions, the pattern was consistent: the first set contained the largest proportion of students who became less honest; next came the second set; and last were the astronomers, with the smallest proportion of students who became less honest.

Whaples (1995) presents evidence that students' opinions change as they take introductory economics, with a greater percentage of students coming to regard market outcomes as fair.

Walstad (1997) analyzed the relationship between economic knowledge and public opinion on selected economic issues. Economic knowledge, whether measured by a general score or the knowledge of a particular issue, is shown to be the most consistent and influential factor affecting public opinion.

Allgood and Walstad (1999) examined the effects of economics instruction on high school economics teachers and their students. They concluded that a three-year master's program in economics has beneficial effects on both the understanding of participating teachers and their students. They used two outcome measures: a standardized test and a measure of the degree to which teachers "think like economists."

Cassidy and Franklin (1996) studied whether business students' perception of risk can be affected by completing an introductory risk management and insurance course. Their results indicate that risk perceptions did change after taking the insurance course.

This subsection discussed the effect of education on students' perception, attitude, belief, and behavior. It emphasized that graduates have certain characteristics which are learned in academia. More specifically, current finance graduates obtain functionalist finance education in academia which forms their perception, attitude, belief, and behavior. The next subsection looks at the process of the growth of career opportunities for finance graduates and finance graduates' role in the creation of financial reality.

Graduates and their Employment in Corporations and Financial Institutions

One of the major changes in the structure of capital markets since the Second World War has been the growth of corporations and financial intermediaries with their increasing ownership of corporate stock.

In addition to this growth, the internationalization and diversification of the largest companies after the war encouraged the separation of the corporate treasurer's department from divisional financial management with an emphasis on the efficient use of corporate funds. Corporate treasurers are increasingly sophisticated users of capital markets and are continuing to do some of the traditional roles of investment bankers. Investment banks now share control of capital markets with new financial intermediaries and the giant corporations.

The expansion of financial markets (individuals, corporations, and financial intermediaries participating in them) has had a number of consequences:

First, the number of people engaged in the finance profession, such as brokerage, analysis, and fund management, has grown substantially.

A second consequence of the development of new financial intermediaries and the expansion of existing ones is the decline of traditional barriers between segmented markets and the development of new forms of competition, including new financial instruments, among financial institutions. This creates the concern for establishing specialized competence and service as a means of differentiating skills and expertise.

Thirdly, the growing number of people involved in the finance profession is increasingly employed by firms competing for assets and profits in an organized and systematic manner.

These consequences have resulted in the increasing specialization of tasks. This in turn has encouraged hiring people who have been equipped with the established body of knowledge, such as university graduates with doctoral, masters, and bachelor degrees in finance, and people with professional certificates, such as Certified Financial Analysts.

Practice and Creation of Reality of Finance

Financial education helps to shape financial practice by influencing the perception, attitude, belief, and behavior of finance graduates who become finance practitioners upon graduation.

Norgaard (1981) notes that, in the 1960s, finance through research was developing its distinct identity, which had a substantial effect on textbooks during the 1960s.

Weston (1967) states:

> … textbook literature lags journals by three to five years, general business practice probably lags the good textbooks by another two or three years. … great progress has been made in the utilization of new tools of analysis in the financial operations of business firms. (p. 539)

Gilbert and Reichert (1995) in their survey of the practice of financial management conclude that modern analytical models and techniques being taught in universities are finding their way into relatively widespread use among large US corporations. Their comparison with earlier surveys reveals that corporations in general have noticeably increased their use of sophisticated financial management techniques.

For instance, Payne, Carrington Heath, and Gale (1999) note that in an earlier study Istvan (1961) found that 82 per cent of the firms in his sample used criteria that ignore time value of money, such as payback method or accounting rate of return. They also note that in a later study Kim, Crick, and Kim (1986) report that 70 per cent of the firms in their sample use discounted cash flow methods, such as the internal rate of return or net present value, as their primary evaluation tool, with most preferring the internal rate of return.

Moreover, Kester et al (1999) note that:

1. Klammer (1972) found that only 19 per cent of his sample of large industrial companies used discounted cash flow techniques to evaluate and rank projects in 1959, and that the percentage increased to 57 per cent in 1970.
2. Hendricks (1983) reported that the percentage was 76 per cent in 1981.
3. Trahan and Gitman (1995) found that in 1992 both the majority of responding Fortune 500 large firms and the majority of responding *Forbes 200* best small companies used discounted cash flow techniques.
4. Bierman (1993) reported that 99 per cent of the respondents in his 1992 survey of the 100 largest *Fortune 500* companies used the internal rate of return or the net present value as either the primary or secondary evaluation measure.
5. The use of other techniques than the discounted cash flow techniques, such as payback, as the primary evaluation measure has declined.

As modern finance theories have been expanding on numerous topics and with emphasis on details, their applications in practice have been following suit. Consequently, academics have looked into such applications by corporations and conducted surveys. Such surveys, overtime, have correspondingly become more focused on either a single detailed topic or a comprehensive set of general topics with their coverage continued to be national or extended to become international.

For instance, with respect to the general topic of capital budgeting Petry and Sprow (1993) note that the past surveys have focused on capital budgeting with the early ones emphasizing types of methods used, trends in their use, cut-off rates, decision rules, risk management, and firm performance. They continue to note that some of the more recent articles have become more specialized, including inflation adjustments, real estate, the relationship of sophisticated techniques to firm performance, and research and development. In their own study, Petry and Sprow (1993) include the new topic of mergers and acquisition and perform a comprehensive multi-subject approach to give more consistency to the information obtained.

There are studies that have surveyed other specialized applications of finance theories by corporations—for example, Mukhrejee and Hingorani (1999)—or have done international comparisons—for example, Payne, Carrington Heath, and Gale (1999) and Kester et al (1999). The increasing number of academic surveys of corporate applications of numerous finance theories, without and with international coverage, is itself a reflection of the increasing use of finance theory in practice. Merton (1995) summarizes this trend: "With all their seemingly abstruse mathematical complexity, the models of finance theory have nevertheless had a direct and significant influence on finance practice. Although not unique, this conjoining of intrinsic intellectual interest with extrinsic application is a prevailing theme of research in modern finance." (p. 7)

Some of the practitioners are financial theorists, who form their subsequent theories based on their own behavior and the behavior they observe in others, behavior which was shaped by earlier theories.

Theory forms part of the reality that the theory intends to describe. In this way a theory comes to have a life of its own and, therefore, may be experienced as external to the theorist. Thus, for example, how is the validity of Monetarist or Keynesian theory affected by the fact that they are employed to both be acted upon and describe reality? Does the knowledge about the efficient market theory not make the markets more efficient by detecting the anomalies? Are characteristics of economic rationality (such as acquisitiveness; selfishness; competitiveness) inherently natural to human beings, or are they products of theories? Are forecast budgets merely "best estimates" of what will happen, or they are also targets used to motivate managers to adopt particular courses of action. In this respect, it is not the forecasting ability of a budget that is important rather it is the desirability of the situation that it helps to create.

Also note the following example. Many US companies have, in recent years, protested their high tax burden. They refer to the expense items on their financial statements which show effective tax rates in excess of 40 per cent. Yet the payment of these expenses is deferred, often for many years. If the current expenses associated with these future payments were estimated in present value terms, the current effective tax rate would fall considerably. The businesses take this stand because financial statements can be used politically to resist government regulation and to lobby for a more favorable business climate. Therefore, financial statements may be seen as creators of business reality rather than objective descriptions of historical facts.

The difficulty with the functionalist assumption that truth comes from facts is that it does not recognize that theory creates some of the facts. Functionalists assume a subject-object split. That is, we (the subjects) can observe and analyze reality (the object) in a completely detached objective manner. Functionalists do not agree that observers (subjects) are a product of the reality (objects) they observe, which means that the observers' models of observation and perception are products of the reality as well. Moreover, functionalists do not agree that the object (reality) is changed by the results of the subject's analysis and theorizing.

How can social scientists discover the truth about the workings of the socio-economic world if their theories have helped to create the reality they are examining? An example is provided by McGoun:

> When we ask whether the CAPM is right or wrong we are assuming that there is some underlying reality there and that we can find out something about it. I would argue that reality, in this case, is really what we think it is—that if we all believe in the CAPM, it works; if we do not, it does not work. I feel the same thing about option pricing. If you look at the coincidence of the publication of the option-pricing formula, that sale of computers that actually have it programmed in, and the start of organized options exchanges, we really have to question whether we have explained something or whether we have created something. (Frankfurter, Carleton, Gordon, Horrigan, McGoun, Philippatos, and Robinson 1994, p. 201)

Social sciences are different from the natural sciences due to the relationship which exists between researchers and the phenomena they study. The social science research changes the phenomena under investigation more than does the research in the natural sciences. For instance, astronomic theory does not alter movement of the planets in the way that behavioral theory affects social conduct. However, social activity is shaped by culturally shared frameworks of conceptual understanding and, at the same time, the chief product of social science is the conceptual understanding. Consequently, as social theories and concepts are communicated with the lay discourse, they reconstitute the very reality social theorists seek to investigate. This is particularly true in management sciences, where theories function as instruments of managerial control. As a practically oriented science, it furnishes advice about potential interventions in organizational affairs, and so the concepts are especially accessible to managerial audiences. The relationship between management theory and managerial practice is, consequently, a dialectical one, whereby theory not only reflects but also structures its own subject matter.

Conclusion

The purpose of this chapter was to provide an explanation for the way the reality in the world of finance comes to conform to the theory of finance. It set out to show that financial behavior is not independent of the theory of finance. It recalled the discussion in Chapter 2 regarding theories, Ph.D. programs, journals, and conferences in academic finance, which lead to the conclusion that they adhere, almost exclusively, to the functionalist paradigm. Then, the chapter discussed the role of finance graduates as employees of universities, corporations and financial institutions in the practice of finance. In this way, the chapter provided an explanation for the way the reality of finance comes to be formed, among other things, by the theory of finance.

Chapter 6

Development of Academic Finance: Four Paradigmatic Views

Any adequate analysis of the current state of affairs in mainstream academic finance necessarily requires fundamental understanding of the world views underlying explanations of the course of the development of science, in general, and finance, in particular. This chapter provides four explanations, each based on one of the four paradigms or world views. It emphasizes that these four explanations are equally scientific and informative; they look at the process of the development of academic finance from a certain paradigmatic viewpoint.

The functionalist paradigm has provided the framework for current mainstream academic finance, and accounts for the largest proportion of theory and research in its academic field. This has been a topic for debate, both in the past and present. However, there has been no comprehensive account of: "How and why academic finance has reached its current state of affairs?"

More specifically, there was a heated debate in the not too distant past.[1] This has been captured by Kavesh (1970) in his address to the American Finance Association, which was made with reference to exchanges between Sauvain, Durand, and Weston. Kavesh (1970) stated:

> But disciplines change, new thinking evolves, controversies flair. In finance one can almost sense the shifts by leafing through the volumes. The early years were filled with descriptive articles, with a heavy "institutional" flavor largely reflecting the type of research being carried out in those days. ... Slowly, the mathematical and model-building revolution was revealed in the pages of the *Journal*. And feelings (pro and con) ran high. Balance and perspective were sought then—and are sought now—but to many it was the battle between the "new" vs. "old" finance. Some readers complained about the lack of "relevance" in the newer approaches; others confessed that they could no longer understand what was in the *Journal*. Younger members wanted more "rigor." (p. 5)

Sauvain (1967) stated:

> We learn from them and they learn from us. ... Sometimes their mathematical logic leads them to examine an aspect of a problem that we hadn't even thought about or to see a problem in an entirely different light. ... They can learn from us. Some of these bright young men spent so much time studying mathematics and theory that they learned too

---

1 Horrigan reminds us: "Our sense of finance history is really astonishing. We all seem to think that finance as a subject started about 1960, even though we know its origins go back a lot further than that." Frankfurter, Carleton, Gordon, Horrigan, McGoun, Philippatos, and Robinson (1994), p. 183.

little about finance. Once in a while one of my quantitative colleagues comes to me with a question about some instrument or institution that reveals abysmal ignorance. (pp. 541–542)

Durand (1968) stated:

The new finance men, on the other hand, have lost virtually all contact with terra firma. On the whole, they seem to be more interested in demonstrating their mathematical powers than in solving genuine problems; often they seem to be playing mathematical games. (p. 848)

Weston (1967) stated:

Yet the developments in both theory and practice since the end of World War II provide a basis for predicting that our research will reflect an increasing ratio of analytical-theoretical materials with quantitative testing of models to studies dealing with institutions and instruments. (p. 540)

More recent debate continues along the same lines. Findlay and Williams (1985) state:

The real world decision making implications are also limiting, as practitioners are ever more inclined to employ "theoretical" as antonym for "practical" or "useful." (p. 1)

Gordon (1994) states:

The existing body of literature in neo-classical theory is utterly ridiculous. It does not explain dividend policy; it does not explain capital structure policy; it does not explain anything. It just says that there are imperfections. That is all it does. (p. 197)

Frankfurter and Lane (1992) state:

The next section of this essay is a brief critique of the principal dividend models. It is argued that all these models share the common problem of not being able to explain observed behavior. (p. 116)

Frankfurter and Wood (1995) state:

To our surprise we learn that academic theories that were advanced in financial economics during the last 40 years to rationalize the practice, completely fail to consider its evolution. … Our advice, nevertheless, is to study more carefully dividend policies as a cultural phenomenon, rather than to expend efforts in mathematical model building. (pp. 1 and 41)

Merton (1995) states:

With all their seemingly abstruse mathematical complexity, the models of finance theory have nevertheless had a direct and significant influence on finance practice. (p. 7)

The debate continues. An essential question that arises, in this context, is: "How and why academic finance has reached where it is now?" Ironically, there is no all-encompassing explanation of the development of mainstream academic finance.[2] Such a treatment necessarily should uncover the underlying worldviews and their fundamental assumptions. This is in contrast to the above-mentioned historical debates, which only touch upon the surface of this important phenomenon.

This chapter provides four explanations, each based on one of the four paradigms. The functionalist paradigm views science as the outcome of the search for objective truth; the interpretive paradigm views science as being socially constructed; the radical humanist paradigm views science as an element of the dominant ideology; and the radical structuralist paradigm views science as being class determined. It emphasizes that these four explanations are equally scientific and informative; they look at the process of the development of academic finance from a certain paradigmatic viewpoint.

This chapter takes the case of development of academic finance as an example and emphasizes that, in general, any phenomenon may be seen and analyzed from different viewpoints and that each viewpoint exposes a certain aspect of the phenomenon under consideration. Collectively, they provide a much broader and deeper understanding of the phenomenon. Therefore, academic finance can benefit much from contributions coming from other paradigms if it respects paradigm diversity.

Functionalist View

Scientific progress is the cumulative discovery of objective truth.[3] Knowledge grows linearly as new data are added to the existing stock of research findings.

Science must be both objective and truthful. However, when a theory becomes more truthful and has more explanatory power, the probability that its predictions become true gets smaller.

Progress in science satisfies the following two conditions. First, a new theory which constitutes a progress vis-à-vis another must be at variance with it. It must lead to some conflicting results. This reflects the revolutionary nature of progress in science. Second, progress in science must be conservative. A new theory must explain not only what is explained by all previous theories, but also new phenomena.

A theory that fails must be discarded. This is the condition of falsifiability, as opposed to verifiability. A new theory is verifiable if:

1. It is based on a new and unifying idea about observable relations;
2. It is testable; that is, it has testable implications which have not been observed yet; and
3. It is successful in going through novel and severe tests; that is, success in new predictions and difficulty in refutations.

---

2 It is the contention of this chapter to fill this void.

3 Much of the discussion which follows is based on Popper (1979) and Frankfurter and Philippatos (1992).

The following is a comprehensive set of rules to judge the superiority of theory *B*, the new theory, over theory *A*, the old theory:

1. *B* is a more precise theory than *A*;
2. *B* explains more facts than *A*;
3. *B* explains facts in more detail than *A*;
4. *B* succeeds in more tests than *A*;
5. *B* implies more tests than *A*; and
6. *B* connects and unifies more facts than *A*.

In summary, science is the totality of facts, theories, and methods, which scientists have contributed to it, one element at a time. Scientific development is the gradual process of linearly adding these elements, singly and in combination, to the ever-growing stock of research finding that constitutes scientific knowledge.

McGoun (1992a) in his reflection "On the Knowledge of Finance" states:

> The behavior of most scientists implies their having made certain tacit assumptions regarding scientific activity:
>
> (1) There is a real external environment out there independent of science;
> (2) It is possible, at least in principle, to determine the truth of a scientific statement regarding the external environment;
> (3) Scientists will never state all truths regarding the external environment; and
> (4) Over time, scientists state more precise truths regarding the external environment. (p. 161)

Weston (1994) in providing "A (Relatively) Brief History of Finance Ideas" applies the above principles and provides a general explanation[4] by stating:

> Review and analysis of financial history suggest five generalizations. One, the developments of each historical period and the creators of these developments were responding to the pressing economic, financial, and socio-political problems of the period. Two, financial thought has also responded to the maturation of financial markets, internationalization, and increased competition. Three, the development and/or uses of new tools, new mathematical models, and new methodologies have facilitated the creation of theories to explain financial behavior. Four, practice has reflected the new learning with varying time lags but has also stimulated the development of theory to understand, explain, and predict financial behavior. Five, new ideas have built on the ideas provided by previous knowledge. (p. 7)

In this context, Miller (1986) provides a specific explanation:

> ... finance surely became *the* field in the 60s and 70s. ... What gave the academic field of finance its great impetus in the 60s and 70s was a powerful and almost unique interaction of theory and empirical research. ... My review can at least serve as a reminder ... that the path of progress, ... has a large element of the unanticipated and often of the completely unintended. ... Certainly, the first major breakthrough in modern finance had such

---

4 For a more detailed and specific explanation, see Weston (1966).

consequences. By first, I am not referring to the Modigliani-Miller propositions; they too did have unexpected consequences that I will get to in due course. But they were not first. That honor belongs to the mean-variance portfolio selection model of Harry Markowitz ... (pp. 396–397)

Interpretive View

Philosophers of science have shown that more than one theory can explain a given set of data.[5] Scientific theories are based on paradigms. In the development of any science, the received paradigm is usually successful in explaining most of the observations and experiments of researchers. Further development requires the construction of elaborate equipment, esoteric vocabulary, skills, and concepts. This restricts the scientist's vision, and science becomes rigid. But, by focusing attention on specific areas, a paradigm quite efficiently directs scientists to a precision of the observation-theory match.

Scientists learn concepts, laws, theories, and their applications through education. Further theories and applications will be reflected in the textbooks, from which future scientists will get their education. During university education, from early university courses to doctoral dissertation, students face more complex problems. These are modeled and solved based on previous achievements. Likewise, problems encountered during their subsequent independent scientific research are dealt with in the same manner. Scientists talk easily about a concrete piece of research, but they are not well aware of the established basis of their field, its legitimate problems, and methods. They do successful research, without recourse to hypothetical rules of the game.

However, methodology does not necessarily lead to a unique conclusion about a certain scientific problem. The particular conclusion a scientist arrives at is generally determined by his or her background, personality, and the specifics of the investigation.

In the development of most sciences there has been competition between different views of nature. They have all been scientific, but they have seen the world, and are practicing science in it, differently. Scientific observation restricts the range of admissible beliefs, but is not the only determinant of such beliefs. An arbitrary factor, based on personal and historical elements, is another important determinant of the beliefs of a certain scientific community, at a certain time.

Science assumes that the scientific community chooses the right worldview. Science is cumulative; the extension of the scope and precision of scientific knowledge. However, that factor of arbitrariness has an important effect on scientific development.

A theory does not solve all the problems at a given time, and the solutions provided are often imperfect. This incompleteness and imperfection defines many of the problems that characterize science.

---

5 Much of the discussion that follows is based on Kuhn (1970).

A paradigm provides a map with details to be explained by scientific research. However, since nature is too complex, that map is as essential as observation and experiment to the development of science. A paradigm also provides scientists with essentials for map-making. These are theories, methods, and standards.

In research, scientists select problems that can be solved with available concepts and techniques. That is, these problems are mostly defined by existing knowledge and technique. The scientist does not just look around. He or she knows what is to be achieved, how to design instruments, and how to direct thoughts accordingly. The scientist is a solver of problems, not a tester of paradigms.

Scientific communities strongly defend their paradigm, even at considerable cost. Science often suppresses fundamental novelties because they are subversive. However, since a paradigm is partly arbitrary, novelty cannot be suppressed for an extended period of time. Sometimes a problem cannot be solved by known rules and procedures, even by the experts of the field. On other occasions, a piece of equipment, designed and constructed for research, fails to perform in the anticipated manner, revealing an anomaly. In still other occasions, new and unsuspected phenomena are uncovered. In these and other ways, science goes astray. And when it does, the profession begins the extraordinary investigations, both observational and conceptual, that lead the profession, at last, to an invention of a new radical theory, a synthesis, a new set of commitments, a new basis for the practice of science. The extraordinary episodes, in which that shift of professional commitments occurs, are known as "scientific revolutions." They are the tradition-shattering, as opposed to the tradition-bound, activity of science.

Anomaly, problem, or new theory, appear in the context of paradigm. A more precise paradigm is more sensitive, and provides a riper basis for paradigm change. In the normal mode of discovery, resistance to change has a benefit. It ensures that the paradigm will not be easily surrendered. Resistance guarantees that not only scientists will not be lightly distracted, but also the anomalies that lead to paradigm change will penetrate existing knowledge to the core. This characteristic of science shows that research under a paradigm induces paradigm change.

Naturally, there is a conflict between the paradigm that suffers from the anomaly and the one that explains it. Anomalies come to existence in a game played under one set of rules whose explanation requires the creation of another set. New theories can hardly arise without substantive changes in beliefs about nature. When they become part of science, the nature of science becomes inherently different.

A scientific theory becomes invalid only if an alternative is available to take its place. Experience and experiment are essential to the process of rejecting a scientific theory, but they are not the sole determinants of the decision. The judgement leading to that decision is based on the comparison of both theories with nature and with each other.

Every problem,[6] when seen from another viewpoint, can become a counter instance and, thus, as a source of crisis. This loosens the existing rules, allows for proliferating versions of the paradigm, which ultimately permits a new paradigm to emerge.

---

6 Except those that are exclusively instrumental.

Scientists, in the wake of an anomaly or crisis, change their attitude toward the existing paradigm, and change the nature of their research accordingly. The proliferation of competing versions of paradigms, the eagerness to try anything, the expression of discontent, the recourse to philosophy and debate over fundamentals, are symptoms of a transition to extraordinary research.

A theory is accepted as a paradigm if it seems better than its competitors. But it need not, as it never does, explain all the observations with which it is confronted. Paradigms gain popularity when they are more successful than their competitors in solving a few problems that scientists consider as important. To be more successful is not, however, to be either completely successful with a single or a large number of problems. The success of a paradigm, at the start, is largely based on a promise of success in selected and still incomplete examples. Science takes shape in the actualization of that promise. The actualization is achieved by extending the knowledge of those facts that the paradigm promises, by increasing the match between those facts and the paradigm's predictions, and by further development of the paradigm itself.

The focus area of science becomes minuscule, which restricts vision. However, in this way, the paradigm directs scientists to investigate aspects of nature in such detail and depth that would otherwise be unimaginable.

The scientists who invent new paradigms have, almost always, been either very young or very new to the field. Obviously, these scientists, who are least committed to the traditional rules of science, are more likely to see that those rules no longer define a playable game, and to conceive another set that can replace them.

The historical study of paradigm change indicates similar characteristics in the development of sciences. The choice between competing paradigms proves to be like the choice between competing political institutions, that is, a choice between incompatible modes of community life. Because of its character, the choice is not, and cannot, be determined merely by the evaluative procedures of science. The role of paradigms in paradigm choice is circular. Each paradigm uses its own assumptions to argue in its own defense. The circular argument can only be used for persuasion. It cannot be made logically, or even probabilistically, convincing to those whose view is based on another paradigm.

There are other reasons for the incomplete logical contact in paradigm debates. No paradigm solves all the problems it defines, and no two paradigms leave the same problems unsolved. Therefore, paradigm debates boil down to the question: Which problems are more significant? Such a question involves values, which can be answered only with reference to criteria that lie outside of science. In fact, it is the recourse to external criteria that makes paradigm debate revolutionary.

The community of scientists is the highest entity for choosing a new paradigm. To understand how such revolutionary decisions are made, one needs to examine both the impact of nature and logic, and the techniques of persuasion, within the community of scientists.

They talk through each other. Each hopes to convert the other to his or her way of seeing the science and its problems. The competition between paradigms cannot be resolved by proofs. They cannot fully communicate, unless one group experiences the conversion which is called a "paradigm shift." The transition between competing paradigms cannot be made gradually, forced by logic and neutral experience. It must happen all at once or not at all.

At the time of paradigm change resistance is inevitable and legitimate, and proof looses its importance for justification. However, arguments gain relevance for persuading scientists to change their minds.

A new candidate for paradigm has few supporters at the start. They improve it, explore its possibilities, in order to show the advantages of belonging to its community. If they are successful, the number and strength of the persuasive arguments in its favor increase. More scientists convert, and the exploration of the new paradigm goes on. Gradually the number of experiments, instruments, articles, and books based upon the new paradigm multiply. More and more scientists, convinced of the new paradigm's fruitfulness, adopt the new mode of practicing science. Finally, only a few scientists remain who do not convert, and who cannot be judged as being wrong.

Scientific revolutions are defined as those non-cumulative developmental episodes in which an older paradigm is replaced, in whole or in part, by an incompatible new one. It is a reconstruction of the science on a new foundation; a reconstruction that changes some of the most fundamental theories, methods and applications. When the reconstruction is complete, the community of scientists has changed its view of the field, methods, and goals. This aspect of scientific development is similar to a change in visual gestalt: the marks on paper that were first seen as a bird are now seen as an antelope. The parallel between political and scientific development should be clear.

Paradigms differ in substance, which is directed not only to nature but also on the science itself. They imply methods, problem-field, and standards of solution, which are accepted by the scientific community, at any time. The reconstruction of a new paradigm requires a redefinition of the scientific field. Some old problems may be passed to another science, or declared entirely unscientific. Others, which were not existent or considered trivial before, may become the very archetype of significant scientific achievement. As the problems change, so does the standard that distinguishes a scientific solution from a metaphysical speculation, word game, or mathematical play. The science that emerges from a scientific revolution is both incomplete and incommensurable with its predecessor. That change affects the structure of post-revolutionary textbooks[7] and research publications.

When paradigms change, the world changes with them. With a new paradigm, scientists adopt new instruments and look in new places. Even more important, after revolutions scientists see new and different things, when looking with familiar

---

7 In this respect, it is interesting to note the following two statements. First, the statement by Harrigan: "I taught corporate finance the first time in 1956 ... At that time, we used a textbook ... It was all descriptive. It was about the practical details of stocks and bonds and investment banks and so forth." Frankfurter, Carleton, Gordon, Horrigan, McGoun, Philippatos, and Robinson (1994), p. 194. Second, the statement by Carleton: "... most of the people— 'financial economists'—who have entered the Ph.D. degree since then (early 1970s) got their degrees in the finance department under programs that involved only a very narrow slice of economics training. Most of us who got into finance at an earlier time had training in economics that was a lot more broadly based than simply neoclassical economics." Frankfurter, Carleton, Gordon, Horrigan, McGoun, Philippatos, and Robinson (1994), p. 193.

instruments, in places they looked before. In other words, after a revolution, scientists respond to a different world. Paradigms determine large areas of experience. The scientist with a new paradigm sees differently from the way he or she had seen before. What individuals see depends both upon what they look at and upon what their previous visual-conceptual experience has taught them to see. The perceived size, color, and so on, of experimentally displayed objects also vary with the subject's previous training and experience.

All in all, the older views of nature were, as a whole, neither less scientific nor more the product of human idiosyncrasy than those current today.

In summary, science is of fundamentally subjective nature. Researchers adhere to different worldviews and generate alternative perspectives. This is because they impose different meanings and interpretations upon data. Competition between rival paradigms translates into advocates trying to persuade others of the superiority of their paradigm. Knowledge is generated through a rigorous examination of ideas. Ideas must usually survive scrutiny by advocates of diverse theoretical positions before they gain the status of truth. New definitions of truth come to being, as products of a socially negotiated consensus between truth makers. This consensus may encourage scientists to view knowledge as objective, but it is, in fact, intersubjectively produced. As for scientific progress, theories that gain dominance are those that win the most converts; they do not negate their predecessors, they need not necessarily have greater explanatory or predictive power. Theories do not gain popularity because they are better than their predecessors, but because they are able to attract adherents and withstand attacks from other positions. Scientific progress is not the outcome of the instrumental acquisition of information about objective reality, but it is the product of a subjective process, in which scientists seek superiority of their paradigm as an end in itself.

Based on the interpretive paradigm, McGoun (1992a) in his reflection "On the Knowledge of Finance," states:

> Financial economists proceed as if their science is no exception. There is financial behavior out there, and financial economists empirically test theoretical statements regarding financial behavior to determine their truths, rigorously search for new theoretical statements regarding financial behavior, and periodically congratulate themselves on their success.
>
> However, the ontology of finance is not what is implied by these assumptions:
>
> (1) Financial behavior is not independent of the science of financial economics. Therefore,
> (2) The truth of scientific statements regarding the determinants of financial behavior is not a matter subject to determination;
> (3) At all times, all current truths regarding the determinants of financial behavior have been stated; and
> (4) Over time, financial economists state neither more nor better but different truths regarding the determinants of financial behavior.
>
> Actors know what determines their financial behavior, and these determinants change as the environment of the actors changes. Part of this environment is the science of financial

economics itself. Financial economics is not a positive science of what is nor it is even a normative science of what ought to be. Rather, it is rhetorical science of contention for what will be. (p. 162)

Frankfurter's interpretation of the general developments in the academic field of finance falls within the interpretive paradigm, when he states:

> I started thinking about what we are really doing, and reached the conclusion that we are following a positivist ... logic. ... This logic was adopted in economics. Finance, of course imitates economics in every sense, following Friedman's famous 1953 book, Essays in Positive Economics.

> His view is merely a statement—a statement for which there is no solid proof. But, everyone accepted the statement because it was made with such fervor that it seemed true. No one questioned its validity. Then, I started looking more closely at what happened around that time. I found, to my surprise, that many people criticized Friedman at the time the statement was made. If I want to criticize positive economics today, I would not be able to come up with anything new that I could add to the criticism that was voiced at that time. In other words, everything was known then and there yet everyone disregarded the criticism and instead followed positive economics, which is basically the underpinning of whatever we do in finance today. All the models follow positivist logic. (Frankfurter, Carleton, Gordon, Horrigan, McGoun, Philippatos, and Robinson 1994, p. 191)

McGoun (1992a) provides a more specific explanation of developments in the academic field of finance:

> Changes occur in the world view or weltbild. Paradigms are overthrown by revolution and/ or research programs degenerate. The influence of science on the intellectual environment is what permits science to advance.

> While it is by no means clear what a scientific revolution is, Modigliani and Miller (1958) would certainly be a strong candidate for having effected one in financial economics. According to Ross (1988), "If the view of the progress of science that interprets it as one of paradigms has merit, then surely the work of Miller and Modigliani provides a laboratory example of a violently shifted paradigm." (p. 127)

> For better or worse, the process of simplification, the mathematization, and the arbitrage structure of their proof all have had a profound impact on the way in which financial economics has proceeded since. In turn, they are intellectually indebted to their predecessors for their graphs, their diagrams, their notation, and whatever was referenced in their footnotes. (pp. 166–167)

Radical Humanist View

In contemporary social life rational domination is the primary mode of organization.[8] Neutrality, objectivity, and an observer who is not part of phenomenon being studied, provide the basis for the social order that replaces earlier forms of social organization

---

8 Much of the discussion that follows is based on Held (1980).

reflecting criteria like birth, class, ethnicity, and gender. Bureaucratic values, replace traditional values, and provide the foundation for certain elements of society to dominate others, through the control of the definitions of rationality.

Claims, perspectives, and philosophies are ideological, if they conceal social contradictions in favor of a dominant class or group. For instance, they are ideological, when they present over all social interests but conceal the interests of the ruling class; or when they present societal outcomes as natural but they are the result of particular social relations; or when they present the social situation as harmonious but it is conflict ridden. Ideologies are not illusions, but embodied in social relations. Ideologies often consist of packages of symbols, ideas, images and theories, through which people experience their relation to each other and the world. Ideologies mystify social relations, or adequately reflect distorted ones. Therefore, the aim should be to expose contradictions between society's performance and legitimating ideologies.

Rationalization may encompass the following two meanings. First, it refers to the mathematization of experience and knowledge. That is, the extension of the rationality of the model of natural sciences to all scientific practices, including the conduct of life itself. Second, it refers to means-end relationship. That is, the attainment of a given end by the use of the precise calculation of means.

Rationalization most often refers to the extension of means-end rationality, which is often called technological rationality, instrumental reason, or subjective reason. The emergence and advance of instrumental reason led to the progressive undermining of traditional world views; Reformation and Protestantism played important roles in the formation of conditions necessary for capitalist development; and capitalism provided a major impetus to the further development of instrumental reason and bureaucratization, resulting from the division of labor.

Individualism, or self-interest, was nurtured in the sixteenth and seventeenth centuries. Its underlying philosophies were committed to the view that the individual is rational and capable of independent thinking. Its fulfillment was held to be dependent on social and economic conditions in which the individual would be free to work and think in a setting of his or her choice. Free competition and liberalism were thought to be sufficient. Over time, however, the notion of individual achievement was expressed in terms of labor productivity figures. That is, performance was motivated, guided, and measured by standards external to the individual. Capital accumulation required the expansion of instrumental reason, which created a common framework for all occupations. Compliance and subordination to pre-set goals and standards were required of all individuals. Furthermore, as standardized techniques advanced, and technological rationality expanded over the whole of society, they developed values only for the better functioning of the apparatus. Propositions regarding production, organization, rules of the game, business methods, science and technique, are evaluated with reference to the means-end relationship, and if, as means, they are suitable for reaching the end, which remains unquestioned.

Specialization atomizes individuals. The continued extension of division of labor leads to the fragmentation of tasks. Under these circumstances, there are fewer opportunities for mental and reflective labor. Knowledge of the total work process is not easily available. The majority of occupations tend to become isolated units, which require co-ordination and management from above. Centralized control mechanisms, private and public bureaucracies, appear as necessary for, and a guarantee of, a rational order.

The private and public bureaucracies, thus, seem to emerge on an objective and impersonal ground. The objective and impersonal qualities of technological rationality make them look more reasonable, and provide the bureaucratic groups the universal dignity of reason. The rationality, embodied in the giant capitalist enterprises, makes it appear as if individuals, when obeying them, obey objective rationality. The private bureaucracy creates a delusion that there is harmony between special and common interests. Under these circumstances, there is a decline in the acceptability of critical thinking by society.

Reason gains its only meaning with reference to the process of coordinating means to predetermined ends. Instrumental reason gains its privileged status, since it is embodied in the concept of rationality. The confounding of calculatory with rational thinking creates the perception that whatever cannot be measured and reduced to numbers is illusion or metaphysics. The difference between phenomena is judged only as the difference in quantity or efficiency. The individual, instead of having qualities of resistance and autonomy, has qualities of compliance and adjustment. But the individual's lack of freedom is not usually experienced as such. It is not considered as the work of some hostile force. Rather, it is considered as the result of reason. Individuals do not come to know that, in fact, subjective reason is pursued and put to profitable use.

All individuals who seek the maintenance of their lives have to act rationally. That is, they have to behave according to the standards which insure the functioning of the apparatus. This reinforces types of behavior that are adaptive, passive, and acquiescent, whereby the mechanisms of social control are strengthened.

The Enlightenment gained its success based on modern science, that is, with the mathematization of nature, and it gave an enormous impetus to science. The new science defined a purely rational world as the only true reality. It portrayed the world as a scientific universe, which could be systematically comprehended only by science itself. Every object, which could be represented by mathematical theorems, became a possible subject of study. The development of a universal, mathematically formulated science, and its emergence as the model for all science and knowledge, represents the era of positivism.

Positivism counters the influence of purely a priori thinking and establishes the authority of observation. Positivism makes few distinctions between the methods appropriate to the physical and human sciences. The study of society is equated with that of nature. Both are seen as governed by natural necessity. Therefore, individuals should take a positive attitude toward the prevailing state of affairs. Positive philosophy affirms the existing order, against negating it. Science does not deny the necessity of progressive reforms. But the form of these changes is always determined by the established order.

Science sees all social movements as subject to law-like regularities; it regards many social institutions as unchangeable through rational will. Political action, therefore, must direct itself to fixed and general limits. Central issues in social struggle should be resolved by scientific investigation. Thus, critical thinking surrenders to ideology. Scientific system surrenders metaphysics and political imagination to the existent.

Certain principles of positive philosophy ensure the existing order. They are the principles which justify the authority of observation, against alternative forms of reason and imagination. Only seeing the given, follows from the positivist view that phenomenon must be observed. Human activity is categorized as objective necessity. Sociology, as a positive science, has no relation to value judgements, and facts and values are quite separate entities. Therefore, there is no objective basis, independent of science and its findings, to criticize society. "What is" is "what ought to be!" But, this stance cannot be justified by positive philosophy. Since, questions of "ought," that is, of value judgement, are irrational, by the separation of fact and value. Positive philosophy builds upon prejudgments and evaluations, which it cannot rationally justify.

The goal of radical humanists is to be able to judge between competing analyses of reality and to expose elements of ideology. Radical humanists view science and evaluation as united. One must be able to evaluate aspects of reality, for instance, ideology and myths, in order to analyze it accurately. A positivist approach cannot do this, because it has no basis to assess competing frames of reference.

For emancipation, it is essential to nullify the influence of scientism in philosophy, and other spheres of thought. Scientism implies that science is not one type of possible knowledge rather it is "the" knowledge. Positivism provides scientism with the most sophisticated defense. Positivism came to life as a critique of ideology (of religion, dogma, speculative metaphysics, and so on), however, it became a central element of technocratic consciousness and the key aspect of modern ideology.

Radical humanists must discard the illusion of objectivism from knowledge. This illusion conceals the processes in which facts are constructed, and prevents consciousness of the interlocking of knowledge with interests. Knowledge is formed in virtue of three interests: (1) information that increases our power of technical control of objects in the environment; (2) interpretations that make possible the orientations of action within common traditions by furthering mutual, intersubjective understanding; and (3) analyses that free consciousness from its dependence on hypostatized power.

The third interest, the emancipatory interest, is securing freedom from hypostatized forces and conditions of distorted communication. This interest is based in individuals' capacity to decide rationally, to self-consciously reason, in light of available knowledge, rules, and needs. Human history is made with will and consciousness. But, once it is noted that history reflects domination, repression, and the ideological framing of action, it becomes clear that self-understanding is often limited by unacknowledged conditions. If the rational capabilities of human beings are to be nurtured, a particular type of knowledge becomes necessary, to guide the elucidation and abolition of these conditions. The form of knowledge most appropriate for this purpose is self-knowledge generated through self-reflection. By bringing to consciousness the determinants of the self-formative process, structures of distortion can be revealed, isolated and, under the proper, specifiable conditions, eradicated.

Emancipatory interest in knowledge is the driving force to achieve self-understanding and autonomy of action. It is the human beings' ability to reflect on their own development, and to act with greater consciousness and autonomy, which sets the basis for the emancipatory interest in knowledge.

To summarize, there are three knowledge-related interests and three categories of knowledge. Each of the interests initiates a distinct methodological approach to the generation of knowledge. Each is rooted in life, which is basic to the survival and development of human beings. It is only in light of these interests that knowledge can be comprehended.

Interests, power bases, and institutional settings, affect the concern and practices of social scientists. It is not sufficient to recognize, as with interpretive paradigm, that knowledge communities are guided by, and defensive of, paradigms. Beyond this, paradigms must be dealt with within the larger social context, through ties to interest and power bases in organizations, institutional complexes, and so on.

In academic finance, there are instances where reference is made to the ideological nature of mainstream academic finance. The following constitutes a sample of three: Frankfurter (1995) states:

> Neoclassical economics, with its notion of the existence of an almighty, all-encompassing market, is the ideological base, and positivist thinking, as articulated by Friedman's (1953) classical essay, is the methodological base. (p. 26)

Gordon states:

> It may be wondered why neoclassical economics theory remains widely accepted when many of its important theorems are so false as to be ridiculous. The answer is that the theory is an ideology and not a science. In fact, neoclassical economic theory provides a more attractive vision of the future and rationalization of the status quo than our great religions. (Frankfurter, Carleton, Gordon, Horrigan, McGoun, Philippatos, and Robinson 1994, p. 180)

Bettner, Robinson, and McGoun (1994) state:

> The famous capital markets scholars have founded ideological dynasties (The Chicago School, The Rochester School, etc.) and even received Nobel Prizes. Though their joint control of the editorial boards of the major finance journals and the political and social processes which underlie doctoral education, capital market researchers can ensure the perpetuation of their methods as the sole form of legitimate inquiry, and guarantee their own future success. (p. 2)

Whitley (1986) specifically explains how business finance was transformed into financial economics to meet the self-interest of both academics and the professional finance community.

> In seeking to explain how the study of business finance became transformed into "financial economics" so quickly in the USA, it is necessary to combine a discussion of academic expansion, the growth of technocratic beliefs in the efficacy of science, economists' imperialism, … and changes in financial markets, especially the rise of new financial intermediaries.

The high prestige of the natural sciences after the Second World War, ... encouraged the widespread belief in the late 1940s and 1950s that "science" could be applied to managerial and business problems and scientific research into these problems should be supported.

This belief in the methods and procedures perceived to be typical of the natural sciences, ... also encouraged the growth of the "behavioral sciences" and the expansion of economics in the 1960s. The apparent success of Keynesian inspired macro-economic advice and relatively steady growth rates of the US economy in the 1950s and 1960s reinforced the belief that economics and social affairs could be "managed" through the use of expert advice based on scientific research, and that the appropriate way of conducting such research was exemplified by the use of mathematical procedures and models in economics and O.R. ... This belief was expressed in some detail in the studies of business education in the USA ... The Ford foundation accompanied these suggestions with the allocation of considerable funds for doctoral research and faculty development to encourage business schools to become more "scientific" by applying mathematics, statistics and the social sciences to business problems.

As part of this general "scientification" of business education and research, the study of business finance has become transformed since 1960. From being largely descriptive and focused on the operations of particular financial institutions, it has developed a highly mathematical and formal approach and concentrated on valuation processes in perfect markets.

... the study of finance has become highly organized around a particular style of research and analysis drawn from orthodox, neo-classical economics. ... Indeed, the dominant intellectual standards and goals are remarkably similar to those of Anglo-Saxon (positive) economics and research appears to be similarly organized and controlled as a "partitioned bureaucracy."

Partitioned bureaucracies are highly rule-governed scientific fields which manifest a considerable degree of technical task uncertainty in dealing with empirical phenomena at the same time as a much greater degree of control over analytical work and objects.

This partitioning remains effective as a means of coping with uncertainty as long as the reputational system as a whole is dominated by the standards and goals of those undertaking analytical studies and retains sufficient economic and social support for their standards to govern access to material rewards.

The expansion of the US equity markets, of individuals and institutions participating in them and of financial intermediaries have had a number of consequences. First, the number of people engaged in brokerage, analysis and fund management has grown substantially.

Secondly, ... More people are now engaged in investment analysis and management than in the 1940s and more of them are coordinated and controlled in hierarchical organizations. These consequences have encouraged attempts at "professionalization" among financial analysts.

A third ... was the ... new forms of competition—including new financial instruments —between financial institutions.

The expansion of job opportunities in investment analysis and management, ... and competition between, funds managers provided a benign setting for the expansion and transformation of business finance teaching and research. (pp. 171–85)

Radical Structuralist View

To survive and reproduce themselves, human beings transform reality, where material reality is the most important.[9] In a society, which is defined with reference to social relations, this transformation takes place through the social division of labor. That is, the social product results from a collective activity. The social division of labor implies that these groups enter into relations with each other to produce, while they use means of production. That is, they enter into production relations. These groups, formed in terms of production relations, are called social classes. A complete definition of a social class encompasses economic, political, and ideological elements, with dialectical relationships. Production relations, under capitalism, are antagonistic and asymmetric. They are antagonistic, since they unite two antagonistic poles, defined as owner/appropriator/non-laborer and non-owner/expropriated/laborer. They are asymmetric, since in this relation the owner is the principal, or determinant, and the non-owner is the secondary, or determined. Therefore, social classes, who are the carriers of contradictory aspects of social relations, are antagonistic too. They exist in a context of class struggle, and constantly attempt to dominate each other.

Transforming material requires knowledge of doing it. Gaining knowledge of doing it requires dealing with it, i.e., transforming it. This is the materialist basis of epistemology. That is, only those who are engaged in material transformation have the possibility of knowing reality. In other words, science has a materialist nature, i.e., the principle of the determination of the concrete in thought by the real concrete. This starts with the development of knowledge by material production. Therefore, only classes, identifiable in terms of production relations, have the objective possibility of an independent knowledge of reality. Furthermore, the class which deals with a larger portion of reality has the greater objective possibility of gaining a correct knowledge of it. Under capitalism, the proletariat,[10] which deals with an increasing portion of social reality, has the objective possibility of knowing it correctly. In the context of the constant attempt that classes make to dominate each other, the need for classes to know reality in order to transform, can only realize itself through a multiplicity of world views. Since all of them are struggling for domination, it can only realize itself through ideological class struggle. Knowledge is, thus, in the most fundamental sense, ideological, since it formulates views of reality and solves problems from a class point of view.

The materialist position presupposes the existence of material reality and non-material reality, that is, social relations. This recognizes the existence of both material and non-material real concretes, and the primacy of social relations of

---

9 Much of the discussion that follows is based on Carchedi (1983).

10 The proletariat is defined as all the individuals who participate in the transformation of material, that is, in the transformation of the social product, while not owning the means necessary for this transformation.

material transformation, that is, production relations, over other social relations and phenomena, as well as over material transformation.

The primacy of real transformation over the production (transformation) of knowledge implies that the production of knowledge is a process of mental, active transformation, and not of reflection of the real concrete in thought, and is class determined. In other words, there are different interpretations of the same reality and all of them are objective, though not necessarily correct. The different interpretations are antagonistic. This is because they are conditions of domination, on the level of knowledge, of antagonistic classes. In other words, they are conditions of reproduction or supersession of inherently antagonistic structures.

There is complementarity between class determination of knowledge, plurality of objective knowledge, and the possibility for one of them to provide a correct, but not in the sense of a reflective, vision of reality. More specifically, knowledge is both objective, and class determined, since these problems are raised and solved from class points of view. This implies, first, that the solution of problems is an aspect of class domination. That is, problems are never solved to the advantage of the whole society, of all classes, but only to the advantage of one, or some, of them. Second, it implies the incompatibility of different types of knowledge, because they are class determined. Therefore, knowledge is the correct solution, as checked by the process of practical and logical verification, of problems from a class point of view. It is, therefore, not reflective. Problems, in principle, can be correctly solved by the class that has the largest contact with reality. The principle of class determination of knowledge, and thus of the incompatibility of different kinds of knowledge, prevents verification in terms of comparison with socially neutral theories or data. However, the materialist basis of epistemology ensures the possibility for one class to produce a knowledge that is not only class determined, but also able to be correct because of that class's position within the social structure. This perceives reality, and thus problems, in terms of contradictions, and has at its disposal a theory that justifies its claim to be able to solve not only localized but also general contradictions.

The proletariat believes that each class generates its own knowledge, as a condition of domination over other classes. From the proletariat's point of view, absolute or judgmental relativism is ruled out, because it is the proletariat that has the objectively determined possibility of gaining a correct knowledge of reality.

Class affiliations affect the concern and practices of social scientists. It is not sufficient to recognize, as with interpretive paradigm, that knowledge communities are guided by, and defensive of, paradigms. Beyond this, paradigms must be dealt with within the larger social context, through ties to social classes.

In relation to the development of the general field of management, Burrell and Morgan (1979) provide an interesting reference and explanation:

What is interesting for our present purposes is the form taken by Braverman's attack upon many of the contemporary schools within management theory, an attack which is predicated upon an analysis of advanced capitalism in terms of its basic economic structure, using conceptualizations derived from Marx's Capital. With the aid of detailed examples, Braverman carefully links the developments of these schools with changes in the societal means and relations of production. In essence, he portrays management theory as a superstructural manifestation of the workings of the economic base of capitalist societies. He implies that "as a branch of management science," it "views all things through the eyes of the bourgeoisie." ... Moreover, they become an important motive force in this process in their own right. Thus, ... through their intervention, they actively and in a concrete way ensure its survival and continued good health. (pp. 381–2)

Conclusion

This chapter discussed four explanations for the course of the development of science, in general, and finance, in particular. Each explanation was based on one of the four paradigms. The functionalist paradigm views science as the outcome of the search for objective truth; the interpretive paradigm views science as being socially constructed; the radical humanist paradigm views science as an element of the dominant ideology; and the radical structuralist paradigm views science as being class determined. The chapter emphasized that these four explanations are equally scientific and informative; they look at the process of the development of academic finance from a certain paradigmatic viewpoint.

This chapter took the case of development of academic finance as an example and emphasized that, in general, any phenomenon may be seen and analyzed from different viewpoints and that each viewpoint exposes a certain aspect of the phenomenon under consideration. Collectively, they provide a much broader and deeper understanding of the phenomenon. Therefore, academic finance can benefit much from contributions coming from other paradigms if it respects paradigm diversity.

Knowledge of finance is ultimately a product of the researcher's paradigmatic approach to this multifaceted phenomenon. Viewed from this angle, the pursuit of financial knowledge is seen as much an ethical, moral, ideological, and political activity, as a technical one. Academic finance can gain much by exploiting the new insights coming from other paradigms.

Chapter 7

Mathematical Language of Academic Finance: Four Paradigmatic Views

It is well known that neoclassical economists develop and refine their theory using the language of mathematics. The defense of the use of mathematics as a neutral language means that the debates within literary criticism about the non-neutrality of language have an important contribution to make in reconsidering the use of mathematics.

Any adequate analysis of the nature of language and its role necessarily requires fundamental understanding of the worldviews underlying the expression of views with respect to the nature of language and its role. Four general views with respect to language and its role, corresponding to the four paradigms, are discussed. The functionalist paradigm views language as an instrument for reference to sense data or systematic treatment of ideas. The interpretive paradigm views language as being socially constructed, that is, people create language by their daily usage. The radical humanist paradigm views language both as inhibiting the growth of human beings and as the solution to the removal of such an inhibition. The radical structuralist paradigm views language as being created by economic substructure. These four views with respect to the nature of language and its role are equally scientific and informative; each looks at the nature of language and its role from a certain paradigmatic viewpoint.

This chapter takes the case of language as an example and emphasizes that, in general, any phenomenon may be seen and analyzed from different viewpoints and that each viewpoint exposes a certain aspect of the phenomenon under consideration. Collectively, they provide a much broader and deeper understanding of the phenomenon. Therefore, academic finance can benefit much from contributions coming from other paradigms if it respects paradigm diversity.

Functionalist View

Functionalist paradigm views with respect to the nature of language and its role are discussed in this section.[1]

---

[1] Classics in this literature are Ayer (1936), Carnap (1964, 1967), Russell (1914, 1918, 1926), and Schlick (1930, 1932).

Rationalist and empiricist epistemologies are closely tied to the nominalist legacy, with its distinctive separation of logic and reality or of conceptual apparatus and sense data. Logically refined empiricism and rationalism demonstrate the possibility of translating pure mathematics into logic and, conversely, of transcribing logical reasoning into a mathematical or quasi-mathematical language or symbol system. A radical version of empiricism or realism holds that all knowledge ultimately derives from direct sense experience.

From the nominalist perspective, conceptual-linguistic categories are viewed as tools or instruments for empirical analysis, tools which are relatively independent of their subject matter.

The dual stress on logic and empiricism places epistemological emphasis on the way sense experience can be adequately captured in language. That is, the way words or sentences can be properly "hooked up" with concrete sense data or "immediate objects" of sensation. It shows the dependence of conceptual and linguistic significance on direct experience, i.e., an uncompromising attachment to empirical semantics or to what some language theorists call a "referential theory of meaning."

The most expedient or straightforward manner of preserving the referential meaning of language is to use such terms as "this, that, and the other" as direct designations or what is termed "proper names" for the experienced phenomena, since ordinary descriptions are liable to exceed the bounds of acquaintance.

Rigorously stated, the logical-atomist position involves not only a loose correlation or parallelism but rather an actual "isomorphism" of linguistic terms and statements, on the other hand, and the structure of reality (seen as compound of sense data), on the other.

The same principle carries over into the character of atomic sentences and their constituent parts. In line with the requirement of sense immediacy, such sentences should be simply structured, containing basically "names" for particular sense data together with terms designating their properties and various inter-relations between data. Basic or atomic statements should be composed of only one or a few names, linked with a single predicate or relational term, and should assert merely that a named entity has a given property or stands in a specified relation with other entities. The central advantage of properly constructed atomic sentences is their amenability to empirical testing. That is, given the sense correlates of their constituent parts such sentences can readily be verified or falsified by direct experience. Even more complex strings or compounds of sentences are in principle subject to the same empiricist yardstick—provided these compounds can be broken up or reassembled into a series of atomic units, each of which satisfies the requirement of immediate sense correlation.

The central aim is to design logically precise and univocal linguistic instruments which can serve as "meta-languages" for the analysis of reports or "object languages" employed by sciences in various sense-data domain. Such meta-languages are logical syntactical structures fashioned for strictly analytical or "philosophical" purposes. The objective is to provide a system of concepts, a language, with the help of which the results of logical analysis can be exactly formulated. More specifically, philosophy is to be replaced by the logic of science. That is, to be replaced by the logical analysis of the concepts and sentences of the sciences, for the logic of science is nothing other than the logical syntax of the language of science. In implementing this objective, two linguistic levels can be delineated. The first is more "simple in form" covering a "narrow field of concepts," while the second is "richer in modes of expression" by which all sentences both of classical mathematics and of classical physics can be formulated.

Apart from strictly syntactical-analytical propositions, the "meaning" of any statement is determined by the conditions or methods of its verification. That is, a statement makes sense only if, and to the extent that, its empirical reference can be firmly corroborated.

Two broad types of legitimate assertions can be differentiated. On the one hand statements which are true solely by virtue of their form (tautologies) and also the negations of such statements (contradictions). On the other hand statements whose truth or falsehood is predicated on the "protocol sentences" and which are therefore "(true or false) empirical statements." The first category in this account say or report "nothing about reality" and contain "the formulae of logic and mathematics," while the second group of sentences is content-laden and basically co-extensive with "the domain of empirical science." Accordingly, since all statements are of an empirical nature and belong to factual science, "philosophy" is identified basically with "method." In other words, the method of logical analysis is seen as the yardstick for inquiring into logical foundations of a properly scientific philosophy in contrast to metaphysics. Rationalism and empiricism are marked by the intensive cultivation of logical and mathematical modes of reasoning, a cultivation leading to the identification of "philosophy" with logical analysis.

Rationalists view "mind" as an arsenal or source of substantive knowledge, of a knowledge which, in contrast to purely contingent sense impressions, can claim in some sense "a priori" or "universal" status.

Despite the contrast between their epistemological approaches, both empiricism and rationalism are linked by a common linguistic commitment: the search for univocity or a stable set of significations. Empiricists stabilize meanings through recourse to a formal-logical idiom whose terms are expected somehow to match sense data. Rationalists pursue a similar aim by focusing on language itself and, assuming a connection between language and thought, on the inherent structure and capacities of "mind." Instead of using external "reference" as a stabilizing loadstone or anchor, the moorings of language in the second case are found in pure syntax, grammar, and other "internal" factors.

Interpretive View

Interpretive paradigm views with respect to the nature of language and its role are discussed in this section.[2]

Language is an inter-subjective phenomenon in which words function as games tokens, with the incredibly rich variety of the game being matched by the variety of

---

2 The classic in this literature is Wittgenstein (1953).

functions served by the tokens. Words are not a translation of something else that was there before they were. Language is connected to the world by social convention and training, not as a form of representation. The proper study of language is a pure cultural anthropology.

The basic picture is this: first, naturally given, biologically driven patterns of interaction, then simple language-games that are embellishments of these, and then a proliferation of more complex language-games that grow sequentially out of those early simple ones. Simple language customs grow out of proto customs, or interaction patterns, and the simple customs change, grow and combine into the multitude of complex language customs that we participate in daily. And at the far end of that evolution are language-games of extreme complexity, requiring for their mastery years of special study, such as theoretical physics or neuroscience. But those abstract and abstruse bits of regimented language retain their roots in the primitive. Learning physics requires one to learn to count. Language-games should be thought of as language complete in themselves and as complete systems of human communication. The multiplicity of language-games is not fixed once and for all. New types of language, new language-games come into existence, and others become obsolete and get forgotten. The changing styles speak of changing needs, fashions, and circumstances.

A language-game does not have its origins in consideration. Consideration is part of a language-game. Training and instinct provide the starting point of all our explanations and the terminus of all our justifications. Explanation is only possible after training bas been successful. Words are ultimately connected to the world by training, not by translation. If language is to be a means of communication, there must be agreement not only in definitions but also in judgements.

Linguistic responses can only be understood in the way they are integrated into patterns of activity. Only in the stream of thought and life do words have meaning. Meaning is located in the function that words have as "signals" passed back and forth between people in the course of purposeful and shared activity. Even if proper names can be said to have meaning, it still is not possible to use "the formula:" meaning equals thing named. Here the term "language-game" is meant to bring into prominence the fact that speaking of language is part of an activity or of a form of life.

An object does not obtain a name except in the context of a language-game. The emphasis on the word-object link needs to be supplemented by an awareness of the context in which the word is used. Since a word mediates activities, then the dominance of "the formula" will be broken. In place of such theories, emphasis needs to be placed on the idea of "use." For a large class of cases the meaning of a word is its use in the language. Words are to be brought back from their metaphysical to their everyday use.

The established meaning of a word does not determine its future applications. The development of a language-game is not determined by its past verbal form. Meaning is created by acts of use. Use determines meaning; meaning does not determine use. Meaning extends as far as, but no further than, the finite range of circumstances in which a word is used.

Meaning is not a formal method of hypothesis verification deliberately conducted to exact a specific end product. Rather, it is a process wherein the individual's awareness of how "the way of telling anything" relates to "what the thing is" and impacts on the process itself.

Meaning is interactive. What could count as accord with the "rule of meaning" in language can be found only in the relations of rules and their usage, that is, the life which is given to interpretations of linguistic rules by practice. Not only rules, but also examples are needed for establishing a practice. Our rules leave loopholes open, and the practice has to speak for itself.

Instead of producing something common to all that is called language, these phenomena have no one thing in common which makes everyone use the same word for all, but that they are related to one another in many different ways. And it is because of this relationship, or these relationships, that we call them all "language."

A sign does not stand in a projective relation with the meaning that it represents. The various phenomena of language must not necessarily have a unity. The uniform appearance of a word or sentence (for example, in speaking, spelling, and so on.) assures us of no uniformity or generality pervading many and various ways of using it, which are dependent upon spatial and temporal factors or what might be called context. Language consists ultimately of nothing more than the multiplicity of "family resemblances" among linguistic phenomena (concepts), each bearing the same signifier. There are similarities among phenomena bearing the same signifier, but it is in the differences among uses that meaning can be grasped.

In all things there can be noticed ("seen" or "heard") both similarities and differences, and these ultimately lead to the specific notion of "resemblances" among people, words, and meanings.

Language consists of "overlapping of many fibers," in contrast to the essentialist view that it consists of "some one fiber running through its whole."

The context-based modeling of meaning shows that in order to discern and describe the actual use of language in a given circumstance without dependence upon recourse to an *a priori* frame of interpretation, grammar (in this philosophical sense) obviously must include the description of a language-situation. Language thus becomes the means by which reality is represented as it is approximated and signified by people. The grammar of language is thus not merely linguistic but also extra-linguistic (for example, social, cultural, and historical).

What one sees across uses of a word is not a concept "common to all," but rather the way that words are related to one another in many different ways. What defines the parameters of meaning is the resemblance of words sharing a common cultural location. The fact that similarity can be generalized only into resemblance, not identity, combined with the idea that we compose our reality, leads to the idea that with every moment we begin again, composing anew.

We create the resemblances of word meanings in contexts, in which we compose their meanings. There is no *a priori* foundation for meaning or understanding. This is constitutive of linguistic meaning. As a result, the meaning remains latent, impossible to translate into something else.

Radical Humanist View

Radical humanist paradigm views with respect to the nature of language and its role are discussed in this section.[3]

This view links types of knowledge with underlying human orientations termed "cognitive interests." Those interests reflect a categorical structure of human existence or experience. Existence exhibits three main dimensions: those of man's relations with nature, with his fellow man, and with himself. In the first dimension cognition aims at the appropriation of nature's bounty of human goals (and thus is guided by a "technical interest"). The second domain is animated by the purpose of reaching reciprocal understanding among individuals (in accordance with a "practical interest"). In the last area the quest for knowledge involves a search for self-knowledge, a search necessitating a struggle against both internal and external "blinders" or constraints (thus reflecting an "emancipatory interest"). Language as speech plays a role primarily in the last two fields: first, as an instrument of communicative interaction, and secondly, as a "therapeutic" medium facilitating the transition from a distorted-repressive to a rational and liberated mode of self-knowledge.

In order to participate in normal discourse the speaker must have at his disposal, in addition to his linguistic competence, basic qualifications of speech and symbolic interaction which is called *communicative competence*. The latter term denotes basically the "mastery of an ideal speech situation," that is, a situation manifesting the "ideal" or universal parameters of communication.

To be fully operative, the structure of communication requires "ideally" competent speakers. That is, speakers who are able to perform all types of speech act without discrimination or constraint. Pure inter-subjectivity exists only when there is complete symmetry in the distribution of assertion and denial, revelation and concealment, prescription and conformity among the partners of communication. These three symmetries represent, incidentally, a linguistic conceptualization of what are traditionally known as the idea of truth, freedom, and justice.

Although legitimate for some purposes, the bifurcation between langue and parole is not sufficient reason for the view that the pragmatic dimension of language from which one abstracts is beyond formal analysis. Whereas a grammatical sentence fulfills the claim to comprehensibility, a successful utterance must satisfy three additional validity claims: it must count as true for the participants insofar as it represents something in the world; it must count as truthful insofar as it expresses something intended by the speaker; and it must count as right insofar as it conforms to socially recognized expectations.

On the functional level, the chief types of language use are: a "cognitive," an "interactive," and an "expressive" type. The first emphasizes propositional content, the second concerns the interpersonal speaker-hearer relations, and the third relates with the intentional self-disclosure. Correlated with these functional categories are distinct types of speech acts, labeled "constative," "regulative," and "expressive" act (or "avowals"). The difference between functional modes and speech acts derives

---

3 Classics in this literature are Habermas (1970a, 1970b, 1971, 1973, and 1979).

from stressing one of the validity claims universally inhabiting speech, from the fact that in the cognitive use of language we raise truth claims for propositions and in the interactive use we claim (or contest) the validity of a normative context of interpersonal relations, while the expressive use relates to the truthfulness with which a speaker utters his intentions or the transparency of a subjectivity representing itself in language. The forth claim of comprehensibility is equally raised in all three functional modes and utterances; for every speech act must fulfill the presuppositions of comprehensibility.

The entire model highlights the universal structural features of communicative pragmatics, by showing how grammatical sentences are embedded, by way of universal validity claims, in three relations to reality. Relations corresponding to the pragmatic functions of representing facts, establishing legitimate interpersonal relations, and expressing one's own subjectivity.

The structure of domination embedded within our language and everyday discourse needs to be stressed. The structure of language, its nature and use, provide a key with which to unlock many insights into the fundamental mode of operation of different social formations.

Recent developments in linguistics and ordinary language philosophy demonstrate that the "problem of language" has replaced the traditional "problem of consciousness." The theory of "communicative competence" deals with these developments. It borrows conceptualizations from hermeneutics in order to provide the link between the political macro-structure and speech acts within a context of symbolic interaction. It develops the concept of an "ideal speech situation," in which "symbolic interaction" is possible since genuine consensus is arrived at between parties in communication and is recognized as a consensus without the operation of power. This "ideal speech situation" is contrasted with one characterized by "communicative distortion," in which a supposed consensus is arrived at through discourse within the context of an unequal power distribution.

The theory of "communicative competence" illustrates the difference between these two situations through the concepts of "work" and "interaction." These are seen as being fundamentally different categories of social life, with purposive rationality dominating the former and symbolic interaction the latter. "Work" is viewed as the dominant form of social action within capitalist industrialized society. This social form is seen as based upon a purposive rationality which stresses the importance of goal attainment, defined in terms of means-ends relationships. The system develops technical rules to guide action and modes of thinking, and places stress upon the learning of skills and qualifications. Social life is compartmentalized and language is "context-free." The rationalization of the system of action as a whole lies in the growth of productive forces and the extension of power of technical control. "Work" is seen as a form of "communicative distortion" characterized by asymmetrical choice in the use of speech acts which reflects an unequal power relationship.

"Interaction," on the other hand, is based on communicative action between men in which shared norms develop and are reflected in an inter-subjectively shared ordinary language. Implicitly, "interaction" is seen as more typical of societies in the pre-capitalist era, with their low levels of specialization and relatively undeveloped division of labor. "Interaction" subsumes "labor" as a cohesive and integral part of social life. Within this social form there are reciprocal expectations about behavior, violations of which attract widely based social sanctions. The norms and values which govern social affairs are acquired through a process of role internalization. The rationalization of this system of action lies in "emancipation," "individuation," and the "extension of communication free of domination." "Interaction" is seen as based upon "ideal speech" situations in which man is emancipated from "work" and domination.

Radical Structuralist View

Radical structuralist paradigm views with respect to the nature of language and its role are discussed in this section.[4]

The interrelationship of the basis and superstructures can be elucidated to a significant degree through the material of the word. Looked at from this angle, the essence of this relationship comes down to *how* actual existence (the basis) determines sign and *how* sign reflects and refracts existence in its process of generations.

The properties of the word as an ideological sign are what make the word the most suitable material for viewing the whole of this relationship in basic terms. What is important about the word is that the word is implicated in literally each and every act or contact between people. It stands to reason, then, that the word is the most sensitive *index of social changes*. The word has the capacity to register all the transitory, delicate, momentary phases of social change.

Production relations and the sociopolitical order shaped by those relations determine the full range of verbal contacts between people. In turn, from the conditions, forms, and types of verbal communication derive not only the forms but also the themes of speech performances.

Social psychology is first and foremost an atmosphere made up of multifarious *speech performances* that engulf and wash over all persistent forms and kinds of ideological creativity. Social psychology exists primarily in a wide variety of forms of the "utterance," of little *speech genres* of internal and external kinds.

Each period and each social group has had its own repertoire of speech forms for ideological communication in human behavior. Each set of cognate forms, that is, each behavioral speech genre, has its own corresponding set of themes.

An interlocking organic unity joins the forms of communication (for example, on-the-job communication of the strictly technical kind), the form of the utterance (the concise, businesslike statement) and its theme. Therefore, *classification of the forms of utterance must rely upon classification of the forms of verbal communication*. The latter are entirely determined by production relations and the sociopolitical order.

Every sign is a construct between socially organized persons in the process of their interaction. Therefore, *the forms of signs are conditioned above all by the social organization of the participants involved and also by the immediate conditions of their interaction*. When these forms change, so does sign. In this way the *problem of the relationship between sign and existence* find its concrete expression.

---

4 Classics in this literature are Harvey (1982), Marx (1954, 1959), and Sweezy (1964).

Every ideological sign, in coming about through the process of social intercourse, is defined by the *social purview* of the given time period and the given social group. So far, note has been made of the form of the sign as shaped by the forms of social interaction. Now, another important aspect of sign will be dealt with, that is, the *content* of the sign and the evaluative accentuation that accompanies all content.

Every stage in the development of a society has its own special and restricted circle of items which alone have access to that society's attention and which are endowed with evaluative accentuation by that attention. In other words, *only that which has acquired social value can enter the world of ideology, take shape, and establish itself there.* Only items within that circle will achieve sign formation and become objects in semiotic communication.

In order for any item, from whatever domain of reality it may come, to enter the social purview of the group and elicit ideological semiotic reaction, it must be associated with the vital socioeconomic prerequisites of the particular group's existence. It must somehow, even if only obliquely, make contact with the bases of the group's material life.

Let us agree to call the entity which becomes the object of a sign the *theme* of the sign. Each fully-fledged sign has its theme. So, every verbal performance has its theme. An ideological theme is always socially accentuated. The theme of an ideological sign and the form of an ideological sign are inextricably bound together. Ultimately, the same set of forces and the same material prerequisites bring both the one and the other to life.

Indeed, the economic conditions that inaugurate a new element of reality into the social purview, that make it socially meaningful and interesting, are exactly the same conditions that create the forms of ideological communication, which in turn shape the forms of semiotic expression.

Existence reflected in sign is not merely reflected but *refracted*. This refraction of existence in the ideological sign is determined by an intersecting of differently oriented social interests within one and the same sign community, that is, *by the class struggle*.

Class does not coincide with the sign community, that is, with the community, which is the totality of users of the same set of signs for ideological communication. Thus, different classes use one and the same language. As a result, differently oriented accents intersect in every ideological sign. Sign becomes an arena of the class struggle.

This social *multi-accentuality* of the ideological sign is a very crucial aspect. By and large, it is thanks to this intersecting of accents that a sign maintains its vitality, dynamism, and the capacity for further development. A sign which has been withdrawn from the pressures of the social struggle inevitably loses force, degenerating into allegory and becoming the object not of live social intelligibility but of philological comprehension.

The very same thing that makes the ideological sign vital and mutable is also, however, that which makes it a refracting and distorting medium. The ruling class strives to impart a supra-class, eternal character to the ideological sign, to extinguish or drive inward the struggle between social value judgements which occurs in it, to make the sign uni-accentual.

In actual fact, each living ideological sign has two faces. Any current curse word can become a word of praise and any current truth must inevitably sound to many other people as the greatest lie. This *inner dialectical quality* of the sign comes out fully in the open only in times of social crises or revolutionary changes. In the ordinary conditions of life, the contradiction embedded in every ideological sign cannot emerge fully. This is because the ideological sign in an established, dominant ideology is always somewhat reactionary and tries to stabilize the preceding factor in the dialectical flux of the social generative process, so accentuating yesterday's truth to make it appear as today's. That is responsible for the refracting and distorting peculiarity of the ideological sign within the dominant ideology.

This, then, is the picture of the relation of the basis to superstructure. The material of the verbal sign allows one most fully and easily to follow out the continuity of the dialectical process of change, a process which goes from the basis to superstructure.

Conclusion

This chapter discussed four views with respect to the nature of language and its role. The four views correspond to the four paradigms. The functionalist paradigm views language as an instrument for reference to sense data or systematic treatment of ideas. The interpretive paradigm views language as being socially constructed, that is, people create language by their daily usage. The radical humanist paradigm views language as both inhibiting the growth of human beings and as the solution to the removal of such an inhibition. The radical structuralist paradigm views language as being created by economic substructure. These four views with respect to the nature of language and its role are equally scientific and informative; each looks at the nature of language and its role from a certain paradigmatic viewpoint.

This chapter took the case of language as an example and emphasized that, in general, any phenomenon may be seen and analyzed from different viewpoints and that each viewpoint exposes a certain aspect of the phenomenon under consideration. Collectively, they provide a much broader and deeper understanding of the phenomenon. Therefore, academic finance can benefit much from contributions coming from other paradigms if it respects paradigm diversity.

Knowledge of finance is ultimately a product of the researcher's paradigmatic approach to this multifaceted phenomenon. Viewed from this angle, the pursuit of financial knowledge is seen as much an ethical, moral, ideological, and political activity, as a technical one. Academic finance can gain much by exploiting the new insights coming from other paradigms.

Chapter 8

Mathematics and Academic Finance: Four Paradigmatic Views

An analysis of the nature of mathematics and its role in sciences necessarily requires a fundamental understanding of the worldviews underlying the views expressed with respect to the nature of mathematics and its role. Four general views with respect to mathematics and its role in sciences, corresponding to four broad worldviews, are discussed. The functionalist paradigm views mathematics as discoveries about a special realm of objects that exist prior to our knowledge of them. The interpretive paradigm views mathematics as a social invention and mathematical proofs as only one part of a larger social process whereby mathematicians come to feel confident about a theorem. The radical humanist paradigm views mathematics as constituting the core of science and that the rationality of science and technology is immanently one of control: the rationality of domination over nature and man. The radical structuralist paradigm views mathematics as being historically specific and class determined, that is, to satisfy the requirements of a social class in an historical period. These four views with respect to the nature of mathematics and its role are equally scientific and informative; each looks at the nature of mathematics and its role from a certain paradigmatic viewpoint.

This chapter takes the case of mathematics as an example and emphasizes that, in general, any phenomenon may be seen and analyzed from different viewpoints and that each viewpoint exposes a certain aspect of the phenomenon under consideration. Collectively, they provide a much broader and deeper understanding of the phenomenon. Therefore, academic finance can benefit much from contributions coming from other paradigms if it respects paradigm diversity.

Functionalist View

Functionalist paradigm views with respect to the nature of mathematics and its role in science are discussed in this section.[1]

Mathematics is regarded as a language, a universal instrument of representation. The universe is mathematical in structure and behavior, and nature acts in accordance with general laws. Mathematics is a neutral medium into which all statements of each theory, and the statements of all theories, can be translated without modifying them. Mathematics, in this way, is devoid of content. That is, as a result of the conceptual

---

1 For classics in this section, see Frege (1959) and Russell (1919). Also, see Ewald (1996), Hale (1999), Peressini (1999), and Urquhart (1999).

neutrality of the methods and procedures of mathematical formalization, the object of analysis are unaffected by their mathematical manipulation.

Mathematics is uniquely capable of interpreting theory with its ability to separate the rational from the vague intuitional, the essential from the inessential. It is the unique standard of logic, consistency, and proof. Once intuitions are formed, mathematical models can be constructed which prove or disprove the logical consistency of the theory. Other languages are incapable of doing this because the operations of mathematics have an essential truth that other languages do not possess. Mathematics is more important than other languages in that it is uniquely capable of generating truth statements and that it has no impact on what is being thought and communicated. Mathematical statements are based on the necessity of arriving at conclusions as a result of following mathematical rules.

Mathematics eliminates the noise by agreeing on the meaning of symbols that otherwise would vary from one use to another. That is, everyone agrees to recognize the same symbol.

The notion of mathematics as a special code is linked, in turn, to the twin pillars of traditional epistemology: empiricism and rationalism.

Empiricists consider mathematics as a universal instrument of representation. It is used as a tool to express the statements of a discourse which already, always has an essential grasp on the real. It is the universal language by which statements about objects of different economic and social theories can all be expressed.

Theory is compared to the facts in order to examine its validity. The role of mathematics is to express the various intuitive statements of the theorist in a neutral language such that they can be measured against reality.

This is based on the traditional subject-object dichotomy: the passive subject and the active object impressing itself on the knowing subject. The theorists know how the world works by observing it. They then translate the description into a model to check its consistency, its logical thoroughness, and so on. Mathematics merely represents, in a different language, that which was already present in the pre-mathematical intuition.

Rationalists consider logic as the foundation of mathematics and use mathematics for logical abstraction. Thus, the use of formal, mathematical methods is a necessary, although not sufficient, condition for arriving at scientific propositions. Mathematical models are conceived as abstract images or ideal representations of a complex reality. The process of theorizing is identified with the initial elaboration of, and deductive operations on, a set of mathematical models.

Here the subject becomes the active participant in discovering knowledge by operating on the theoretical model of reality. In this sense, the logical structure of theory—not the correspondence of theory to the facts—becomes the privileged or absolute standard of the process of theorizing. Reality, in turn, is said to correspond to the rational order of thought. The laws that govern reality are deduced from the singular set of mathematical models in and through which the essence of reality can be grasped.

Both empiricists and rationalists conceive of mathematics as a neutral language and as the language singularly privileged over all others. They represent two sides of the same epistemological coin: although each reverses the order of proof of the other, both empiricism and rationalism presume the same fundamental terms and some form of correspondence between them. In this sense, they are variant forms of an essentialist conception of the process of theorizing. Both of them invoke an absolute epistemological standard to guarantee the singular, unique scientific production of knowledge.

Interpretive View

Interpretive paradigm views with respect to the nature of mathematics and its role in science are discussed in this section.[2]

Mathematics is regarded as an anthropological phenomenon. The foundations of mathematics are the psychological, social, and empirical facts upon which the structure of knowledge is actually raised. Mathematics is the product of instinct, training, and convention. Mathematics is invented rather than discovered.

The compelling force of mathematical procedures does not derive from their being transcendent, but from their being accepted and used by a group of people. The procedures are not accepted because they are correct, or correspond to an ideal; they are correct because they are accepted. Mathematical truth is established by agreement, that is, it is agreed upon as a rule. The basis and cause of these agreements are not matters to be settled by *a priori* reflection. They must be investigated empirically: One might give an ethnological account of this human institution.

The belief in mathematical essence is a reified perception of social processes. The conventional aspects of the techniques become transmitted in the consciousness into something mysterious. This is the form taken in our consciousness by the social discipline imposed upon their use. It is as if the work that society puts into sustaining a technique returns to its users in the phenomenological form of an essence. The reality behind mathematical techniques is the reality that society has a use for certain techniques: it is an ethnological fact—it is something to do with the way the society lives.

Simple calculations are grounded in certain techniques and the physical and psychological facts that make the techniques possible. But calculations do not state these conditions; they take them for granted.

Of all the indefinitely large number of techniques for manipulating objects that exist, society selects those that provide useful patterns. The operations and techniques that are chosen, and which become memorable patterns, are the ones that become central to the training given to children.

What mathematical techniques for manipulating objects and symbols do is to produce one structure out of another. They are used as paradigm identity but their experimental character disappears when one looks at the process simply as a memorable picture. They are used to define the essential features of a change and see them as yielding relations which are not merely contingent: The calculations are regarded as demonstrating an internal property, a property of the essence.

---

2 For classics in this section, see Wittgenstein (1964, 1967, 1976). Also, see Carson (1999), Divers (1999), Ewald (1996), Joseph (1998), Lehrer (1999), and Urquhart (1999).

The emergence of the mathematical out of the physical occurs when the empirical manipulations are put to a certain use; when they become part of a certain technique, and when they become subject to certain conventions and norms.

Starting from the idea of a calculation as a kind of experiment that becomes frozen into a criterion of identity, one may imagine a gradual widening of the range of experimental procedures so treated. The range of models that might be taken up from experience, and turned into paradigms of identity, has no known limits. What can be said, however, is that available models are exploited by assimilating novelties and problematic cases to them. Models are made applicable to new cases by analogies seen between them. A proof goes in fact step by step by means of analogy—by the help of paradigm. Mathematical conviction might be put in the form of recognizing "this as analogous to that." The word "recognize," here, does not mean acknowledging a pre-existing fact: it indicates the acceptance of a convention. The reason proofs are of interest is that it is so easy to reproduce them again and again in different objects. The proof exhibits the generation of one from others.

The proof changes society's concepts. It makes new connections, and it creates the concept of these connections. A sentence asserting an internal relation between two objects, such as mathematical sentences, is not describing objects but constructing concepts. One does not have to accept the conventions thus created. What is regarded by one person as essential may be regarded by another as inessential. They may put an opposite construction on it. But if one does that one is enabled to recognize one thing as analogous to another. One should not look at a proof as a procedure that is compelling, but as one that is guiding.

Radical Humanist View

Radical humanist paradigm views with respect to the nature of mathematics and its role in science are discussed in this section.[3]

Mathematics is regarded as constituting the core of modern science with its rational, methodical, calculating nature. Modern science has lead to the rationalization of society. Rationalization means the extension of the areas of society subject to the criteria of rational decision. It refers to either the organization of means or choice between alternatives. Planning can be regarded as purposive-rational action at a higher order. It aims at the establishment, improvement, or expansion of systems of purposive-rational action themselves.

The rationalization of society is linked to the institutionalization of scientific and technical development. To the extent that science and technology spread through social institutions and transform them, old legitimations are destroyed.

Rationalization realizes not rationality as such but rather, in the name of rationality, a specific form of unacknowledged political domination. This type of rationality removes the total social framework of interests in which strategies are chosen, technologies applied, and systems established from the scope of analysis.

---

3 For classics in this section, see Marcuse (1964, 1968, 1970). Also, see Garrison (1999), Smith and Plotnitsky (1997), and Sherratt (1999).

Moreover, this rationality extends only to relations of possible technical control and therefore requires a type of action that implies domination, whether of nature or of society. By its very nature, purposive-rational action is the exercise of control. Rationalization is the institutionalization of a form of domination whose political character becomes unrecognized. However, the technical reason of a social system of purposive-rational action does not lose its political content.

The concept of technical reason is ideological. Not only the application of technology but the technology itself is domination, of nature and men. Purposes and interests of domination are not imposed upon technology subjectively and from the outside; they enter the very construction of the technical apparatus. Technology is a historical social project. It reflects what a society and its ruling interests intend to do with men and things.

The growth of the forces of production following from scientific and technical progress surpasses all historical proportions. The ruling class takes advantage of it for legitimizing the existing relations of production. These present themselves as the technically necessary organizational form of a rationalized society. At this stage of their scientific-technical development the forces of production appear to reinforce the relations of production. They no longer function as the basis of a critique of prevailing legitimations in the interest of the ruling class, but become instead the basis of legitimation.

The scientific method, with mathematics at its core, which led to the increasing domination of nature, provided the pure concepts as well as the instrumentalities for the increasing domination of man by man through the domination of nature. Now, domination recreates and extends itself not only through technology but as technology, and this provides the legitimation of the expanding political power, which affects all aspects of culture.

Rationalization demonstrates the technical impossibility of one being autonomous, of determining one's own life. This inability appears neither as irrational nor as political, but rather as submission to the technical apparatus which enlarges the comforts of life and increases the productivity of labor. Technological rationality thus protects the legitimacy of domination and leads to a rational totalitarian society.

Nature, scientifically comprehended and mastered, reappears in the technical apparatus of production which sustains and improves the life of the individuals while subordinating them to the masters of the apparatus. Then the change in the direction of progress, which would require severing this link, would also affect the very structure of science, that is, the scientific project. Its hypotheses, without losing their rational character, would develop in an essentially different context, would arrive at essentially different concepts of nature, and would establish essentially different facts.

Radical Structuralist View

Radical structuralist paradigm views with respect to the nature of mathematics and its role in science are discussed in this section.[4]

Mathematics is regarded as one of constituents of the social superstructure. It is determined by the social base and affected as one of the constituents of the social superstructure. Mathematics, in turn, influences the social base and the other constituents of the social superstructure. As a matter of fact, mathematics has been influenced by and has influenced agriculture, commerce, manufacture, warfare, engineering, philosophy, physics, and astronomy.

Take the case of calculus, perceiving that it deals with the most profound kernel of the dialectical process, with the essence of change. The invention of calculus, much as the birth of all modern science, followed closely on the birth of capitalism. The great renaissance of commerce and industry in Europe, accompanied by the rise of the capitalist class in the fifteenth, sixteenth, and seventeenth centuries, began to exercise a tremendous influence on mathematics. With the discovery of analytic geometry and the function concept and the invention of calculus, mathematics was transformed from a science of constant quantities to the mathematics of varying quantities.

The introduction of mechanical tools of production, from windmills and cranes to water pumps and machines to drill stones, the development of oceanic navigation, new military techniques, and the natural sciences in general demanded new knowledge—necessitating means of analyzing and calculating motions, that is, projections, free fall, planetary motion, accelerated motion, and so on.

The mathematics of varying quantities constituted the mathematical response to this external stimulation, further enriched by the study of problems arising from the technical, inner development of mathematics, such as the study of abstract curves and surfaces, including the so-called tangent problem. The mathematics of varying quantities represents the response of mathematics to a profound problem—the analysis of motion.

The socioeconomic pressure to discover adequate mathematical methods makes it easy to understand that the invention of calculus could not have been the work of one or another isolated genius. It was the culmination of the work of four generations of mathematicians. It was through joint work and mutual discussion that they created the differential and integral calculus.

This mathematical tool rapidly won new successes in astronomy and practical applications such as artillery, construction, of fortifications and hydraulics, such as water wheel, turbines, shape of ship hulls, and so on.

The refinements of the concepts of calculus in the nineteenth century similarly continued. The French Revolution and the Napoleonic period created extremely favorable conditions for the development of mathematics, particularly in France, where there was the greatest ideological break with the past era. A whole series of new technical and scientific problems arose from the Industrial Revolution, such as the problem of construction of machine parts, transmission of force, friction, precision

---

4 For classics in this section, see Struik (1948, 1987). Also, see Charlton (1996).

mechanics, and energy. This brought about a closer linkage between physicists and a number of mathematicians with material production.

At the same time, the concentration of workers in growing industrial cities gave rise to problems of supply of food, water, home heating materials, and problems of street lighting, construction of building, etc. The resolution of these and other problems—to service the process of capitalist production—obliged the natural sciences and mathematics to develop in the corresponding direction.

In general, to a materialist mathematics can be significant and relevant only when it reflects processes of the real world. Its application gains more relevance in a comprehensive study of a phenomenon.

In economics, mathematics may be used to avoid computational errors, to express the economic phenomena in an algebraic form, to grasp the dynamics of economic processes, to deepen the analysis of political economy, and to raise the scientific level of political economy because a science is really developed only when it successfully made use of mathematics.

Conclusion

This chapter briefly discussed four views expressed with respect to the nature of mathematics and its role in sciences. The four views correspond to the four paradigms. The functionalist paradigm views mathematics as discoveries about a special realm of objects that exist prior to our knowledge of them. The interpretive paradigm views mathematics as a social invention and mathematical proofs as only one part of a larger social process whereby mathematicians come to feel confident about a theorem. The radical humanist paradigm views mathematics as constituting the core of science and that the rationality of science and technology is immanently one of control: the rationality of domination over nature and man. The radical structuralist paradigm views mathematics as being historically specific and class determined, that is, to satisfy the requirements of a social class in an historical period. These four views with respect to the nature of mathematics and its role are equally scientific and informative; each looks at the nature of mathematics and its role from a certain paradigmatic viewpoint.

This chapter took the case of mathematics as an example and emphasized that, in general, any phenomenon may be seen and analyzed from different viewpoints and that each viewpoint exposes a certain aspect of the phenomenon under consideration. Collectively, they provide a much broader and deeper understanding of the phenomenon. Therefore, academic finance can benefit much from contributions coming from other paradigms if it respects paradigm diversity.

Knowledge of finance is ultimately a product of the researcher's paradigmatic approach to this multifaceted phenomenon. Viewed from this angle, the pursuit of financial knowledge is seen as much an ethical, moral, ideological, and political activity, as a technical one. Academic finance can gain much by exploiting the new insights coming from other paradigms.

Chapter 9

Money and Academic Finance:
Four Paradigmatic Views

An analysis of the nature of money and its role necessarily requires a fundamental understanding of the worldviews underlying the views expressed with respect to the nature of money and its role. Four general views with respect to money and its role, corresponding to the four broad worldviews, are discussed. The functionalist paradigm views money as belonging to a world in which individuals behave as rational participants in market transactions, and making distinctions only of price and quantity, a dispassionate sphere where all monies are alike. The interpretive paradigm views money as being socially constructed, i.e., people earmark money, incorporate money into personalized webs of friendship, family relations, interactions with authorities, and dealing with shops and businesses. The radical humanist paradigm views money as the very essence of our rationalizing modern civilization, which necessarily replaces personal bonds with calculative instrumental ties, and corrupts cultural meanings with materialist concerns. The radical structuralist paradigm views money as capital and its roles in the generation of surplus value, exploitation of labor, and the systemic crises of the capitalist system. These four views with respect to the nature of money and its role are equally scientific and informative; each looks at the nature of money and its role from a certain paradigmatic viewpoint.

This chapter takes the case of money as an example and emphasizes that, in general, any phenomenon may be seen and analyzed from different viewpoints and that each viewpoint exposes a certain aspect of the phenomenon under consideration. Collectively, they provide a much broader and deeper understanding of the phenomenon. Therefore, academic finance can benefit much from contributions coming from other paradigms if it respects paradigm diversity.

Functionalist View

Functionalist paradigm views with respect to the nature of money and its role are discussed in this section.[1]

Money is regarded as an extremely liquid asset, measured in a standard unit of account, and capable with certainty of discharging debt expressed in that unit. Most liquid assets in the United States consist of short-term claims upon the national government, upon the Federal Reserve banks, upon commercial banks, or upon

---

1 For classics in this section, see Friedman and Schwartz (1963), Keynes (1930, 1936), and Patinkin (1956).

non-bank credit institutions—particularly mutual savings banks, savings and loan associations, and, in the view of some analysts, also credit unions and life insurance companies.

Many economists prefer to define money more informally than is proposed above: simply as that which constitutes means of payment.

Most societies until recently have thought of their units of account as expressing the value of a stated weight of gold or silver; but since paper money came into general use in the nineteenth century, units of accounts have become more and more abstract.

One of the key problems of present-day economics is the role of money and other liquid assets in the structure of economic decisions—particularly in the decisions of firms and households to save and to invest in durable real assets, such as factories, machinery, houses, and vehicles. Broadly speaking, the funds available to a firm or household for investment within a stated period consist of its saving during the period—taking saving gross, to include depreciation charges and the like—plus its net borrowing, plus any reduction it may make in its holdings of liquid assets. In any stated situation, there is usually something to be gained for the firm or household by investing more, something to be gained by reducing rather than increasing debt, and also something to be gained—in the form of increased consumption, or of increased distribution of a firm's profits to its owners—by saving less. Given the size of current income, the more ample the stock of liquid assets, the more it is possible to realize all these benefits simultaneously. The scarcer the liquid assets, the more it is necessary to choose to forgo one benefit in order to reap another. Thus, adequacy of liquid assets in the possession of a firm or household is viewed as incentive to invest, while inadequacy of liquid assets is viewed as an incentive to save and to curtail investment.

Monetary economists have developed an interesting array of hypotheses about the motives for holding money. Prior to the great depression of the 1930s, emphasis was placed primarily on *the transactions motive*: the need to hold a stock of money so as to smooth out the irregularities of inflow and outflow and to carry the holder past a foreseen trough in his money holdings. There is also *the speculative motive*: the benefit of holding money while one waits for an expected fall in the price of some asset one may be interested in buying. Also, *the precautionary motive*: the benefit of holding money to mitigate uncertainty.

Except for very short-term aspects of the transactions motive, all these motives for holding money can be served as least moderately well by holding some type of non-monetary liquid assets. Money as ordinarily defined consists of elements— paper currency and checking deposits—which yield no money income, while non-monetary liquid assets do yield such income. Hence, it pays the holder to substitute other liquid assets for money up to the point at which the next remaining unit of money has a net advantage equal to the interest income forgone.

A theoretical consequence of this fact is that the demand for money can also be considered in opportunity-cost terms. Developing a Keynesian insight, many monetary economists center their analysis on a liquidity-preference function, which treats the stock of money the public chooses to hold as an inverse function of the interest rate which could be earned on alternative uses of funds.

On the supply side, the central bank is able to facilitate the expansion of bank assets, and thus of the money stock, or to apply pressure toward contraction. The

Federal Reserve System has authority within wide limits to vary legal reserve requirements. Furthermore, the total mass of reserves can be increased by Federal Reserve open-market purchases of government securities or decreased by open-market sales. The commercial banks borrowing from the Federal Reserve can be altered by varying the official discount rate or by official moral suasion.

Monetary economics offers a wide range of competing views about the impact of monetary forces on prices and economic activity. To a large extent differences of views relate to the interpretation of somewhat ambiguous historical and statistical evidence. In principle, the adherents of each of today's monetary schools admit the conceivability of a world in which the other school's favorite channel of monetary influence would be of the highest importance, but each school tends to argue that realistically and quantitatively its favorite channel of influence is the most important by a decisive margin. Furthermore, the different schools disagree sharply with regards to monetary policy. Hence, a correct impression can probably be given by contrasting several distinct types of theory—disregarding the minor concessions made by each school to the others.

Current schools of monetary economics may be categorized according to their preferences in devising models that explain the general level of economic activity and prices in a market economy. At one extreme stands the "modern quantity theory" school, typified by Milton Friedman. This theory is based on the following equation:

$$MV = PQ$$

where: M is the quantity of money, V is the velocity of circulation, P is the average price level, and Q is the total quantity of output. It pictures changes in the stock of money as the dominant force in any explanation of the course of money payments and draws the policy inference that the prescription for steady economic growth without inflation is to adhere to a steady growth rate in the money stock about equal to the growth of the economy's productive potential. In this theory, velocity is treated neither as a constant nor as an exogenous variable but as endogenous to the system of interrelations used in the theory. Nevertheless, the forces that govern velocity are not pictured as lending themselves to any sort of policy intervention which might usefully supplement the regulation of the quantity of money.

At the other extreme stand models that analyze the behavior of economic activity and the price level without including any variable that corresponds to the stock of money. It would be hard to name any economists who would make it a matter of principle to go to this extreme. But the stress, in teaching and in popularized statements about economic policy, on investment as an exogenous variable, and on the determination of economic activity by investment, is so heavy that this extreme view is likely to be taken as the sum of academic wisdom about macroeconomics by a large proportion of those who have been exposed to economic pedagogy or advice. The associated view of economic policy is that fiscal policy is what matters and monetary policy is immaterial.

Much more representative of professional opinion, as the academic monetary economists would like it to be understood, is what may be called the interest rate school. On the theoretical side, the models typical of this view present the rate of interest as a major influence on investment and, through investment, on economic activity. In policy terms, this school treats the interest rate as the monetary influence on economic activity and does not concern itself with any direct influence of the stock of money on economic activity. In relation to fiscal policy, the position of this school is likely to be eclectic, looking to an interaction of interest rate policy with such fiscal-policy variables as public expenditure and tax rates. In the analytical models of this school, a peripheral liquidity-preference function expresses a relation between the money stock and the interest-rate. The policy implication drawn may be that the interest rate can be regulated through the stock of money, or that if an appropriate rate of interest is adopted the stock of money can be allowed to adapt itself to this rate without disturbing other aspects of the economy.

Despite the lively controversy among schools, it is hard to see their views as philosophically irreconcilable. Pure models of one or another of the types just sketched illuminate the implications of various hypotheses, can help guide the search for evidence, and may offer useful special-purpose models for work on economic diagnosis and economic policy.

Interpretive View

Interpretive paradigm views with respect to the nature of money and its role are discussed in this section.[2]

Money can be regarded as having the power to transform non-pecuniary values, but the reciprocal transformation of money by values or social relations is as important. Money used for rational instrumental exchange is another type of socially created currency, which is subject to particular networks of social relations and its own set of values and norms.

People adopt a set of controls over money and establish differential earmarks when and where they are engaged in social interactions. Some examples are:

1. Creating or dissolving social ties *by* courtship expenses, child-support payments, and alimony.
2. Making strong attempts to control others *by* bribes, token currencies in penal or mental institutions, and restricted bequests at death.
3. Establishing or maintaining inequality *by* welfare payments for the poor, monies for children, and women's pin money.
4. Maintaining delicate status distinctions *by* tips to mailpersons or nurses.
5. Dealing with risk and uncertainty *by* contributions of money to secure divine or magical intervention.
6. Managing intimacy *by* loans or money gifts to friends or kin; payments to sexual partners; and legal monetary compensation for moral or emotional damages.
7. Establishing or managing individual or group identity *by* contributions

---

2 For classics in this section, see Geertz (1973), Lea, Tarpy, and Webley (1987), Parry and Bloch (1989), Radford (1945), Shipton (1989), and Zelizer (1994).

to causes or organizations based on race, ethnicity, gender, or sexual orientation; donations to religious organizations; and donor-named bequests to universities.

8. Marking rites of passage *by* fees, gifts, donations at weddings, funerals, and baptisms.
9. Establishing or maintaining honor *by* blood money.
10. Managing inadmissible conflicts of interest *by* payments for birthing or parenting—surrogate mother's fees, black-marked payments, adoption fees, board payments to foster parents; and payments for organs or blood.
11. Maintaining clandestine social relations *by* blackmail, drug-dealing payments, payoffs to spies, and payments to concubine.

The earmarking of money is thus a social process. That is, money is attached to a variety of social relations rather than to individuals.

Between the 1870s and 1930s, people invented elaborate and extensive systems of earmarking, precisely as a national market system was being consolidated in America, as industrial capitalism flourished, as consumerism boomed, and as the government worked hard to achieve a centralized, uniform legal tender. The modern consumer society turned the spending of money not only into a central economic practice but into a dynamic, complex cultural and social activity. They sorted the seemingly homogeneous legal tender into distinct categories, and they created other currencies that lacked backing from the state.

Families differentiated and segregated their monies, setting food money apart from rent money, school money, or charity money, as well as funds for burial, weddings, Christmas, or recreation. Family members did not always agree on earmarking arrangements, as they struggled over how to define, allocate, and regulate their monies. Wife's money differed fundamentally from her husband's or her child's, not only in quantity but in how it was obtained, how often and how it was used, even where it was kept. Disputes were not always settled cordially: women, men, and children often lied, stole, or deceived each other in order to protect their separate currencies. Families thus constructed distinct forms of monies, shaped by a powerful domestic culture and by changing social relations between husbands and wives, parents and children. They were also influenced by class: middle- and working-class domestic dollars were not exact equivalents.

Households and businesses reshaped money into its supposedly most alien form, that of a sentimental gift, expressing care and affection. It mattered who gave gift money and who received it, when it was given, how it was offered, and how it was spent. Gift money circulated as a meaningful, deeply subjective, non-fungible currency, closely regulated by social conventions. At Christmas, wedding, christenings, or other religious and secular events, cash was turned into a dignified, welcome gift, almost unrecognizable as market money and clearly distinguished from other domestic currencies.

Authorities created a different category of currencies when they intervened in the earmarking of monies. Concerned with seemingly incompetent consumers, a number of institutions and organizations entered earmarking systems of dependent populations. In the case of the poor, public and private welfare authorities became deeply involved in creating charitable currencies designed to teach their clients the proper uses of money. What social worker did with the poor resembled the efforts of other institutions to regulate spending patterns, as in the case of prisons, reformations, or orphan asylums, as well as a range of workplace and company towns.

Monies are commonly earmarked by constraining their *uses:* a child's income is designed for specific appropriate purchases, to be spent only for the child's entertainment or clothing; gift monies are usually intended for specified objects or activities; cash relief often restricted to budgeted expenses approved by social workers. Monies are also distinguished by designating particular *users* for specified currencies: a weekly allowance is for children, not adults; pin money is a female, not a male, currency; tips are acceptable for waiters, not for lawyers. Or monies are set apart by linking certain *sources* of money to selected uses: income earned by the wife may be reserved for her children's education while her husband's income pays mortgage; inherited monies may be spent differently from earned income or a windfall profit. Currencies are further distinguished by creating different *systems of allocation:* the calculation and distribution of household income, gift monies, or cash relief, for instance, are based on contrasting domestic principles, affective guidelines, and welfare philosophies. Finally, people not only earmark legal tender but, in some instances, either transform selected material objects into currencies (cigarettes, subway tokens) or create new restricted currencies (gift certificates, food stamps).

There are a number of different techniques to create distinction among and distinguish multiple monies. They include restricting the uses of money, regulating modes of allocation, inventing rituals for its presentation, modifying its physical appearance, designating separate locations for particular monies, attaching special meanings to particular amounts, appointing proper users to handle specified monies, and earmarking appropriate sources of money for specified uses. Indeed, the standard practice of budgeting constitutes a special case of earmarking: the subdivision of funds available to an organization, government, individual, or household into distinct categories, each with its own rules of expenditure.

Social differentiation of money is pervasive, not only in the corners of the economy but everywhere; different kinds of social relations and values shape and reshape monies. Not just individuals but organizations and even the government distinguish among forms of legal tender or other monies. Multiple monies are a central feature of advanced capitalist economies.

These areas of social life did not resist commodification, but, they readily absorbed monies, transforming them to fit a variety of values and social relations. The homogenization of money was unsuccessful because people who were the objects of these efforts had their own ideas about earmarking monies.

The Federal Reserve recognizes as part of the national money supply not only cash, currency, demand deposits, and travelers checks, but also, among other financial assets, overnight repurchase agreements, eurodollars, money market mutual-fund shares, savings bonds, commercial paper, bankers' acceptances, and liquid treasury obligations. In fact, a whole series of monies and near monies have come into existence, such as the billions of dollars in privately issued credit card money, home-equity lines of credit, or the money lent to individuals and businesses by the so-called non-banking financial institutions such as General Electric Credit Corporation. It becomes clear that calculating how much money exists is nearly impossible.

Radical Humanist View

Radical humanist paradigm views with respect to the nature of money and its role are discussed in this section.[3]

Money as a social institution cannot be understood separated from the total social framework within which it is embedded. Money provides an insight into the total workings of a society and the structure of a society provides the context within the importance and nature of money as a social phenomenon can be grasped.

Neither the individual nor society can be understood without starting from social interactions and without grasping that social structures are forged out of the process of sociation.

The forms of social life—groups, families, networks, exchange relations and so forth—which emerge out of the endless sociation of individuals assume a logic of their own, which over time becomes separated from the content of human interaction. Culture becomes reified as structures which are congealed. That is, the humanly created forms of life assume an autonomy and independence from the human beings who initially created them in the process of sociation. Money is the classic illustration of this congealing of content into reified form. The activity of exchange among individuals is represented by money in a concrete, independent, and, as it were, congealed form.

The dual nature of money, as a concrete and valued substance and, at the same time, as something that owes its significance to the complete dissolution of substance into motion and function, derives from the fact that money is the reification of exchange among people, the embodiment of a pure function.

The analysis of how the form of exchange is detached from its content, of how money becomes a determining, autonomous feature of social relations has three components: (1) the historical transition from simple barter to a complex monetary system; (2) the dominance of abstract money is a representation of the prominence of abstract, impersonal social relationships; (3) money creates greater interpersonal freedom through impersonal exchange relations, but at the same time makes human life more subject to bureaucratic, quantitative regulation.

A simple system of barter or exchange gradually gives way to a situation in which some third element of measurement enters into the exchange of commodities. The value of two commodities in exchange is measured in terms of some other commodity which is held to be precious, such as shells, cloth, or metals. Money, as a measurement of value, develops from precious metals, to coins of silver or gold, to leather money, and finally to paper money. In this development, money increasingly assumes a pure function as the mere symbol of value, rather than itself being of

---

3 For classics in this section, see Lukacs (1971), Marx (1970), Simmel (1978), and Weber (1978).

value. This development is made possible by the changing nature of society and in particular by the growth of trust.

The expansion of the society, backed up by the state, law and custom, together with social stability and trust, and in association with an expanded social division of labor, are the necessary precondition for money to lose its intrinsic value and to acquire a purely functional significance. The centralization of social power in the institution of the state and the individuation of citizens are symbolically represented by the growing abstraction and impersonality of paper money. The existence of a stable monetary system means that exchange can take place between persons or groups which are not related or connected socially or physically.

The growth of trust and economic credit come to replace morality, since a person's worth is judged entirely in terms of their capacity to pay. Money is an unnatural power which converts the morally bad into the morally good, the anti-social into the social, and the ugly into the beautiful. Money assumes an autonomy and power over social relations so that money becomes the incarnation of social power. Money ceases to be a means and is transferred into an end itself.

Money is the bond binding a human being to human life, binding society to a human being, binding a human being and nature and man. That is, money is the bond of all bonds. At the same time it dissolves all ties. It is the universal agent of separation. It is the true agent of separation as well as the true binding agent—the universal power of society.

Money, then, appears as this overturning power both against the individual and against the bonds of society, and so on, which claim to be essences in themselves. It transforms fidelity into infidelity, love into hate, hate into love, virtue into vice, vice into virtue, servants into master, master into servant, idiocy into intelligence, and intelligence into idiocy. With this characteristic, money is thus the general overturning of individualities, which turns them into their contrary and adds contradictory attributes to their attributes.

Money, as the existing and active concepts of value, confounds and exchanges all things. It is, therefore, the general confounding and compounding of all things, the confounding and compounding of all natural and human qualities.

Money is the symbol of the reduction of quality to quantity. Money is totally indifferent to values. Only money is free from any quality and exclusively determined by quantity. With money, all qualitative distinctions between goods were equally convertible into an arithmetically calculable system of numbers.

As money became nothing but mere money its freedom was apparently unassailable and its uses unlimited. This objectification of modern life had a dual effect. On the one hand, a money economy broke the personal bondage of traditional arrangements by allowing every individual the freedom of selecting the terms and partners of economic exchange. But the quantifying character of money had a more negative aspect. The complete heartlessness of money is reflected in our social culture, which is itself determined by money.

Money makes every minute detail of human endeavor have a price fixed upon it. Because of the divisibility of money into small change, there is in principle no limit to the quantification of human activity. Money is, therefore, a fundamental aspect of the process of rationalization in modern societies, especially as that process is manifest in economics as a science, and economic predictions by systematic means.

While money increases the range of economic dependencies through its infinite divisibility, flexibility, and exchangeability, social interaction on the basis of money exchanges removes the personal element in social relations as a result of the abstractness and indifference of money. Although money liberates people from personal dependencies, it also makes the quantitative regimentation of individuals more precise and reliable as an aspect of standardization, regulation, quantification, and social control.

There are a number of dimensions to the rationalization process. Rationalization involves the separation of mental and manual workers from the means of production. It makes rational calculation of capitalist activities possible, increases managerial rationality, and creates the most favorable conditions for discipline for the expropriation of the workers. In short, rationalization includes alienation as the basis of calculation and discipline. Rationalization also involves intellectualization. This process involves the subordination of all areas of life to systematic scientific inquiry and management, at least in principle. In turn, this means the dominance of the expert over traditional authorities in the sphere of morality, social relations, and interpersonal behavior. Rationalization is manifest in the progressive dominance of bureaucratic models of social organizations, the dominance of bureaucratic personnel, and the surveillance of the individual by the state. Rationalization results in individuality being swamped by individuation. These aspects of rationalization finally produce secularization. Absolute values, whether those of religion or natural law, collapse in front of the wave of relativism generated by modern society, in front of the ethic of calculation and as a result of the prevalence of instrumental rationality.

Radical Structuralist View

Radical structuralist paradigm views with respect to the nature of money and its role are discussed in this section.[4]

Money is regarded as a key component in the engine of the capitalist system and its central role is illustrated in the schematic representation of the circuit of productive capital:

$$M \rightarrow C \rightarrow MP, LP \rightarrow P \rightarrow C' \rightarrow M'$$

where: M represents money advanced for the purchase of commodities (C) in the form of the means of production (MP) and labor power (LP), which through production (P) are transformed into new commodities (C'). When sold, these new commodities realize a sum of money (M') which exceeds the value of that originally advanced. Capital is said to have been "valorized" when it increases in value through production, generating "surplus value" through the difference between the value of the money capital originally advanced and the value contained within the

---

4 For classics in this section, see Harvey (1982), Marx (1954, 1959), and Sweezy (1964).

transformed commodities. If surplus value generated from the circuit of production is then advanced for the purchase of more commodity inputs, then the cycle can be repeated and so the realization of surplus capital continues.

Distinction can be made among three forms of capital, which are defined in relation to the role they play within the circuit of productive capital. Thus, *productive capital* is the form of capital which exists when it is articulated within the productive circuit itself. That is, when capital is translated into commodity inputs, which are in turn transformed into new commodities within the production process.

Banking capital, or *financial capital*, is the form of capital which is advanced in the form of money prior to production. This is interest-bearing capital, and is advanced by money-owners in return for an eventual share of the surplus value produced within production.

The third form of capital is *commercial capital*. This form of capital exists only in exchange relations, and is extended through the purchase and resale of commodities at a higher price. It does not enter production, nor is it advanced for production to take place. Therefore, commercial capital does not contribute directly towards the creation of surplus value.

Commercial capital is considered to be extended at the expense of productive capital by securing a share of surplus value. This is done either via arbitrage—buying cheaper and selling dearer—or charging of a fee for facilitating the circulation of commodities. A sub-form of commercial capital that is that of *money-dealing capital*.

Both financial and commercial capital can exist outside the circuit of productive capital. Indeed, in the forms of usurer's capital and merchant's capital, respectively. However, since these types of capital cannot actually produce value in their own right, the creation of value within the capitalist mode of production is essential for the expansion and extension of both financial and commercial capital. In turn, financial and commercial capital exist in a symbiotic relationship with one another, for they provide the means by which the circulation of capital is speeded up, thereby increasing the rate at which money is borrowed and lent out—so extending financial capital—and the rate at which commodities are bought and sold—so extending commercial capital.

Money performs two very important functions within the process of capital accumulation: the medium of exchange and the measure of value. Money operates as a medium of exchange at two critical points in the circuit of productive capital, facilitating first the exchange between $M \rightarrow C$, and then the exchange between C' $\rightarrow M'$. Therefore, money lubricates the circuit of productive capital, providing both free exchange between a wide range of commodities and a universally recognizable medium. However, money is much more than just a signatory to an exchange of commodities. To be medium of exchange, money must also be a measure of value otherwise the process of exchange would not be possible. Money acts as a universal equivalent against which the values of commodities can be judged. Money adopts the recognized role of the universal equivalent by way of its representation as the socially recognized incarnation of human labor expanded in the production process. Human labor is conceived as the sole generator of surplus value, representing the difference between the money advanced and the money realized through the sale of commodities transformed within the production process. Money, therefore, possesses all the hallmarks of a true commodity. It has an intrinsic value, which is the amount of human labor expended in production. It has an exchange value, in relation to the value of other commodities, and it has a use value, as a medium of circulation in the process of exchange. However, its role as the universal equivalent and as a measure of value confers upon money a status above all other commodities. As such it is the ultimate expression of social power: commodities are not exchanged in pursuit of other commodities, but are exchanged in the pursuit of money.

This characteristic endows money with a dominant role within the circuit of productive capital and within the cycle of capitalist accumulation as a whole. But this dominant role is also responsible for a systemic weakness within the capitalist system of production, the cause of which is buried within the nature of money. The dual roles of money, as a lubricant of circulation and exchange and as an independent expression of value, are ultimately contradictory, for if money begins to fail while acting as a lubricant of exchange it will be withdrawn from circulation. That is, for the circuit of capital to operate effectively, money must constantly be made available to allow the initial purchase of commodities which are thrown into production. Money must also be available to allow the exchange of transformed commodities back into money. Money will only be invested in production for as long as M is successfully transformed into M', through the generation of surplus value and ensuring an increase in the store of money. If, for any reason, the circuit of productive capital begins to fail, leading to a decline in the production of surplus value, then money may be withdrawn from the circulation altogether and hoarded for its utility as an independent expression of value. This withdrawal will, of course, preclude its use as a medium of circulation. The diversion of money away from the circuit of productive capital will therefore lead to a crash in the capitalist system as a whole, which becomes unable to reproduce itself. Such crises in capitalism are systemic, and can be traced back to the contradictory nature of the dual roles of the money commodity, to its dominance as the denominator of social power and to its ability to exist as a valuable commodity outside of and external to the production cycle.

Financial capital asserts its dominance over productive capital. This is linked to a more fundamental contradiction within the structure of the capitalist system. This contradiction manifests itself in a tension between on the one hand the central dynamic within the system towards the production of output for the realization of surplus value, and on the other, the ability of this output to be consumed by society as a whole, that is, the limit of the market.

The tendency to revolutionize the methods of production leads to an over-accumulation of capital. Production proceeds until the supply of commodities exceeds the demands and capacities of the market, causing a fall in prices. For those capitalists that have introduced new methods of production, this may not be a problem, since new production processes may reduce the costs of production sufficiently that a fall in the sale price of commodities can be accommodated without lowering profit levels.

Therefore, the extension of productive capacity beyond the limit of the market first causes prices, then profits, to fall. Bankruptcies escalate and the overall productive system begins to collapse as the owners of money refuse to introduce it into the circuit of productive capital. Money-owners, in the realization that the chances of them obtaining a return on money invested are increasingly unlikely, choose instead to hoard their money for its self-contained value. It is this ability of money to possess a value that is autonomous from the circuit of productive capital that lends financial capital its supremacy over productive capital within the capitalist accumulation cycle.

Crises of the sort described above are cyclical and systemic within capitalism. However, the period of time between crises has tended to increase, and this can be attributed in part to the growth of "credit money." The development of credit money has been important in postponing financial crashes, because credit money extends the limits of the market by granting purchasing power to those who do not possess money but expect to gain possession some time in the future.

Conclusion

This chapter briefly discussed four views expressed with respect to the nature of money and its role. The four views correspond to the four paradigms. The functionalist paradigm views money as belonging to a world in which individuals behave as rational participants in market transactions, and making distinctions only of price and quantity, a dispassionate sphere where all monies are alike. The interpretive paradigm views money as being socially constructed, that is, people earmark money, incorporate money into personalized webs of friendship, family relations, interactions with authorities, and dealing with shops and businesses. The radical humanist paradigm views money as the very essence of our rationalizing modern civilization, which necessarily replaces personal bonds with calculative instrumental ties, and corrupts cultural meanings with materialist concerns. The radical structuralist paradigm views money as capital and its roles in the generation of surplus value, exploitation of labor, and the systemic crises of the capitalist system. These four views with respect to the nature of money and its role are equally scientific and informative; each looks at the nature of money and its role from a certain paradigmatic viewpoint.

This chapter took the case of money as an example and emphasized that, in general, any phenomenon may be seen and analyzed from different viewpoints and that each viewpoint exposes a certain aspect of the phenomenon under consideration. Collectively, they provide a much broader and deeper understanding of the phenomenon. Therefore, academic finance can benefit much from contributions coming from other paradigms if it respects paradigm diversity.

Knowledge of finance is ultimately a product of the researcher's paradigmatic approach to this multifaceted phenomenon. Viewed from this angle, the pursuit of financial knowledge is seen as much an ethical, moral, ideological, and political activity, as a technical one. Academic finance can gain much by exploiting the new insights coming from other paradigms.

Chapter 10

Corporate Governance
and Academic Finance:
Four Paradigmatic Views

An analysis of corporate governance necessarily requires a fundamental understanding of the worldviews underlying the views expressed with respect to the nature and role of corporate governance. Four general views with respect to corporate governance and its role, corresponding to four broad worldviews, are discussed. The functionalist paradigm views corporate governance as ways of reducing agency costs. The interpretive paradigm views corporate governance as a social construction which should be analyzed within the larger social process. The radical humanist paradigm views corporate governance from a truly democratic standpoint. The radical structuralist paradigm views corporate governance as being historically specific and class determined, that is, to satisfy the needs of a social class in an historical period. These four views with respect to the nature and role of corporate governance are equally scientific and informative; each looks at the nature of corporate governance and its role from a certain paradigmatic viewpoint.

The paper takes the case of corporate governance as an example and emphasizes that, in general, any phenomenon may be seen and analyzed from different viewpoints and that each viewpoint exposes a certain aspect of the phenomenon under consideration. Collectively, they provide a much broader and deeper understanding of the phenomenon. Therefore, academic finance can benefit much from contributions coming from other paradigms if it respects paradigm diversity.

Functionalist View

Functionalists' views with respect to the nature and role of corporate governance are presented in this section.[1] Researchers who adhere to this paradigm believe that corporate governance is a technical matter and focus on this aspect of the corporate finance in their research.

The field of corporate governance is based on the existence of potential agency problems that arise from the separation of ownership and control in modern

---

1 For classics in this literature, see Becht, Bolton, and Roell (2002), Charreaux (2004), Cutler (2004), Denis (2001), Denis and McConnell (2003), Farinha (2003), Hawley and Williams (1996), Keasey, Thompson, and Wright (1997), Moreland (1995), Shleifer and Vishny (1997), Weimer and Pape (1999), and Zingales (1998). The following segment is based on Denis (2001) and Moreland (1995).

corporations. Corporate governance deals with the institutional and market mechanisms that encourage self-interested managers to maximize the value of the residual cash flows of the firm on behalf of its shareholders. A manager who owns less than all of the residual cash flow rights of the firm has potential conflicts of interest with the outside shareholders. Financial economists have tried to define, measure, and minimize these conflicts in order to maximize shareholder value.

There are three basic sources of such conflicts: managers' desire to remain in power, managerial risk aversion, and free cash flow.

Managers' desire to remain in power: When the current management team is not desirable by the shareholders then a conflict of interest between managers and shareholders exists.

Managerial risk aversion: A shareholder usually holds a diversified portfolio so that a relatively small portion of his wealth is invested in any company. However, the manager has the majority of her human capital tied up in the firm. Therefore, a manager will lose more than a shareholder if a project fails. This results in the conflict of interests with respect to investment policy.

Free cash flow: Free cash flow is defined as the cash flow generated by the firm in excess of the amount required to invest in all positive net present value projects. Shareholders prefer that the free cash flow be paid to them. However, a manager may prefer to either retain the cash flow or invest it in negative net present value projects, which results in a conflict of interests.

There are three general ways to increase the likelihood that management acts in the interests of shareholders: bond them contractually to do so, monitor them to ensure that they do so, and provide them with incentives such that it is in their own interest to do so.

Bonding solutions: By writing a contract, shareholders might be able to make management do some of what the shareholders consider to be desirable.

Monitoring solutions: The potential monitors of a firm's top management are the board of directors, creditors, large shareholders, and competing management teams.

Incentive alignment solutions: Shareholders can benefit from anything that makes management benefit from an increase in the value of the firm's common stock, such as management's ownership of the company's stocks and stock options.

Corporate governance mechanisms might reduce the agency effect. Their four basic categories are: legal and regulatory mechanisms, internal control mechanisms, external control mechanisms, and product market competition.

Legal and regulatory mechanisms: This is the system of laws and regulations that govern the firm. Cross-country differences in ownership structure, capital markets, financing, and dividend policies are all related to the degree to which investors are legally protected from expropriation by managers and controlling shareholders.

Internal control mechanisms: This consists of the board of directors, the compensation plans that they devise, the firm's ownership structure, and the firm's debt structure.

The law requires every US corporation to have a board of directors. Management may form the board with individuals sympathetic to management's interests. To avoid this, many firms are reducing board size and increasing the proportion of outside directors.

Executive compensation intends to align the interests of the management with those of the shareholder. The most common way is the management's ownership of the firm's common stocks or stock options.

The ownership structure considers shareholders who hold significant equity stakes in a firm. They have the ability and the incentive to monitor and influence what is happening in the firm and play a crucial role in successful corporate governance systems.

Debt obligates the management to return specified amounts of cash to debt-holders at specified times. Thus, debt reduces the free cash flow problem discussed earlier. Furthermore, the requirement to make ongoing cash payments gives management greater incentive to operate efficiently so as to produce greater cash flow.

External control mechanisms: An acquirer can operate a firm more efficiently and realize a profit. The threat of losing control provides some managers with the incentive not to deviate too far from value-maximizing behavior.

Product market competition: Management wastefulness or inefficiency will be reflected in poor performance in its product markets, and a cost of capital that is high due to the lack of the protection that a good system of corporate governance will afford investors. In the extreme, such poor performance can result in financial distress, perhaps even bankruptcy.

Different corporate governance systems which are prevailing in different countries are converging. When the Angle-Saxon countries, such as the US, UK, Canada, and Australia, are compared with many countries of continental Europe, such as Germany, and Japan, it is noted that changes in financial markets, financial institutions, investors' attitude, and the degree of global competition are leading to convergence in corporate governance.

Interpretive View

Interpretive paradigm's views with respect to the nature and role of corporate governance are presented in this section.[2] Researchers who adhere to this paradigm believe that corporate governance is socially constructed and therefore consider the social context in their corporate finance research.

Corporate governance is about the understanding of and institutional arrangements for relationships among various economic actors and corporate participants who may have direct or indirect interests in a corporation, such as shareholders, directors, managers, employees, creditors, suppliers, customers, local communities, government, and the general public.

---

2 For articles written in the interpretative tradition, see Allen (2001), Analytica (1992), Branson (2005), Hollingsworth and Boyer (1997), Hollingsworth and Lindberg (1985), Hollingsworth, Schmitter, and Streek (1994), Letza, Kirkbride, and Sun (2004), Lee, Michie, and Oughton (2003), Maruyama (1991), Morgan (1997), Plumptre and Graham (1999), Powell (1990), Roy (1997), Streek and Schmitter (1985), Turnbull (1978, 1994a, 1994b, 1997), Whitley (1991), and Whyte and Whyte (1988). The following segment is based on Lee, Michie, and Oughton (2003) and Letza, Kirkbride, and Sun (2004).

The finance view is the dominant corporate governance model, which focuses on a universal agency problem and how to solve the problem. The economic approach employed in such analyses is culture-free, historically separated, and contextually unrelated. This approach is based on the notions of profit maximization, increasing market value, economic rationality, and efficiency. Underpinning the finance view is the continuous search for the optimal governance structure which constitutes the most efficient form.

The finance view ignores the fact that corporate governance is a social process, which is not isolated from social and non-economic conditions and factors such as power, legislation, social relationships, and institutional contexts.

The social approach to corporate governance is process based rather than being static. It explains the temporary, transient, and emergent patterns of corporate governance on a historical and contextual basis in a given society. Corporate governance is completely changeable and transformable and there is no permanent or universal corporate governance principle which covers all societies, cultures, and corporations. It recognizes that corporate governance systems in different parts of the world have developed from their own unique cultural, historical, and social circumstances. It acknowledges that each system will continue to evolve.

It is a balanced approach that never assumes that any single or extreme model can perfectly work in practice. A firm is neither a purely private nor a purely public affair. A firm not only consists of physical assets, but also of human beings, that is, shareholders, and other stakeholders.

It is a relational approach that views the social reality as fundamentally interconnected, interdependent, and mutually influential. Business relationships are thought of as corporate interrelationships and social interactions. In this way, shareholders' interest and stakeholders' interests are interdependent. In general terms, a firm is not independent of its constituents. Any view or model that separates the corporation and its stakeholders, or shareholders and stakeholders, in fact oversimplifies the phenomenon of corporate reality and makes the social reality artificial. Dichotomous approaches or binary values have limited applicability to the complex social world.

It is a pluralistic approach that realizes corporate governance is not only shaped and influenced by economic logic (such as economic rationality and efficiency), but also by politics, ideologies, philosophies, legal systems, social conventions, cultures, modes of thought, methodologies, and so on. Accordingly, a purely economic and financial analysis of corporate governance is indeed too narrow.

It is a dynamic and flexible approach that continuously evaluates and adjusts the method of governance in practice. It does not intend to design and specify any ideal model in advance that can be offered as a once-and-for-all solution. In a business setting, it involves the design and management of the organization through juxtaposition of competing viewpoints in a constant process of dynamic tension with no preset.

It is an enlightening approach that attempts to transcend the habitual, inertial, static, and stagnant ways of thinking about corporate governance.

A social approach might emphasize the following four basic premises. First, the institutional context constraints or supports economic organization, economic behavior, and economic performance. Second, there is a wide variation in institutional systems in different societies. Third, changes in nationally specific institutional configurations are influenced and shaped by path dependency, institutional complementarity, and sociocultural embeddedness. Fourth, there are also recognizable patterns at the supranational level—for instance, Anglo-Saxon, Communitarian, and emerging economy systems—despite the significant variance and specificity of national contexts. It should be noted that social norms, informal institutions, and non-market processes may facilitate social exchange not only because there are inadequate formal institutional arrangements and mechanisms to adjudicate disputes, but also because voluntary compliance and cooperation based on internalization of shared moral principles cannot be generated exclusively through formal institutions and regulatory rules.

Evidence suggests that there are four distinct forms of governance: market, hierarchies, the clan or community, and associations. While the finance view recognizes only the former two forms, the latter two forms may offer more value in corporate governance, especially in non-Anglo cultures.

The finance view of corporate governance endorses convergence towards one best Anglo-American model. In the social view firms are socially constructed and their organizational forms are shaped by the social, political, and economic systems in which they are embedded. Different kinds of enterprise structures become feasible and successful in particular social contexts, resulting in different types of corporate governance systems as well as different sources of competitiveness.

Radical Humanist View

Radical humanists' views with respect to the nature and role of corporate governance are presented in this section.[3] Researchers who adhere to this paradigm believe that corporate governance is socially and politically constructed and therefore consider the social and political context, and its resultant political domination, in their corporate finance research.

One of the most important issues in corporate governance is whether a given population has had the opportunity to go through a truly democratic process to choose what it deems to be the most appropriate form of corporate governance. This is crucial in determining what constitutes good corporate governance. Therefore, the most fundamental concern is to ensure that models of corporate governance are freely chosen through a fair and democratic process.

The economic and corporate governance reforms that have been carried out in developing countries have moved them towards an Anglo-American model of governance. These reforms have been founded on the interests of international and domestic business and political elites. The processes involved in economic globalization, in which the developing countries have largely been forced to lose

---

3 For articles written in the radical humanist tradition, see Branston, Cowling, and Sugden (2006), Beck, Demirguc-Kunt, and Levine (2001), Chomsky and Herman (1988), Coffee (1999), Ellerman (1999), Gourevitch (2003), Marsh (1995), McCall (2001), Monks and Minow (1995), Pagano and Volpin (2001a, 2001b), Parenti (1995), Pound (1993), Rajan and Zingales (2003), Reed (1999, 2004), and Roe (1990, 1994, 1997, 2000, 2002). The following segment is based on Reed (2004).

their public policy autonomy, have made the Anglo-American model the most readily available option for reform.

There are several possible factors that may help to explain the fact that the implementation of the governance reforms is directing the developing countries to an Anglo-American model. One factor is the past experience of the developing countries themselves. Some countries have had strong historical ties to the Anglo-American model that make further movement in the same direction appear natural. Another factor is the lack of success which coincided with their previous interventionist policies, which has been used to gain credit for non-interventionist liberal policies. Moreover, to the extent that the previous interventionist policies supported uncompetitive firms, liberal financial markets present themselves as an important alternative tool for promoting more competitive firms. While it is not clear whether past failures are directly attributable to the interventionist policies, it is indisputable that key domestic business and political actors have presented past failures as a justification for liberalization and moving towards an Anglo-American model. Another factor is the ability of business elites in developing countries to exert their influence in order to convert any resistance against processes of globalization to the benefit of large domestic firms. Generally, business interests advocate the Anglo-American model and oppose the adoption of any other models of governance, especially models that provide a role for stakeholders, e.g., employees.

Another reason for the move towards an Anglo-American model is the developing countries' borrowing in relation with the international financial institutions. As a condition for negotiating and renegotiating loans, international financial institutions require developing countries to implement structural adjustment programs. These programs are founded on the same premises as those of the Anglo-American model of governance. For instance, the requirement of fiscal cutbacks forced the governments to reduce credit supplies, which diminished the role of bank finance, reduced direct bank influence in governance, and led to a much greater role for equity financing. The promotion of equity financing, and shareholder interests, was also encouraged through the requirements for states to deregulate financial markets and reduce controls on foreign portfolio investment. States were also required to drastically diminish their interventionist industrial policies and substantially reduce direct participation in production. While it is not clear why the structural adjustment programs have been required, there is no doubt that they have paved the way for the developing countries to move towards the Anglo-American model.

Structural adjustment programs emanate from the business and political elites' general approach to economic reforms. This approach advocates liberalizing reforms in most areas. This approach has shaped not only International Monetary Fund and World Bank policies, but also the neo-liberal path that the processes of globalization have followed. The neo-liberal nature of the globalization has promoted an Anglo-American model of corporate governance. In the neo-liberal environment, where domestic firms have had to increasingly raise capital in equity markets, as a result of the decline in bank capital, and states have been encouraging foreign portfolio investment to finance domestic firms, and states have been promoting foreign direct investment to generate employment and simulate key sectors of the economy shareholder interests have had to be given priority. The approach has necessitated a liberalization of capital markets, changes to company law, abolition of interventionist industrial policies, etc. In summary, the Anglo-American model of corporate governance is the micro-level counterpart of the macro-level neo-liberal global economy model.

The general approach has come to prominence by the lobbying efforts of large transnational corporations in developed countries with respect to the governments of the dominant economic powers. The transnational corporations have influenced the national states through the creation of strong business lobbies and the unofficial multilateral bodies. The dominant economic powers, in turn, have influenced multilateral organizations, whose members are almost exclusively the developed countries. Through such organizations, the dominant economic powers have reached a basic agreement among themselves, and laid the basis for key changes in the international economy, without much regard for domestic public opinion or the concerns of developing countries, and only then have invited the developing countries for participation. These practices in the process of globalization largely reflect the interests of transnational corporations of developed countries.

In this way, businesses, especially transnational corporations, subvert the formally democratic structures of nation states to determine the nature of governance reforms in developing countries in line with their own interests.

Radical Structuralist View

Radical structuralists' views with respect to the nature of corporate governance and its role are presented in this section.[4] Researchers who adhere to this paradigm believe that corporate governance has its base in social classes.

The early entrepreneur, as both the owner and the controller of business, was clearly identifiable as a business leader. In a public corporation, it became possible for the owners, that is, shareholders and providers of capital, not to have any effective control over the actual operations of the corporation.

There is a need to examine the consequences of these changes for the exercise of power and control within the business systems of the advanced industrial economies. This involves an examination of not only the narrow view of power within specific business enterprises, but also of the power of business enterprises to affect economic development and state policies. In turn, these explorations lead to fundamental concerns about the nature of the class relations that are associated with the exercise of corporate power, that is, finance capital.

An enterprise must abide by the company, property, and commercial law in operating its business. However, enterprises are complex social entities and the legal framework is only an approximate guide to how they actually operate. Similarly, the relations among different categories of employees are regulated by their employment

---

4 For articles written in the radical structuralist tradition, see Aaronovitch (1961), Brennan (2005), Bukharin (1918), Bukharin and Preobrazhensky (1920), Child (1969), Ghilarducci, Hawley, and Williams (1997), Lenin (1917a, 1917b), Menshikov (1969), Miliband (1969), Perlo (1957), Rochester (1936), Scott (1997), Stoney and Winstanley (2001), Zeitlin (1974), and Zeitlin and Norich (1979). The following segment is based on Scott (1997).

contracts and by relevant laws. However, their actual interactions cannot be deduced from their legally defined roles. For instance, the relations among managers, directors, and shareholders are both complex and variable. Indeed, corporate governance has increasingly been concerned with these broader social relations.

Organized capitalism is the outcome of the growth of industrial concentration and combination from the apex of competitive capitalism to the monopoly form. The formation of the joint stock company played an essential role in this monopolization of capital. This is because it allowed enterprises to grow not only through internal capital accumulation but also through merger and amalgamation with other enterprises. Moreover, different enterprises are more closely linked through cartels, trusts, interweaving shareholdings, and interlocking directorships. These larger enterprises have greater economic power in their markets.

In this situation, banks have become critically more important as shareholders, mobilizers of capital, organizers of cartels, and providers of directors. This resulted in bank control and bank influence. Monopoly in banking has obtained economic power over industrial enterprises and consequently banking and industry have been gradually interrelated into this new form of capital, finance capital. That is, banking and industry are related to each other through shareholdings, credit relations, and interlocking directorships. The credit system has been expanded through the new and varied roles for savings banks, insurance companies, investment trusts, pension funds, and other new forms of savings and investment. The finance capital is under the control of banks and is a form of capital that is not restricted to any one particular sphere of economic activity. Industrial enterprises are increasingly dependent on bank loans and other forms of finance capital for expansion, and in this way they consolidate the dominance of finance capital over productive capital.

The numerous competing enterprises of liberal capitalism are replaced with the system of finance capital in which there are a much smaller number of distinct and competing financial groups or empires of high finance. These are sets of connected enterprises within which the control by dominant over subordinate is established. At the core of each financial group is a close group of monopolies that pursue a common policy in order to exercise control over a large number of industries in various branches of the economy. Interlocking directorships, cross-shareholdings, and other types of connection have created associations of capital in order to set a common direction and avoid conflicts of interest. The ties that connect the monopolies have become tighter and more complex. The control of industries is increasingly centralized in centers of finance capital power.

The core of finance capitalists are the rentier capitalists. They are dependent on the incomes they earn from their shareholdings and are, therefore, parasitic upon those who actually manage productive capital. They are from wealthy families and sit on the boards of major banks and industrial companies. They form a financial oligarchy, a term that refers to a few hundred or at most a few thousand men of wealth who comprise the dominant social class. Therefore, the dominant social class in organized capitalism is a class of rentiers, that is, finance capitalists, rather than a class of entrepreneurial capitalists.

Finance capitalists determine the general policies that are implemented by their subordinate managers, engineers, and clerks. Finance capitalists hire and fire managers, and appropriate the proceeds of production. They play a central role in perpetuation of capitalist relations of production.

The relationship between capital and the state is central to the social structure. Organized capitalism establishes interlocking relationships between finance capital and state and increases state intervention. This helps to promote domestic profitability and the socialization of unprofitable activities, and it facilitates the international expansion of national monopolies. The state takes on increasingly more economic functions, such as the maintenance of profitability, the creation of demand, and the redistribution of national income.

Internationally, state monopoly capitalism involves in imperialism and militarism. Confronted with declining profitable investment opportunities in their national economies, financial capital begins to export capital by investment in other national economies. It establishes colonies in order to secure the production of the minerals, raw materials, and agricultural products which are needed by industrial enterprises in the imperial centers. In the consequent division of labor, the industrial development of colonies is subordinated to the need of the imperialist powers.

Conclusion

This chapter briefly discussed four views expressed with respect to the nature and role of corporate governance. The four views correspond to the four paradigms. The functionalist paradigm views corporate governance as ways of reducing agency costs. The interpretive paradigm views corporate governance as a social construction which should be analyzed within the larger social process. The radical humanist paradigm views corporate governance from a truly democratic standpoint. The radical structuralist paradigm views corporate governance as being historically specific and class determined, that is, to satisfy the needs of a social class in an historical period. These four views with respect to the nature of corporate governance and its role are equally scientific and informative; each looks at the nature of corporate governance and its role from a certain paradigmatic viewpoint.

This chapter took the case of corporate governance as an example and emphasized that, in general, any phenomenon may be seen and analyzed from different viewpoints and that each viewpoint exposes a certain aspect of the phenomenon under consideration. Collectively, they provide a much broader and deeper understanding of the phenomenon. Therefore, academic finance can benefit much from contributions coming from other paradigms if it respects paradigm diversity.

Knowledge of finance is ultimately a product of the researcher's paradigmatic approach to this multifaceted phenomenon. Viewed from this angle, the pursuit of financial knowledge is seen as much an ethical, moral, ideological, and political activity, as a technical one. Academic finance can gain much by exploiting the new insights coming from other paradigms.

Chapter 11

Markets and Academic Finance: Four Paradigmatic Views

An analysis of markets necessarily requires a fundamental understanding of the worldviews underlying the views expressed with respect to the nature and role of markets. Four general views with respect to markets, corresponding to four broad worldviews, are discussed. The functionalist paradigm views markets as efficient ways of resource allocation and income distribution. The interpretive paradigm views markets as a social construction which should be analyzed within the larger social process. The radical humanist paradigm views markets from a truly humanistic and democratic standpoint. The radical structuralist paradigm views markets as being historically specific and class determined, that is, to satisfy the needs of a social class in an historical period. These four views with respect to the nature and role of markets are equally scientific and informative; each looks at the nature of markets and their role from a certain paradigmatic viewpoint.

The paper takes the case of markets as an example and emphasizes that, in general, any phenomenon may be seen and analyzed from different viewpoints and that each viewpoint exposes a certain aspect of the phenomenon under consideration. Collectively, they provide a much broader and deeper understanding of the phenomenon. Therefore, academic finance can benefit much from contributions coming from other paradigms if it respects paradigm diversity.

Functionalist View

Functionalist paradigm's views with respect to the nature and role of markets are presented in this section.[1]

Markets play a central role in allocating resources and distributing income. Their performance depends in part on their structure. On the suppliers' side, monopoly and competitive market structures define the extremes. Market structure also varies on the buyers' side. When there is only one buyer, "monopsony" prevails, and when there are few buyers, "oligopsony" prevails. When there is a monopolist and a monopsonist, the structure is a "bilateral monopoly." There are other possible combinations as well.

---

1 For this literature, see Burt (1983), Friedman (1962), Granovetter (1981, 1985), Hayek (1960), Lippmann (2004), Mises (2005), Spencer (2003), Stinchcombe (1983), Sumner (1968), and White (1981). This section is based on *New Palgrave Dictionary of Economics*.

Among economic models, the theory of perfect competition holds the dominant position. Economists have used the logic of perfectly competitive markets very widely and successfully. In contrast, all other market models—referred to as "imperfectly competitive," which includes monopoly, monopolistic competition, dominant-firm price leadership, bilateral monopoly and other situations of bargaining, and all the varieties of oligopoly theory—have been used comparatively very little.

Arrow, Debreu, and MacKenzie are the founders of the formal analyses of Walrasian general equilibrium, and Debreu's Theory of Value (1959) is still the standard treatment of this subject. In this theory, competition finds a behavioral definition. There is a set of consumers, a set of firms, and a set of commodities. One price for each commodity is introduced, and then a perfectly competitive behavior is defined. Each consumer selects transactions that maximize their utilities, subject to a budget constraint. It is assumed that each consumer can buy or sell unlimited quantities at the specified prices and that the consumer's purchases or sales do not affect the profits they earn. Furthermore, it is assumed that each firm selects the inputs and outputs that maximize its net receipts, and that the firm's purchases and sales do not affect prices. Finally, equilibrium is defined as a price vector such that perfectly competitive choices of each agent at these prices aggregate to a feasible allocation, that is, markets clear.

Mathematical proof of this model results in three fundamental theorems. These set conditions on agents' tastes, agents' endowments, and technology under which competitive equilibrium exist (existence), equilibrium allocations are Pareto-optimal (efficiency), and, with an initial reallocation of resources, any Pareto optimum can be supported by a competitive equilibrium (unbiasedness). The combination of efficiency and existence theorems formalizes Adam Smith's argument of the invisible hand that the self-interested behavior serves the common good. The unbiasedness theorem states that the competitive price mechanism does not favor any especial group—capitalists, workers, resource owners, consumers, and so on. The efficiency theorem requires the assumption that not all consumers are satiated. The existence and unbiasedness theorems require the assumption of the absence of any increasing returns to scale as well.

Debreu's model embodies most of the conditions arising in less formal treatments of perfect competition. For instance, the homogeneity and the divisibility of commodities are assumed. But, free entry and large numbers of producers and consumers play no explicit role in Debreu's model. That is, all the theorems would hold if there were only one buyer and one seller of any commodity.

The above property that the results of Debreu's model are independent of the number of producers and consumers reflects the fact that Debreu's model is an equilibrium theory. That is, a theory which specifies what happens only if agents behave as specified and that prices are the equilibrium, market-clearing values. The model neither considers what happens if prices were not at their Walrasian levels, nor specifies how prices are determined. Furthermore, not even Walrasian auctioneer and tatonnement (no trade at non-equilibrium prices) support this equilibrium through a consistent price formation with rational actors. That is, an agent would have incentive to misrepresent their demands, by responding consistently to each price announcement by the auctioneer as if they had a different set of preferences than the real ones, with the goal of arriving at monopolistic prices and outcomes.

The above points are approached by the methods of game theory, especially the theory of non-cooperative games and games in extensive form. Recent research in game theory has significantly improved the partial equilibrium theory of imperfect competition, and it has shown great potential to provide not only a satisfactory general equilibrium theory but also a unified theory of competition that would encompass both perfect and imperfect competition.

Games in extensive form are modeled by specifying the set of agents, the beliefs each has about the characteristics of the other agents, the order in which each acts, the information available to each whenever he/she makes a decision, the possible actions available at each decision point, the outcomes resulting from each possible combination of choices, and the valuations of these outcomes by the agents. In this way, a typical model completely specifies a particular set of institutions.

Then, a solution concept should be specified. In general, there is great freedom in making this specification, but most researchers choose the Nash equilibrium or one of its refinements. It is interesting that adopting the Nash equilibrium does not preclude collusion if opportunities to coordinate and to enforce agreements are modeled as part of the game. Nash equilibrium applies equally to simultaneous or sequential moves, and it does not mean that the agents are necessarily acting simultaneously, in fact, the order of moves is part of the model specification. Finally, the Nash equilibrium does not limit analysis to one-shot situations as it is also applicable to games of repeated play.

Game theory is in the process of unifying the existing theory of imperfect competition. It has provided a common language and analytical framework to understand the earlier work. Also, it has shown that some theories that appeared to be in conflict are in fact consistent in that they arise from a common, more basic model. It is revolutionizing the field of industrial organization.

Interpretive View

Interpretive paradigm's views with respect to the nature and role of markets are presented in this section.[2]

Economies are instituted processes. The understanding of how empirical economies are instituted should be based on the manner in which the economy acquires its unity and stability. That is, the way the economy's parts are interdependent and are perpetuated. This happens through a combination of three patterns which are called forms of integration. These forms occur side by side on different levels and in different sectors of the economy. Therefore, frequently it becomes almost

---

2 For this literature, see Agnew (1986), Appadurai (1986), Boulding (1973), Dannhaeuser and Werner (2006), DiMaggio (1990), Douglas and Isherwood (1982), Ewen (1985), Fligstein (1996), Gudeman (1986), Horowitz (1985), Mantzavinos (2001), Miller (1987), Peiss (1986), Polanyi (1957), Reddy (1984), Sahlins (1976), Schudson (1984), Sen (1977), Taussig (1986), Williams (2006), Wuthnow (1987), and Zelizer (1983, 1987, 1988, 1994). This section is based on Polanyi (1957).

impossible to choose one of them as dominant and use it for a classification of the empirical economy as a whole. However, these forms differentiate between sectors and levels of the economy and offer a means of describing the economic process in comparatively simple terms. In this way, these forms introduce a measure of order into economy's endless variations.

The three empirical patterns are reciprocity, redistribution, and exchange. Reciprocity designates movements between correlative points of symmetrical groupings; redistribution refers to appropriational movements toward a center and out of it again; exchange denotes bilateral movements taking place as between points under a market system. Reciprocity requires symmetrically arranged groupings; redistribution requires the presence of a center in the group; exchange requires a system of price-making markets. Clearly, different forms of integration require different institutional support.

The terms reciprocity, redistribution, and exchange, that is, the three forms of integration, are often interpreted at the personal level. It is important to note that the aggregates of personal behaviors do not by themselves produce such structures. Reciprocity behavior between individuals integrates the economy only if symmetrically organized structures, such as a symmetrical system of kinship groups, prevail. In other words, a system of kinship groups never arises as the result of only reciprocating behavior on the personal level. Similarly, redistribution requires an allocative center in the community. But, such a center is not established merely as a consequence of habitual act of sharing between individuals. Likewise, acts of exchange on the personal level do not produce prices, unless they occur under a system of price-making markets. The supporting pattern may seem to result from the aggregate of the corresponding type of personal behavior, but they are, in fact, contributed by a different type of behavior.

This explains the fact that in the economy behaviors on the personal level usually fail to have the expected societal effects unless there are definite institutional preconditions. Only in a symmetrically organized environment will reciprocative behavior result in a stable economy; only where allocative centers have been organized can sharing behavior on the part of individuals produce a redistributive economy; and only in the context of a system of price-making markets will individuals' exchanges result in formation of prices that integrate the economy. Otherwise, these acts of barter will remain ineffective and therefore will be abandoned. If they randomly happen, they will be harshly reacted to. This is because trading behavior is not an emotionally indifferent behavior and is not, therefore, tolerated in a community whose members hold a different set of opinions and beliefs.

Price-making markets are integrated only if they are part of a network of a system which tends to spread the effect of prices to markets other than those directly affected. The exchange at a set price occurs not because of the market mechanism, but by the integration of the economy with the factors which fix that rate.

Forms of integration neither represent stages of development of human society nor is any sequence in time implied. Several subordinate integration forms may coexist alongside a dominant one, whose relative position may change over time.

Price-making markets, which by themselves constitute the market system, were non-existent before the first millennium of antiquity, and then found their subordinate positions relative to other forms of integration, and did not gain importance until comparatively late in history.

Non-economic factors affect and are affected by markets, rather than a dependence of non-economic factors on the market. The market is not an amoral, self-sufficient institution, rather it is a cultural and social construct. The market has its own set of values and norms and is interdependent with other values and institutions. No market transaction is free from non-economic influences. Therefore, market exchange is neither homogeneous nor ahistorical, but it is variable. Because market exchanges are interdependencies with values and institutional structures, economic exchange can be patterned in different ways.

The construction of market institutions is a cultural project in several ways. Property rights, governance structures, conceptions of control, and rules of exchange define the social institutions required to make markets. Economies are social entities; therefore, they operate according to social principles. Economic actors are involved in political actions versus each other and construct relevant cultures to guide that engagement.

Markets are socially constructed. They reflect the unique political-cultural construction of their firms and nations. The creation of markets reflects societal solutions to the problems of property rights, governance structures, conceptions of control, and rules of exchange. Of course, there are many paths to those solutions.

Radical Humanist View

Radical humanist paradigm's views with respect to the nature and role of markets are presented in this section.[3]

The free market ideology of market liberalism supports the interests of the owners of capital. The ideology and special interests masquerade as economic science and good policy.

Laissez-faire did not come to existence naturally. It was an especial-interest project to be put in place. It was set up and maintained by an enormous increase in continuous, centrally organized and controlled interventionism of the state.

All societies need an economy in order to live. Historically, no economy has ever existed that was controlled by markets, except for laissez-faire. Though the market institution dates back to the later Stone Age, it played a minor role in economic life. Laissez-faire is based on the motive of gain which is only rarely regarded as valid in social history, and certainly never before was used as the foundation for action and behavior in everyday life. Within a generation, the motive of gain influenced all aspects of the human world, including economic, political, intellectual, and spiritual pursuits.

In all previous economic systems the production and distribution of goods were done through a variety of individual motives, which stemmed from the general

---

3 For this literature, see Barber (1977), Bell (1976), Bermant, Brown and Dworkin (1977), Hirsch (1976), Horkheimer (1947, 1974), Kopytoff (1986), Marcuse (1965), Marx (1964), Polanyi (1944), Robbins (1946), Schumpeter (1942), Simmel (1900, 1978), Titmus (1971), Walzer (1983), and Weisskopf (1973, 1977). This section is based on Polanyi (1944).

principles of behavior. These did not create institutions designed for one function only. The motive of gain from exchange, on the other hand, is capable of creating a specific institution, called market. Under this, the economic system is organized in separate institutions and the society must conform so that the market system can function according to its own laws.

It is through the commodity concept that the market system influences various elements of human life. Commodities are objects produced for sale on the market. Accordingly, every element of industry is regarded as having been produced for sale on its own market.

The factors of production are labor, land, and money, which must be organized in markets. But labor, land, and money are obviously not commodities. Labor is a human activity, which is not produced for sale. Labor is part of human life and cannot be detached from the rest of human life, nor can it be stored or mobilized. Labor cannot be used without affecting the owner of this commodity who is a human individual with a specific physical, psychological, and moral identity. Land is not produced by man. Land is a part of life, land is a part of nature, life and nature form an intertwined whole. Land plays a major role in the organizations of kinship, neighborhood, craft, and creed—with tribe and temple, village, guild, and religion. Land performs not only the economic function but also many other vital functions. It provides stability to human life; it constitutes human's habitation; it helps human's physical safety; it is the landscape and the seasons. Money is merely a representation of purchasing power, which is not produced, but is created through banking or state finance. Since profits depend upon prices, then the monetary arrangements, which affect prices, must be vital to the functioning of the market system, which is motivated by profits. More specifically, if the price level falls for monetary reasons for some time, business would be in danger of liquidation, dissolution of productive organization, and massive destruction of capital.

Market economy includes markets for the factors of production: labor, land, and money. Since these factors of production are parts of the elements of human institutions, that is, man and nature, market economy involves a society whose institutions are subordinated to the laws of the market system. Thus, human institutions are disrupted because the market economy is forced upon an entirely differently organized community.

The market does not have a mechanism to warn against the dangers involved in the exploitation of human worker, the destruction of family life, the devastation of neighborhoods, the denudation of forests, the pollution of rivers, the deterioration of craft standards, the disruption of folkways, and the general degradation of existence including housing and arts, as well as the innumerable forms of private and public life that do not affect profits. This explains how a civilization is being disrupted by market institutions whose only purpose is the increase of material welfare.

Society has taken measures to protect itself against the hazards inherent in the market system. Therefore, there have been two movements. One has been based on the principle of economic liberalism, with the aim of establishing a self-regulating market system, by relying on trading classes, and using largely laissez-faire and free trade as its methods. The other has been based on the principle of social protection, with the aim of the conservation of man and nature as well as productive organization, by relying on those most negatively affected by the market—primarily, but not exclusively, the working and the landed classes—and using protective legislation, restrictive associations, and other instruments of intervention as its methods.

To protect humans who provide labor, factory legislation and social laws were required. To protect nature that provides land, land laws and agrarian tariffs were required. To protect manufactures and other productive enterprises, central banking and the management of the monetary system were required. Note should be taken that not only human and nature but also the capitalist production itself has had to be protected against the deleterious effects of the market system.

To protect the factors of production—land, labor, and money—the society has tried to partially remove the factors of production from the total dictate of the market system. New societies have emerged as a result of the disintegration of a uniform market economy. Socialism may be defined as the tendency in a civilization to subordinate the market system to a democratic society. Socialism regulates production and uses markets but subordinates them to the free society.

Radical Structuralist View

Radical structuralist paradigm's views with respect to the nature and role of markets are presented in this section.[4]

Market capitalism is forth in the five consecutive modes of production—primitive communal, slavery, feudalism, capitalism, and socialism—which human society historically evolves through.

Capitalism is not distinguished for its markets rather it is distinguished for the fact that the social relation between producing and exploiting classes is structured in terms of markets, that is, around the sale and purchase of a commodity, a thing, called human labor-power.

When economic problems are reduced to relations between things, or between things and human beings, it would be manifestations of mystification, false consciousness, or reification of human relations. Economic science should uncover relations between human beings which underlie relations between things. Commodity fetishism specifies that in capitalism the social relations between people, that is, producers and exploiters, take the form of relations between things, that is, commodities.

Commodity production and exchange have existed in diverse modes of production. But the laws of commodity production and exchange cannot govern the economy and society as a whole unless the labor-power is turned into a commodity.

Capitalism leads neither to the highest economic growth nor to the highest wellbeing for the greatest number of individuals. This is because it leads to the high

---

4 For this literature, see Amott and Matthaei (1991), Ciscel and Heath (2001), Green (2003), Hartmann (1981), Heath and Ciscel (1988), Heath, Ciscel and Sharp (1998), Kessler-Harris (1981), Luxemburg (1951), Magdoff (2003), Marx (1872, 1932), Marx and Engels (1998), Matthaei (1982), McIntyre and Hillard (1992), Perelman (2006), Sennett (1998), Sweezy (1964), Tilly and Scott (1987), and Zaretsky (1976, 1986). This section is based on New Palgrave Dictionary of Economics.

economic and social price humankind has had to pay for the undeniable progress it produced at a given stage of historical evolution.

The laws of motion of the capitalist mode of production start with the owners of capital search for profit, that is, surplus-value, which is produced by labor-power.

Similar to other commodities, the commodity labor-power has both an exchange value and a use value. Similar to other commodities, the exchange value of labor-power is the amount of socially necessary labor embodied in it, that is, its reproduction costs. This is the value of all goods and services necessary for a laborer to work regularly with the same intensity, and that the number and skill of members of the laboring classes to remain approximately stable. On the other hand, the use value of labor-power is its capacity to create new value, which might be more than its own reproduction costs. Surplus-value is the difference between the use value and the exchange value of labor-power. That is, the surplus-value is the difference between the value created by labor-power and the reproduction costs of labor-power.

The surplus-value is generated in the process of production and it is realized in the process of exchange, that is, through the sale of the commodities. The capitalists desire to sell their commodities at maximum profit. But they cannot be sure of this outcome. They cannot even be sure that there will be enough demand for all their produced commodities. Faced with such uncertainties, they have to constantly strive for operating with more capital. Therefore, part of the surplus-value produced has to be accumulated, that is, be added to the existing capital. Moreover, capitalist firms cut production costs by using more advanced production techniques and more rationalized labor organization.

Competition among firms results in either the firms who prosper or the firms who go bankrupt. The prosperous firms grow and buy bankrupt firms and small- and medium-sized firms. It results in a declining number of firms which survive in each of the key fields of production and an increasing number of workers.

Workers fight for higher real wages, shorter work days, and better work conditions. They form collective organizations for the sale of the commodity labor-power, that is, trade unions.

Periodic economic crises of overproduction have been unavoidable under capitalism. These crises interrupt expanded production or economic growth because there is not sufficient demand for the amounts of commodities produced. Consequently, there will be collapse of firms, firing of workers, contraction of orders for raw materials and machinery, reduction of sales of consumer goods, and so on. Through this economic contraction, prices, production, income, value of capital will be reduced. At the end of the declining spiral, stocks of commodities will be reduced more than purchasing power and production can pick up again. At the same time, the average rate of profit increases and stimulates investment. This occurs because of the increase in the rate of surplus-value—through a decline of wages—and the reduction in the value of capital. Employment, production, and national income expand, and the economy enters a new cycle of economic revival, prosperity, overheating, and the next crisis.

Neither the capitalists' self-regulation nor the government intervention has been able to suppress the cyclical crisis of capitalist production. They cannot succeed in achieving that goal. The cyclical crisis is linked to the production of profit and private property because each firm's attempt at maximizing profit leads to a lower rate of profit for the system as a whole. Similarly, it is linked to the separation of value production and value realization.

Prevention of the crises of overproduction requires elimination of all basic sources of disequilibrium in the economy. This, in turn, requires the elimination of generalized commodity production, of private property, and of class exploitation, that is, the elimination of capitalism.

Capitalism as a socio-economic order carries within itself the seed of its own destruction. Meanwhile, capitalism corrodes all traditional values and institutions such as love, family, and patriotism. Everything passes through markets and all social bonds are dissolved through money.

Conclusion

This chapter briefly discussed four views expressed with respect to the nature and role of markets. The functionalist paradigm views markets as efficient ways of resource allocation and income distribution. The interpretive paradigm views markets as a social construction which should be analyzed within the larger social process. The radical humanist paradigm views markets from a truly humanistic and democratic standpoint. The radical structuralist paradigm views markets as being historically specific and class determined, that is, to satisfy the needs of a social class in an historical period. These four views with respect to the nature of markets and their role are equally scientific and informative; each looks at the nature of markets and its role from a certain paradigmatic viewpoint.

This chapter took the case of markets as an example and emphasized that, in general, any phenomenon may be seen and analyzed from different viewpoints and that each viewpoint exposes a certain aspect of the phenomenon under consideration. Collectively, they provide a much broader and deeper understanding of the phenomenon. Therefore, academic finance can benefit much from contributions coming from other paradigms if it respects paradigm diversity.

Knowledge of finance is ultimately a product of the researcher's paradigmatic approach to this multifaceted phenomenon. Viewed from this angle, the pursuit of financial knowledge is seen as much an ethical, moral, ideological, and political activity, as a technical one. Academic finance can gain much by exploiting the new insights coming from other paradigms.

Chapter 12

Technology and Academic Finance: Four Paradigmatic Views

An analysis of technology necessarily requires a fundamental understanding of the worldviews underlying the views expressed with respect to the nature and role of technology. Four general views with respect to technology, corresponding to four broad worldviews, are discussed. The functionalist paradigm views technology as a factor of production and therefore views technological progress as having corresponding effect on economy's output and growth. The interpretive paradigm views technology as a social construction which should be analyzed within the larger social process. The radical humanist paradigm views technology as ideology and being used for domination over the majority of people in society. The radical structuralist paradigm views technology as the most revolutionary among the forces of production, whose growth has taken human society from primitive commune, to slavery, to feudalism, to capitalism, and towards socialism. These four views with respect to the nature and role of technology are equally scientific and informative; each looks at the nature of technology and their role from a certain paradigmatic viewpoint.

The paper takes the case of technology as an example and emphasizes that, in general, any phenomenon may be seen and analyzed from different viewpoints and that each viewpoint exposes a certain aspect of the phenomenon under consideration. Collectively, they provide a much broader and deeper understanding of the phenomenon. Therefore, academic finance can benefit much from contributions coming from other paradigms if it respects paradigm diversity.

This chapter takes the case of technology as an example and emphasizes that, in general, any phenomenon may be seen and analyzed from different viewpoints and that each viewpoint exposes a certain aspect of the phenomenon under consideration. Collectively, they provide a much broader and deeper understanding of the phenomenon. Therefore, academic finance can benefit much from contributions coming from other paradigms if it respects paradigm diversity.

Functionalist View

Functionalist paradigm's views with respect to the nature and role of technology are presented in this section.[1]

---

1 For this literature, see Domar (1946), Hahn (1965), Hahn and Matthews (1964), Harrod (1939), Hicks (1965), Kaldor (1956), Mitra (1976), Pasinetti (1981), Robinson (1956, 1962), Solow (1956), Sraffa (1960), Uzawa (1961), and von Neumann (1937). This section is based on New Palgrave Dictionary of Economics.

Capital goods are heterogeneous commodities due to their different technical characteristics. Capital goods are one of the factors of production. In contrast to labor and land, capital goods are not given, because they are themselves produced. Capital goods are both an output and an input and, therefore, the size and variation of the capital stock are determined endogenously. That is, as a factor of production, capital stock is not a given but it is the result of an economic process in which it participates as one of the determinants. Consequently, the formation of capital stock or investment is the major channel through which all other determinants—such as technical progress, change in labor supply, or the exploitation of natural resources—influence the long-run growth of an economic system.

Classical economists became interested in the analysis of economic growth because of their philosophical concern with growth in national wealth, consumption, and the material basis of society. They regarded the principle of national advantage as an essential criterion of economic policy. Accordingly, their purpose of analysis was to identify the forces in society that promoted or hindered economic growth in order to provide a basis for policy and action to influence those forces.

Classical economists provided an account of the mechanisms underlying the growth process and major forces that influence economic growth. Their important achievement was the recognition that the main driving force behind economic growth is the investment of a part of the social product towards accumulation of capital stock. Such capital accumulation forms as a result of the reinvestment of a portion of profits.

At the core of the problem of economic growth lies the explanation of the forces underlying the process of the accumulation of capital stock. Closely associated with the accumulation of capital stock is the technical change, as expressed in the division of labor and changes in methods of production.

The most common analysis of the accumulation of capital has viewed the problem as the expansion of the productive potential of an economy with a given technology, which may be improved in the process. This approach leads to analyses based on the idea of steady growth.

Accumulation of capital is the result of plowing back part of the surplus generated from production. Accordingly, accumulation of capital is the investment of part of society's net product—the surplus of output over consumption and the requirements for maintaining the existing capital stock—in order to expand productive capacity to take advantage of new or developing markets. The study of the accumulation of capital in the steady state growth of the economy explains both the availability of the surplus and the motivation for plowing it back.

Most of the modern work studied accumulation of capital in the context of steady growth. Economic growth can have a specific target, or can continue indefinitely. The former is the subject of "turnpike" studies—that is, in order to reach a target set of outputs, first the economy most rapidly shifts to the balanced growth path, the "turnpike," and grows along it, and changes to the desired set of outputs when it reaches the right size. The latter is the subject of models in which equilibrium paths of perpetual growth are determined and their properties examined. In other words, given a system of production, the above two approaches answer the question how that system can be organized in order to grow either over some finite period of time to reach some target set of outputs or over the indefinite future. In either case the accumulation of capital, which is the core of economic growth, will result from the investment of part of the surplus, and will be analyzed either as a case of steady growth or as a deviation from steady growth.

Classical economists provided a complex structure of ideas expressing a deep understanding of the nature of the economic system, the sources of its expansion, and the barriers or limits to its expansion. However, their ideas were constrained by the conditions of their agrarian economy, that is, without significant change in methods of production. Without technological progress, the limited quantity and diminishing fertility of the soil results in the limit to growth by increasing the cost of production of agricultural commodities. Their analysis underestimated the role of technological progress in transforming the conditions of productivity both in agriculture and in industry.

Neo-classical economists explicitly incorporate technological progress in their analysis. The neo-classical model determines a path of steady and stable full-employment growth. For example, when the rate of growth of labor, measured in efficiency units—the natural rate of growth—exceeds the rate determined by the propensity to save and the capital-output ratio—the rate that will just balance aggregate demand and aggregate supply—the real wage will tend to fall. This leads firms to substitute labor for capital. Consequently, the capital-output ratio will decline, raising the rate of growth. If the production function is well-behave—linear and homogeneous, positive first and negative second derivatives, marginal product of capital tends to infinity as capital-labor ratio tends to zero, and tends to zero as capital-labor ratio tends to infinity—then there will exist an equilibrium growth path. Technological progress which leaves the capital-output ratio unchanged (Harrod-neutral) will not affect the steady-growth path; and technological progress which leaves the ratio of the marginal products of capital and labor unchanged (Hicks-neutral) will change the path, but the economy will adjust smoothly to the new equilibrium.

In neoclassical theory, equilibria tend also to be optimal, but in general the steady growth path will not be. Along an optimal path per capita consumption is at a maximum. Consumption is output minus investment. Investment must grow at a constant rate in order to fully employ the growing labor force. If the marginal product of capital is more than is required to equip the labor force, consumption rises; if it is less, consumption falls. Hence when the marginal product of capital just equals the additional investment required to equip the growing labor force, consumption will be at a maximum. The "Golden Rule of Growth" means consumption per head is maximized and obtains when the rate of profit equals the rate of growth.

Interpretive View

Interpretive paradigm's views with respect to the nature and role of technology are presented in this section.[2]

---

2 For this literature, see Bijker (1990), Bijker, Hughes, and Pinch (1987), Bijker and Law (1992), Jasanoff, Markle, Petersen, and Pinch (1995), Klein and Kleinman (2002), Pinch

The social construction of technology shows how social processes influence the content of technology, that is, when a technology is deemed to be working. The social construction of technology illustrates that technology and the facts about its working, which are established through processes of engineering design and testing, are social constructs.

The conceptual framework of the social construction of technology consists of five related components.

The first component of the social construction of technology framework is the *relevant social group*. The understanding of technological development requires the understanding of the technological artifacts, that is, materials and processes. The social construction of technology, which is fundamentally a sociological approach towards technology, approaches and analyzes artifacts in the context of society. Society is conceptualized and related to artifacts through the notion of relevant social groups. These are social groups who play a role in the development of a technological artifact. Such social groups share a meaning of the artifact. This meaning is then used to explain particular development paths which the artifact takes. Some examples of social groups are as follows: engineers, advertisers, public-interest groups, and consumers. The understanding of a complex technology involves a whole array of such social groups. Although the only defining characteristic of a social group is its homogeneous meaning given to a certain artifact, the intention is not just to make general statements about any of the social groups, such as consumers and producers. For each relevant social group, its detailed description is needed in order to be able to define the functioning of the artifact with respect to that social group.

Relevant social groups have particular interpretations and accordingly all members of a social group share the same set of meanings with respect to a given artifact. In other words, they are the agents in this agency-centered approach whose actions reflect the meanings they associate with specific artifacts. Technological development is a social process which involves multiple social groups, each of which has a specific interpretation of a certain artifact, and they negotiate over its design, with different social groups seeing and constructing quite different technological artifact. For instance, if social groups have different definitions of a working technology, then the technological development continues until all groups come to a consensus that their common artifact works. At this stage, the technological development culminates not because the technological artifact works in some objective sense but because all relevant social groups agree that it works for them.

The second component of the social construction of technology framework is the *interpretive flexibility*. It means that different social groups may associate radically different meanings to a certain artifact. That is, there is interpretive flexibility with respect to the meaning given to a given artifact. Interpretive flexibility applies to both a compound artifact and to its separate components.

Interpretive flexibility implies that technology design (and use) is an open process that can generate different outcomes depending on the social circumstances in which they are development. That is, technological artifacts are the outcomes of

(1996), and Pinch and Bijker (1984). This section is based on Klein and Kleinman (2002) and Pinch (1996).

inter-group negotiations. There are several possible outcomes of the design (and use) of technological artifacts, therefore, the final design (and use) that finally results from the process, it could have been different.

The third component of the social construction of technology framework is the *closure and stabilization*. The involvement of several social groups in the technological design (and use) process can lead to controversies since their different interpretations lead to conflicting images of an artifact. Technological design (and use) continues until such controversies are resolved and the technological artifact is considered satisfactory by all relevant social groups. At this point, the process achieves closure and the artifact stabilizes in its final form. Two examples of closure mechanisms are as follows. Rhetorical closure involves a declaration that no further problems exist and that no additional design is necessary. Closure by redefinition involves a redefinition of unresolved problems such that they no longer pose problems to all relevant social groups.

Closure and stabilization obtain when an artifact seems to have fewer problems and become increasingly the acceptable and dominant form of the technology. This may not necessarily lead to all competing technological artifacts disappearing, and often two very different technologies may co-exist. Furthermore, the process of closure or stabilization need not necessarily be final. New problems can arise and the interpretive flexibility of the technological artifact can reappear.

The fourth component of the social construction of technology framework is the *wider context*. This is the wider socio-cultural and political context in which the development of the technological artifact occurs. The background conditions of group interactions, such as their relations to each other, the rules ordering their interactions, and factors contributing to differences in their power fall in this category.

The fifth component of the social construction of technology framework is the *technological frame,* that is, frame with respect to technology. This is a social group's shared cognitive frame of reference that forms social group members' common interpretation of a certain artifact. Similar to a Kuhnian paradigm, a technological frame can include goals, key problems, current theories, rules of thumb, testing procedures, and exemplary artifacts that, tacitly or explicitly, structure group members' thinking, problem solving, strategy formation, and design activities. A technological frame usually promotes certain actions and discourages others. In the process, technological frame acts as a frame of meaning with respect to a particular technology which is shared by several social groups, which, in turn, further guides and shapes the development of the artifact. This helps to shed light on how the structured character of the larger social context is linked to technology design (and use).

Radical Humanist View

Radical humanist paradigm's views with respect to the nature and role of technology are presented in this section.[3]

---

3 For this literature, see Feenberg (1991, 1999), Habermas (1970c), Heidegger (1977), Lukacs (1971), and Marcuse (1964). This section is based on Habermas (1970c).

The concept of "rationality" refers to the form of capitalist economic activity, bourgeois private law, and bureaucratic authority. Rationalization means subjecting different areas of society to the criteria of rational decision, that is, the criteria of instrumental action penetrate into different areas of life. It implies purposive-rational action, which refers to the organization of means of choice between alternatives. In this framework, planning can be regarded as purposive-rational action of the second order. This is because it aims at the establishment, improvement, or expansion of systems of purposive-rational action themselves.

The increasing "rationalization" of society is related to the institutionalization of scientific and technical development. Technology and science progressively permeate social institutions and transform them, and in this way old legitimations are replaced.

The concept of technical reason is ideological. Both the application of technology and technology itself are forms of domination, that is, domination of nature and domination of men. Technical reason is methodical, scientific, calculated, and calculating control. Specific plans of domination are not superimposed on technology subsequently and externally; they enter *a priori* in the construction of the technical apparatus. Technology is always a historical-social phenomenon, that is, it shows what a society and its ruling interests intend to do with men and things.

The technological *a priori* is a political *a priori* to the extent that the transformation of nature involves that of man, and to the extent that the man-made creations affect and are affected by their societal ensemble. It might be said that the machinery of the technological universe is indifferent towards political ends. However, when techniques become the universal form of material production, they affect and modify an entire culture; they project a historical totality, that is, a world.

In the name of rationality, "rationalization" realizes a specific form of unacknowledged political domination. This sort of rationality intends to lead to the correct choice among strategies, the appropriate applications of technologies, and the efficient establishment of systems with presupposed aims in given situations. Therefore, it removes the total social framework of interests in which strategies are chosen, technologies are applied, and systems are established, from the scope of reflection and rational reconstruction. This type of rationality intends to lead only to relations of technical control and therefore encourages actions that imply domination, whether of nature or of society. By its very nature, purposive-rational action is the exercise of control. According to this type of rationality, the "rationalization" of society is the institutionalization of a form of domination. However, the political character of this domination becomes unrecognizable. This is despite the fact that the technical reason of a social system of purposive-rational action does not lose its political content.

The institutionalized growth of the forces of production, which surpasses all historical proportions, follows from scientific and technical progress. This gives the institutional framework the opportunity for legitimation. The idea that the objectively superfluous, repressive character of historically obsolete relations of production can be measured against the growth of productive forces is denied because the existing relations of production are the technically necessary organizational form of a rationalized society. The forces of production, at this stage of their scientific-technical development, enter a new arrangement with the relations of production. Growth in the forces of production are not used as the basis of a critique of prevailing legitimations, instead they are used as the basis for legitimation.

The objectively superfluous repression of individuals is experienced in their intensified subjection to the enormous apparatus of production and distribution, and in their de-privatization of free time. Ironically, however, this repression might not register in the consciousness of individuals because the legitimation of domination is based on the growth of the forces of production and the domination of nature which provide individuals with increasingly comfortable lives.

The rationality embodied in the system of purposive-rational action is limited. In addition, the rationality of science and technology, instead of being reducible to unvarying rules of logic and method, is a substantive, historically derived, and transitory *a priori* structure.

Modern science was *a priori* structured in such a fashion that it could serve as conceptual instrument for productive control. Consequently, theoretical operationalism came to correspond to practical operationalism. The scientific method which led to the progressive domination of nature provided the concepts and instrumentalities for the progressive domination of man by man through the domination of nature. Domination is perpetuated and extended not only through technology but as technology. The latter provides the legitimation of the expanding political power, which encompasses all spheres of culture.

Technology rationalizes the unfreedom of man in being autonomous and in determining one's own life. This unfreedom is recognized neither as irrational nor as political, but rather as submission to the technical apparatus which increases the productivity of labor and enlarges the comforts of life. In this way, technological rationality legitimizes domination and opens on a rationally totalitarian society.

The nature of fusion of technology and domination, rationality and oppression is contained in the material *a priori* of the logic of science and technology and determined by class interest and historical situation. Therefore, social emancipation cannot be conceived without a complementary revolutionary transformation of science and technology themselves.

The transcendental framework within which nature would be made the object of a new experience would replace the functional system of instrumental action. The viewpoint of possible technical control would be replaced by one of preserving, fostering, and releasing the potentialities of nature.

Radical Structuralist View

Radical structuralist paradigm's views with respect to the nature and role of technology are presented in this section.[4]

In order to live, people must have food, clothing, footwear, shelter, fuel, and so on. In order to have these materials, people must produce them. In order to produce

---

4 For this literature, see Croce (2000), Engles (1979), Marx (1969), Plekhanov (1969), Schmitt (1987), and Stalin (1940). This section is based on Stalin (1940).

these materials, people must have the instruments of production. People must be able to produce and use these instruments of production. These embody the technology.

The instruments of production and the people who operate them, together with their experience and skill, constitute the *forces of production* of society.

The forces of production are only one aspect of production. Another aspect of production is the *relations of production*, that is, the relation of men to each other in the process of production. In the production of materials men enter into mutual relations of one kind or another, called relations of production. The relations of production may be free from exploitation, they may be based on domination and subordination, or they may be transitional from one form of relations of production to another.

The relations of production show who owns the *means of production* (the land, forests, waters, mineral resources, raw materials, instruments of production, production premises, means of transportation and communication, and so on), who has command over the means of production, whether the whole of society, or individual persons, or groups, or classes which utilize them for the exploitation of other persons, groups, or classes?

The *mode of production* consists of both the forces of production and the relations of production.

Over time, forces of production develop, most prominently due to the development in technology. At different stages of development of forces of production, societies utilize different modes of production. For instance, different modes of production prevail in the primitive commune, in slavery, in feudalism, in capitalism, or in socialism. A change in the mode of production leads to changes in the whole social system: social ideas, theories, political views, and political.

This means that the history of development of society is above all the history of the development of technology, the history of the development of forces of production, the history of the change in modes of production, which succeed each other in the course of centuries.

The development of instruments of production since the ancient times briefly has been as follows. The development from crude stone tools to the bow and arrow, from the life of hunters to the domestication of animals and primitive pasturage; the development from stone tools to metal tools—the iron axe, the wooden plow fitted with an iron coulter, and so on—and the life of tillage and agriculture; further development in metal tools for the working up of materials, the blacksmith's bellows, the pottery, handicrafts, the separated lines of handicrafts from agriculture, handicraft industry and manufacturing industry; the development from handicraft tools to machines, handicraft machine industry and manufacturing machine industry; the development to the machine system, modern large-scale machine industry.

In conformity with the improvement and development of the technology and the forces of production of society in the course of history, men's relations of production also has improved and developed. The five main types of relations of production are primitive communal, slave, feudal, capitalist and socialist.

Development in technology is the most mobile and revolutionary element in production, which determines the development of society. The development and improvement of the instruments of production has been effected by men who were involved in the process of production. Consequently, the improvement and development of the instruments of production has been accompanied by an improvement and development of men. This has taken effect through their production experience, improvement in their labor skill, and improvement in their ability to handle the instruments of production.

Society's development always begins with the development in technology embodied in the instruments of production. This, in turn, leads to the development in the forces or production. Then, in conformity with them, relations of production change. Note should be taken that the relations of production influence the development of the forces of production. That is, relations of production might accelerate or retard the development of the forces of production. The relations of production cannot fall behind and be in a state of contradiction to the growth of the forces of production. Forces of production can develop only when the relations of production correspond to their character. The relations of production must come, and actually do come, into correspondence with the level of development of the forces of production. Otherwise there would be a fundamental violation of the unity of the forces of production and the relations of production within the system of production. This would mean a disruption of production as a whole, a crisis of production, and a destruction of the forces of production.

For instance, in capitalist countries, the relations of production do not correspond to the character of the forces of production. This is because private capitalist ownership of the means of production does not correspond to the social character of the process of production, that is, with the character of the forces of production. This results in economic crises, which lead to the destruction of productive forces. Furthermore, this incongruity constitutes the economic basis of social revolution, the purpose of which is to destroy the existing relations of production and to create new relations of production which correspond to the social character of the forces of production.

In contrast, in socialism, the relations of production completely correspond to the character of the forces of production. That is, the social ownership of the means of production fully corresponds to the social character of the process of production. Therefore, in socialism, economic crises and the destruction of forces of production are nonexistent.

Conclusion

This chapter briefly discussed four views expressed with respect to the nature and role of technology. The functionalist paradigm views technology as a factor of production and therefore views technological progress as having corresponding effect on economy's output and growth. The interpretive paradigm views technology as a social construction which should be analyzed within the larger social process. The radical humanist paradigm views technology as ideology and being used for domination over the majority of people in society. The radical structuralist paradigm views technology as the most revolutionary among the forces of production, whose growth has taken human society from primitive commune, to slavery, to feudalism, to capitalism, and towards socialism. These four views with respect to the nature of technology and its role are equally scientific and informative; each looks at the nature of technology and its role from a certain paradigmatic viewpoint.

This chapter took the case of technology as an example and emphasized that, in general, any phenomenon may be seen and analyzed from different viewpoints and that each viewpoint exposes a certain aspect of the phenomenon under consideration. Collectively, they provide a much broader and deeper understanding of the phenomenon. Therefore, academic finance can benefit much from contributions coming from other paradigms if it respects paradigm diversity.

Knowledge of finance is ultimately a product of the researcher's paradigmatic approach to this multifaceted phenomenon. Viewed from this angle, the pursuit of financial knowledge is seen as much an ethical, moral, ideological, and political activity, as a technical one. Academic finance can gain much by exploiting the new insights coming from other paradigms.

Chapter 13

Teaching and Academic Finance:
Four Paradigmatic Views

Any adequate analysis of the role of foundational philosophies—or worldviews or paradigms—in educational philosophy must recognize the assumptions that underwrite a given foundational philosophy or worldview.

This chapter discusses the correspondence between the four paradigms—or foundational philosophies—and the major[1] educational[2] philosophies: realism, idealism and pragmatism, reconstructionism, and Marxism. It notes that each educational philosophy favors a certain instructional methodology and when any instructional methods are utilized, they are used within the bounds of the same educational philosophy.

Any philosophy of education is the application of a paradigm—or foundational philosophy—to educational problems. The practice of education, in turn, leads to the refinement of philosophical ideas. The philosophy of education becomes important when educators recognize the need for thinking clearly about what they are doing and to see what they are doing in the larger context of society. Educational philosophy is not only a basis for generating educational ideas, but also a basis for how to provide the desired instruction, that is, instructional methodology.

This chapter shows the correspondence between the four basic paradigms and the educational philosophies: realism, idealism and pragmatism, reconstructionism, and Marxism, respectively. Realism lies in the functionalist quadrant in Figure 1.1 and is located on the right-hand extreme on the objective-subjective continuum. Idealism is located in the interpretive quadrant in Figure 1.1 and is located on the left-hand extreme on the objective-subjective continuum. Pragmatism lies in the interpretive quadrant, but to the right of idealism. Reconstructionism lies in the radical humanist quadrant in Figure 1.1 and belongs to the same position on the objective-subjective continuum as pragmatism. Marxism lies in the radical structuralist quadrant in Figure 1.1 and belongs to the right-hand extreme on the objective-subjective continuum.

---

1 For the basic literature on diverse views see Barrow and Woods (1989), Ellis, Cogan, and Howey (1991), Noddings (1995), Ozmon and Craver (1998), Sadovnik, Semel, and Cookson (1994), and Winch and Gingell (1999).

2 For the more advanced literature on diverse views see Barrow and White (1993), Cahn (1996), Chambliss (1996), Gutek (1996), Kimball and Orrill (1995), Marples (1999), Power (1995), and Rorty (1998).

Realism and Education

Realists strongly promote the study of science and the scientific method.[3] They believe that knowledge of the world is needed for humankind's proper use of it for his or her survival. The idea of survival has important implications for education. It places self-preservation as the primary aim of education.

Realists maintain that knowing the world requires an understanding of facts and classifying the knowledge obtained about them. Schools should teach essential facts about the universe and the method of arriving at facts. Realists place enormous emphasis upon critical reason based on observation and experimentation.

Realists emphasize the practical side of education. Their concept of "practical" includes education for moral and character development, where moral education is founded on knowledge itself. Realists' essentials and the practicalities of education lead themselves further. They proceed from matter to idea, from imperfection to perfection, and all to the good life.

Realists promote the education which is primarily technical and leads to specialization. The idea of specialization is the natural outcome of the efforts to refine and establish definitive scientific knowledge. The expansion of our knowledge can be accomplished by many people, each one working on a small component of knowledge.

Realists support the lecture methodology and other formalized methodologies of teaching. They maintain that such objectives as self-realization can best occur when the learner is knowledgeable about the external world. Consequently, the learner must be exposed to the facts, and the lecture method can be an efficient, organized, and orderly way to accomplish this. Realists insist that any method used should be characterized by the integrity which comes from systematic, organized, and dependable knowledge.

Realists consider the role of the teacher in the educational process to be of primary importance. The teacher presents material in a way which is systematic and organized. He or she promotes the idea that there are clearly defined criteria making judgement about art, economics, politics, and education. For example, in education there are certain objective criteria to judge whether particular educational activities are worthwhile, such as type of material presented, how it is organized, whether or not it suits the psychological make-up of the learner, whether the delivery system is suitable, and whether it achieves the desired results.

Realists expect that institutions of higher education turn out teaching specialists who are knowledgeable, and who can serve as role models for their students. Realists place a lower priority on the personality and character of the teacher than they do on the effectiveness of the teacher to impart knowledge about the world that the learner can use.

Realism results in practices with five formal steps of learning: preparation, presentation, association, systematization-generalization, and application. This is due to the realists' desire for precision and order. These desires are found in such school practices as ringing bells, set time periods for study, departmentalization,

---

3 See, for example, Cromer (1997) and Schrag (1995).

daily lesson plans, course scheduling, increasing specialization in curriculum, pre-packaged curriculum materials, and line-staff forms of administrative organization.

Idealism and Education

Idealists believe that truth cannot be found in the world of matter because it is an ever-changing world.[4] Truth can be attained in the world of ideas, which are of substantial value and endurance, if not perfect and eternal.

Idealists believe that the aim of education should be the search for wisdom and true ideas. This leads to the development of mind and requires character development, as the search for truth demands personal discipline and steadfast character.

The concept of "self" lies at the center of idealistic metaphysics and, therefore, it lies at the center of idealistic education. Self is the prime reality of individual experience and, hence, education becomes primarily concerned with self-realization. Idealists view self in the context of society and the totality of existence.

Idealists believe that human development and education stand in a dialectical relationship with respect to each other. Education is the process of a learner growing into the likeness of a universe of mind, that is, an infinite ideal. Idealists view the student as one who has enormous potential for both moral and cognitive growth. The teacher guides the immature learner toward the infinite. To guide the student, the teacher should possess the necessary knowledge and personal qualities. Idealists favor a more philosophically-oriented teacher.

Idealists favor holistic curriculums. Idealists stress that a proper education includes study of classical writings, art, and science. The aim is to teach students to think and to demonstrate creative and critical thinking. Idealists believe that much of the great literature of the past is relevant to contemporary problems since many of these problems have been debated extensively by great philosophers and thinkers.

Idealists believe that the best method of learning is dialectic. The dialectic is a process in which ideas are put into battle against each other with the more substantial ideas enduring in the discussion. Essentially, it is a matter of disputation and only if ideas emerge victorious there is some reason for believing in them. It is a way of looking at both sides of the question and allowing the truth to emerge. Through this critical method of thinking, individuals can develop their ideas in ways that achieve syntheses and develop universal concepts. Idealists have a high regard for the inner powers of human beings, such as intuition. They believe that dialectic is the proper tool for stimulating intuition.

Idealists favor discussion-oriented learning methodologies. They might use the lecture method, but it is viewed more as a means of stimulating thought than merely passing on information. Idealists also utilize other methods like projects, supplemental activities, library research, and artwork.

Self-realization is an important aim of education and, therefore, idealists stress the importance of self-activity in education. Idealists believe that true learning occurs only within the individual self. The teacher cannot get inside a learner's mind, but he

---

4 See, for example, Freedman (1996) and Hancock (1999).

or she can provide materials and activities which influence learning. It is the response of the learners to these materials and activities that constitutes real education. This action is personal and private, therefore, all education is self-education. The teacher cannot always be present when learning occurs. Therefore, he or she stimulates the student such that the student continues to learn even when the teacher is absent.

Pragmatism and Education

Pragmatism seeks out the processes which work best to achieve desirable ends.[5] Pragmatism examines traditional ways of thinking and doing to reconstruct approaches to life more in line with contemporary conditions.

Pragmatists stress that educational aims grow out of existing conditions. They are tentative and flexible, at least in the beginning. People—that is, parents, students, and citizens—are the ones who have educational aims, and not the process of education.

Pragmatists point out that the philosophy of education is the formation of proper mental and moral attitudes to be used in tackling contemporary problems. When social life changes the educational program must be reconstructed to meet the change.

For pragmatists, the process of education is fulfilled only when the student really understands why he or she does things. School fosters habits of thought, invention, and initiative which assist the individual in growing in the desired direction. School is a place where the other environments which the student encounters—the family environment, the religious environment, the work environment, and others—are combined into a meaningful whole.

Pragmatists do not view education as preparation for life, but as life itself. The lives of learners are important to them. Thus, educators should be aware of the background, interests, and motivations of the learners. Pragmatists believe that educators should also look at learners in terms of their cognitive, physical, emotional, and all their other factors. Pragmatists maintain that individuals should be educated as social beings, capable of participating in and directing their social affairs.

Pragmatists champion a diversified and integrated curriculum. It is composed of both process and content, but it is not fixed or an end in itself. Pragmatists recommend developing a "core" approach to curriculum. Learners can select an area of concentration or "core" for a period of study such that all other subject areas revolve around it. Learners are capable of knowing the general operating principles of nature and social conditions, which serve as general guides for participation.

Pragmatists believe that life is ever-changing and there is a constant need for improvement. Therefore, pragmatic education is based on experimental method which realizes that there are no fixed or absolute conclusions. The students learn the process of discovery and self-sufficiency as much as the facts which are uncovered. One of the approaches suggested by pragmatic educators is the project approach to learning. Students cooperate in pursuing the goals of the project. Projects are

---

5 See, for example, Hickman and Alexander (1998) and Orrill (1999).

decided by group discussion with the teacher as moderator. Pragmatists favor the use of case methodology in class.

Pragmatists adhere to action-oriented education. They suggest an activity-oriented core approach. School can arrange for students to reconstruct past events and life situations in order to better appreciate the difficulties involved in a given actual situation. Learners become involved with the fundamentals of knowledge in a practical and applied way so that the usefulness of knowledge becomes more apparent to them. This approach demonstrates the relationship of various disciplines, shows the wholeness of knowledge, and helps learners to utilize such knowledge in novel and creative ways when tackling problems.

Pragmatism is closely linked with reconstructionism in education in some aspects.[6] However, pragmatists are often critical of the excesses of reconstructionism.

Reconstructionism and Education

Reconstructionists believe that society is in need of constant reconstruction or change in order to adequately deal with social problems to make life better than it is.[7]

Reconstructionists stress that education and schools should be viewed in the much wider societal context. Radical changes in education cannot occur without radical changes in the structure of society itself. Educational reform follows social reforms and rarely, if ever, precedes or causes it. Therefore, an educator must be both an educator and a social activist.

Reconstructionists believe in the ideals of world community, brotherhood, and democracy. Schools should promote these ideals through curricular, administrative, and instructional practices. Schools cannot be expected to reconstruct society by themselves, but by the adoption of these ideals, they can serve as models for the rest of society.

Reconstructionists are critical of the teaching methods presently used at all levels of education. These methods promote traditional values and attitudes underlying the status quo and reinforce resistance to change. For instance, where teachers are viewed as dispensers of knowledge and students as passive recipients of knowledge, students uncritically accept whatever is presented. This results in producing students who think in the same way and who are uncritical of society, the economy, and the political structure.

Reconstructionists hold that teachers should begin by focusing on critical social issues not usually found in textbooks or discussed in schools. Teachers must become critical, analytical, and discriminating in judgement. They should encourage similar development in students. Reconstructionists believe that such a development in class can be brought about by the discussion methodology, including the case methodology. In this way, teachers help develop democratic approaches to social problems by enabling students to deal with social life intelligently. In fact, democratic procedures should be utilized on every level of schooling. This implies that students play an

---

6 They both certainly agree with the philosophy of John Dewey.

7 See, for example, Larochelle, Bednarz, and Garrison (1998) and Popkewitz and Fendler (1999).

active part in the formulation of all objectives, methods, and curricula used in the educational process.

Reconstructionists' favored curriculum is a modification of the core plan advocated by pragmatists. The core may be viewed as the central theme of the school. The core is complemented by related activities such as discussion groups, field experience, content and skill studies, and vocational studies. Finally, there is the synthesizing and unifying capacity. The reconstructionists' curriculum draws the people of the community together in common studies and it extends from the school into the wider community. Thus, it has the capacity to help bring about cultural transformation because of the dynamic relationship between school and society.

Reconstructionists believe that curriculum should be action-oriented by engaging students in projects such as collecting funds for worthy causes, informing the citizenry about social problems, and engaging in petition and protests. Reconstructionists favor students' participation in society, where they can both learn and apply what they learn. A curriculum which engages students in some social activity can produce far more learning than any sterile lecture in a classroom.

Reconstructionists favor a world curriculum which is future-oriented. They encourage reading the literature of other nations that deals with issues on a worldwide basis. They recommend teachers to be internationally oriented and humanitarian in their outlook.

Marxism and Education

Marxists find the definition of education which limits the term to the school system as too narrow since it leaves out the learning which Marxists regard as fundamental.[8] They see the world as it is in order to change it. Therefore, they regard education as those processes which contribute to the formation and changing of a person's consciousness and character. Consciousness is based on the worldview, and character involves how a person behaves in relation to that worldview and society. In this, Marxists not only combine education and socialization, but also impart to them the necessary critical perspective in the light of Marxist goals. By imparting such perspectives in class, Marxists favor the lecture methodology.

Marxists agree that the most obvious agent of education is the school. However, they doubt whether the really important learning takes place there. Other agents include the family, youth organizations, peer groups, work, the mass media, religious institutions, trade unions, political parties, and armed forces. These educative agents are classified as socializing agents. Work is the most important socializing agent for those who perform it.

Marxists' vision of communism as a period when man becomes increasingly self-conscious and self-determining has important implications for education. This performs both as a criterion for judging current efforts and as a guide for setting aims and methods. Communism is the movement that abolishes the present state of affairs, including the activities of both teacher and students throughout the process.

---

8 See, for example, Brosio (1998) and McLaren (1998).

In fact, the relationship is dialectical: a change of social circumstances is required to establish a proper system of education, and a proper system of education is required to bring about a change of social circumstances. This implies that the major concern of education should be moral-political; the development of the socialist consciousness.

Marxists are careful about the ideology an individual adopts. School is the crucial agency within which the conflict of class values is worked out. The ruling class ideology consciously or unconsciously permeates the school system. It is a reflection of the interests of the dominant class, but is also accepted by wide sections of other classes.

Marxists define education in conjunction with productive labor: mental education, bodily education, and technological training. The combination of paid productive labor, mental education, bodily exercise, and polytechnic training will raise the working class far above the level of the higher and middle classes. Polytechnic training is a cognitive activity centered on an interaction of human and non-human nature. The combination of productive labor and mental education is primarily social, an interaction of one human with another human. Marxists see working together on a meaningful task as potentially humanizing. The young, brought up to take their place in the great work of social production, learn to play their part. Moreover, it is obvious that the fact of the collective working group being composed of individuals of both sexes and all ages, must necessarily, under suitable conditions, become a source of humane development.

Marxists' concepts of the relationship of the proletariat and permanent revolution have profound implications for education. Democracy can only be learned through the practice of democracy, and this must apply to schools as well as to all other sectors of society. The rotation of positions of responsibility and control is essential if people are to learn to exercise power. The spread of information in open government and the discussion of matters before policies are formulated are considered as constituting both education and execution. The performance of ordinary, manual labor by government and industrial leaders is an essential educational process, but the converse, government and management by the masses, is also essential if society is to become really classless.

Conclusion

The foregoing discussion noted that foundational philosophies or worldviews underlie educational philosophies, and each educational philosophy favors a certain instructional methodology and when any instructional methods are utilized, they are used within the bounds of the same educational philosophy and foundational philosophy.

Moreover, there does not exist an independent point of reference to be used for evaluation. Any attempt to evaluate or judge the significance of different philosophies may be framed by assumptions or presuppositions that have no *a priori* claim to supremacy over those of other evaluative stances.

This chapter takes the case of teaching as an example and emphasizes that, in general, any phenomenon may be seen and analyzed from different viewpoints and that each viewpoint exposes a certain aspect of the phenomenon under consideration. Collectively, they provide a much broader and deeper understanding of the phenomenon. Similarly, academic finance can benefit much from contributions coming from other paradigms if it respects paradigm diversity.

Knowledge of finance is ultimately a product of the researcher's paradigmatic approach to this multifaceted phenomenon. Viewed from this angle, the pursuit of financial knowledge is seen as much an ethical, moral, ideological, and political activity, as a technical one. Academic finance can gain much by exploiting the new insights coming from other paradigms.

Chapter 14

Conclusion

Social theory can usefully be conceived in terms of four key paradigms: functionalist, interpretive, radical humanist, and radical structuralist. The four paradigms are founded upon different assumptions about the nature of social science and the nature of society. Each generates theories, concepts, and analytical tools which are different from those of other paradigms.

All theories of academic finance are based on a philosophy of science and a theory of society. Many theorists appear to be unaware of, or ignore, the assumptions underlying these philosophies. They emphasize only some aspects of the phenomenon and ignore others. Unless they bring out the basic philosophical assumptions of the theories, their analysis can be misleading; since by emphasizing differences between theories, they imply diversity in approach. While there appear to be different kinds of theory in mainstream academic finance, they are founded on a certain philosophy, worldview, or paradigm. This becomes evident when these theories are related to the wider background of social theory.

The functionalist paradigm has provided the framework for current mainstream academic finance, and accounts for the largest proportion of theory and research in its academic field.

In order to understand a new paradigm, theorists should be fully aware of assumptions upon which their own paradigm is based. Moreover, to understand a new paradigm one has to explore it from within, since the concepts in one paradigm cannot easily be interpreted in terms of those of another. No attempt should be made to criticize or evaluate a paradigm from the outside. This is self-defeating since it is based on a separate paradigm. All four paradigms can be easily criticized and ruined in this way.

These four paradigms are of paramount importance to any scientist, because the process of learning about a favored paradigm is also the process of learning what that paradigm is not. The knowledge of paradigms makes scientists aware of the boundaries within which they approach their subject. Each of the four paradigms implies a different way of social theorizing in general, and finance, in particular.

Scientists often approach their subject from a frame of reference based upon assumptions that are taken for granted. Since these assumptions are continually affirmed and reinforced, they remain not only unquestioned, but also beyond conscious awareness. In this way, most researchers in finance tend to favor the functionalist paradigm.

The partial nature of this view only becomes apparent when the researcher exposes basic assumptions to the challenge of alternative ways of seeing, and starts to appreciate these alternatives in their own terms. To do this, one has to explore other paradigms from within, since the concepts in one paradigm cannot easily be interpreted in terms of those of another.

The diversity of finance research possibilities referred to in this book is vast. While each paradigm advocates a research strategy that is logically coherent, in terms of underlying assumptions, these vary from paradigm to paradigm. The phenomenon to be researched can be conceptualized and studied in many different ways, each generating distinctive kinds of insight and understanding. There are many different ways of studying the same social phenomenon, and given that the insights generated by any one approach are at best partial and incomplete, the social researcher can gain much by reflecting on the nature and merits of different approaches. It is clear that social scientists, like other generators of knowledge, deal with the realization of possible types of knowledge, which are connected with the particular paradigm adopted.

The mainstream academic finance is based upon the functionalist paradigm; and, for the most part, finance theorists are not always entirely aware of the traditions to which they belong. This book recommends a serious conscious thinking about the social philosophy upon which finance is based and of the alternative avenues for development.

Academic finance can gain much by exploiting the new perspectives coming from the other paradigms. An understanding of different paradigms leads to a better understanding of the multi-faceted nature of finance. Although a researcher may decide to conduct research from the point of view of a certain paradigm, an understanding of the nature of other paradigms leads to a better understanding of what one is doing.

Paradigm diversity is based on the idea that more than one theoretical construction can be placed upon a given collection of data. In other words, any single theory, research method, or particular empirical study is incapable of explaining the nature of reality in all of its complexities.

It is possible to establish exact solutions to problems, if one defines the boundary and domain of reality. Functionalist research, through its research approach, defines an area in which objectivity and truth can be found. Any change in the research approach, or any change in the area of applicability, would tend to result in the break down of such objectivity and truth.

The knowledge generated through functionalist research relates to certain aspects of the phenomenon under consideration. Recognition of the existence of the phenomenon beyond that dictated by the research approach, results in the recognition of the limitations of the knowledge generated within the confines of that approach.

It is almost impossible to find foundational solution to the problem of creating specific kind of knowledge. Researchers are encouraged to explore what is possible by identifying untapped possibilities. By comparing a favored research approach in relation to others, the nature, strengths, and limitations of the favored approach become evident. By understanding what others do, researchers are able to understand what they are not doing. This leads to the development and refinement of the favored research approach. The concern is not about deciding which research approach is best, or with substituting one for another. The concern is about the merits of diversity, which seeks to enrich research rather than constrain it, through a search for an optimum way of doing diverse research.

There is no unique evaluative perspective for assessing knowledge generated by different research approaches. Therefore, it becomes necessary to get beyond the idea that knowledge is foundational and can be evaluated in an absolute way.

Different research approaches provide different interpretations of a phenomenon, and understand the phenomenon in a particular way. Some may be supporting a traditional view, others saying something new. In this way, knowledge is treated as being tentative rather than absolute.

All research approaches have something to contribute. The interaction among them may lead to synthesis, compromise, consensus, transformation, polarization, or simply clarification and improved understanding of differences. Such interaction, which is based on differences of viewpoints, is not concerned with reaching consensus or an end point that establishes a foundational truth. On the contrary, it is concerned with learning from the process itself, and to encourage the interaction to continue so long as disagreement lasts. Likewise, it is not concerned with producing uniformity, but promoting improved diversity.

Paradigm diversity is based on the idea that research is a creative process and that there are many ways of doing research. This approach leads to the development of knowledge in many different, and sometimes contradictory, directions such that new ways of knowing will emerge. There can be no objective criteria for choosing between alternative perspectives. The number of ways of generating new knowledge is bounded only by the ingenuity of researchers in inventing new approaches.

The functionalist paradigm regards research as a technical activity and depersonalizes the research process. It removes responsibility from the researcher and reduces him or her to an agent engaged in what the institutionalized research demands.

Paradigm diversity reorients the role of the researchers and places responsibility for the conduct and consequences of research directly with them. Researchers examine the nature of their activity to choose an appropriate approach and develop a capacity to observe and question what they are doing, and take responsibility for making intelligent choices which are open to realize the many potential types of knowledge.

To implement paradigm diversity, some fundamental changes need to be directed to the way research is presently managed in academic finance. In other words, paradigm diversity implies and requires changes. The most fundamental change is to understand the multifaceted nature of finance as a phenomenon.

An understanding of paradigms provides a valuable means for exploring the nature of the phenomenon being investigated. Furthermore, an understanding of other paradigms provides an invaluable basis for recognizing what one is doing.

It is interesting to note that this recommendation is consistent with the four paradigms:

1. It increases efficiency in research: This is because, diversity in the research approach prevents or delays reaching the point of diminishing marginal return. Therefore, the recommendation is consistent with the functionalist paradigm,

which emphasizes purposive rationality and the benefit of diversification.

2. It advocates diversity in research approach: This is consistent with the interpretive paradigm, which emphasizes shared multiple realities.

3. It leads to the realization of researchers' full potential: This is consistent with the radical humanist paradigm, which emphasizes human beings' emancipation from the structures which limit their potential for development.

4. It enhances class awareness: This is consistent with the radical structuralist paradigm, which emphasizes class struggle.

Knowledge of finance is ultimately a product of the researcher's paradigmatic approach to this multifaceted phenomenon. Viewed from this angle, the pursuit of financial knowledge is seen as much an ethical, moral, ideological, and political activity, as a technical one. Mainstream academic finance can gain much from the contributions of the other paradigms.

Bibliography

Aaronovitch, S. (1961), *The Ruling Class* (London: Lawrence and Wishart).

Aggarwal, R. (1993a), "Theory and Practice in Finance Education: Or Why We Shouldn't Just Ask Them," *Financial Practice and Education* 3:2, 15–18.

—— (1993b), "A Brief Overview of Capital Budgeting Under Uncertainty," in Aggarwal (ed.).

—— (ed.) (1993c), *Capital Budgeting Under Uncertainty* (New Jersey: Prentice Hall).

Agnew, J.C. (1986), *The Market and the Theatre in Anglo-American Thought* (Cambridge: Cambridge University Press).

Allaire, Y., Landry, M., Mintzberg, H., and Morgan, G. (eds) (1985), *Actes du Colloque, Perspective de Recherche Pour le Praticien* (Quebec: University of Quebec at Abitibi-Temiscaminque).

Allen, F. and Michaely, R. (2002), "Payout Policy," in Constantinides, Harris, and Stulz (eds).

Allen, W.T. (2001), "The Mysterious Art of Corporate Governance," *Corporate Board* 22:130, 1–5.

Allgood, S. and Walstad, W.B. (1999), "The Longitudinal Effects of Economics Education on Teachers and Their Students," *Journal of Economic Education* 30:2, 99–111.

Altman, E. and Subrahmanyam, M. (eds) (1985), *Recent Advances in Corporate Finance* (Homewood, IL: Irwin).

Amott, T.A. and Matthaei, J.A. (1991), *Race, Gender & Work: A Multicultural Economic History of Women in the United States* (Boston: The South End Press).

Analytica (1992), *Board Directors and Corporate Governance: Trends in the G7 Countries over the Next Ten Years* (Oxford, England: Oxford Analytica Ltd.).

Appadurai, A. (ed.) (1986), *The Social Life of Things: Commodities in Cultural Perspective* (Cambridge: Cambridge University Press).

Appadurai, A. (1986), "Introduction: Commodities and the Politics of Value," in Appadurai, A. (ed.), 3–63.

Ardalan, K. (2000a), "The Academic Field of Finance and Paradigm Diversity," *Southern Business Review* 26:1, 21–31.

—— (2000b), "Worldviews and Explanation of Development of Academic Finance: A Global View," *Journal of Global Business* 11:20, 49–58.

—— (2000c), "Development of the Academic Field of Finance: A Paradigmatic Approach," *Academy of Educational Leadership Journal* 4:1, 44–79.

—— (2001), "On the Role of Paradigms in the Field of Finance," *Academy of Accounting and Financial Studies Journal* 5:1, 1–28.

—— (2002a), "The Research-versus-Practice Controversy in Finance: A Paradigmatic Look," *Southwestern Economic Review* 29:1, 71–84.

—— (2002b), "The Mathematical Language of Academic Finance: A Paradigmatic Look," *International Journal of Social Economics* 29:3, 187–204.

—— (2003a), "Theories and Controversies in Finance: A Paradigmatic Overview," *International Journal of Social Economics* 30:1/2, 199–209.

—— (2003b), "The Lecture-versus-Case Controversy: Its Philosophical Foundation," *Southwestern Economic Review* 30:1, 99–118.

—— (2003c), "Money and Academic Finance: The Role of Paradigms," *International Journal of Social Economics* 30:6, 720–40.

—— (2003d), "On Clinical Research in Finance," *International Journal of Social Economics* 30:10, 1038–48.

—— (2003e), "Alternative Approaches Utilized in the Case Method: Their Philosophical Foundations," *Academy of Educational Leadership Journal* 30:3, 103–20.

—— (2004), "On the Theory and Practice of Finance," *International Journal of Social Economics* 31:7, 684–705.

—— (2005), "Mathematics and Academic Finance: The Role of Paradigms," *International Journal of Social Economics* 32:4, 276–90.

—— (2007a), "Corporate Governance: A Paradigmatic Look," *International Journal of Social Economics* 34:8, 506–524.

—— (2007b), "Markets: A Paradigmatic Look," *International Journal of Social Economics* 34:12, 943–960.

—— (2008), "Technology: A Paradigmatic Look," *American Review of Political Economy*, 6:1.

Ayer, A.J. (ed.) (1930, 1959), *Logical Positivism* (New York: Free Press).

—— (1936, 1946), *Language, Truth and Logic* (London: Gollancz).

Baiman, R., Boushey, H., and Saunders D. (eds) (1999), *Political Economy and Contemporary Capitalism: Radical Perspectives on Economic Theory and Policy* (Armonk, NY: M.E. Sharpe).

Baker, G. (1992), "Beatrice: A Case Study in the Creation and Destruction of Value," *Journal of Finance* 47:3, 1081–1120.

Baker, G. and Wruck, K. (1989), "Organization Changes and Value Creation in Leveraged Buyouts: The Case of O.M. Scott & Sons Co.," *Journal of Financial Economics* 25:2, 163–90.

Ball, R. (1995), "The Theory of Stock Market Efficiency: Accomplishments and Limitations," *Journal of Applied Corporate Finance* 8:3, 19–29.

Barber, B. (1977), "Absolutization of the Market: Some Notes on How We Got from There to Here," in Dworkin, G., Bermant, G., and Brown, P.G. (eds), 15–32.

Barrow, R. and White, P. (eds) (1993), *Beyond Liberal Education: Essays in Honor of Paul H. Hirst* (London: Routledge).

Barrow, R. and Woods, R. (1989), *An Introduction to Philosophy of Education* (London: Routledge).

Becht, M., Bolton, P., and Roell, A. (2002), "Corporate Governance and Control," Working Paper Number 02/2002, European Corporate Governance Institute.

Beck, T., Demirguc-Kunt, A., and Levine, R. (2001), "Law, Politics, and Finance," Working Paper Number 2585, World Bank, Country Economics Department.

Bell, D. (1976), *The Cultural Contradictions of Capitalism* (New York: Basic Books).

Bellofiore, R. (ed.) (1998), *Marxian Economics: Prices, Profits, and Dynamics* (London: Macmillan).

Berg, D.N. and Smith, K.K. (1985), *Exploring Clinical Methods for Social Research* (Beverley Hills, California: Sage Publications, Inc.).

Berg, I. (ed.) (1981), *Sociological Perspectives on Labor Markets* (New York: Academic Press).

Bermant, G., Brown, P.G., and Dworkin, G. (1977), "An Introduction to Markets and Morals," in Dworkin, G., Bermant, G., and Brown, P.G. (eds), 1–14.

Bertin, W.J. and Zivney, T.L. (1991), "The New Hire Market for Finance: Productivity, Salaries and other Market Factors," *Financial Practice and Education* 1:1, 25–34.

—— (1992), "The Determinants of Finance Faculty Salaries: The 1991–1992 FMA Salary Survey," *Financial Practice and Education* 2:1, 19–29.

Bettner, M.S., Robinson C., and McGoun E. (1994), "The Case for Qualitative Research in Finance," *International Review of Financial Analysis* 3:1, 1–18.

Bicksler, J.L. (ed.) (1972), *Methodology in Finance-Investments* (Massachusetts: Lexington Books).

—— (ed.) (1979), *Handbook of Financial Economics* (Amsterdam: North Holland).

Bierman, H. (1993), "Capital Budgeting in 1992: A Survey," *Financial Management* 22:3, 1–24.

Biewener, C. (1999), "The Promise of Finance: Banks and Community Development," in Baiman, Boushey, and Saunders (eds).

—— (2001), "The Promise of Finance: Banks and Community Development," in Gibson-Graham, Resnick, and Wolff (eds).

Bijker, W.E. (1990), *The Social Construction of Technology* (The Netherlands: Eijsden).

Bijker, W.E., Hughes, T.P., and Pinch, T.F. (1987), *The Social Construction of Technological Systems: New Directions in the Sociology and History of Technology* (Cambridge, Massachusetts: MIT Press.)

Bijker, W.E. and Law, J. (1992), *Shaping Technology/Building Society: Studies in Socio-Technical Change* (Cambridge: MIT Press).

Black, F. (1976), "The Dividend Puzzle," *Journal of Portfolio Management* 2:1, 5–8.

Borokhovich, K.A., Bricker, R.J., Brunarski, K.R., and Simkins, B.J. (1995), "Finance Research Productivity and Influence," *Journal of Finance* 50:5, 1691–1717.

Borokhovich, K.A., Bricker, R.J., and Simkins, B.J. (1994), "The Streams of Financial Research and Their Interrelationship: Evidence from the Social Sciences Citation Index," *Financial Practice and Education* 4:2, 110–23.

Boulding, K.E. (1973), "Toward the Development of a Cultural Economics," in Schneider, L. and Bonjean, C. (eds).

Branson, D. (2005), "The Very Uncertain Prospect of "Global" Convergence in Corporate Governance," Working Paper Series, University of Pittsburgh School of Law.

Branston, R.J., Cowling, K., and Sugden, R. (2006), "Corporate Governance and the Public Interest," *International Review of Applied Economics* 20:2, 189–212.

Brav, A. and Heaton, J.B. (2002), "Competing Theories of Financial Anomalies," *Review of Financial Studies* 15:2, 575–606.

Brennan, D.M. (2005), "'Fiduciary Capitalism,' the 'Political Model of Corporate Governance', and the Prospect of Stakeholder Capitalism in the United States," *Review of Radical Political Economics* 37:1, 39–62.

Brennan, M.J. (1995), "Corporate Finance over the Past 25 Years," *Financial Management* 24:2, 9–22.

Brosio, R.A. (1998), "The Continuing Correspondence Between Political Economy and Schooling: Telling the News," *Journal of Thought* 33:3, 85–105.

Bukharin, N. (1918, 1972), *Imperialism and World Economy* (London: Merlin Press).

Bukharin, N. and Preobrazhensky, E. (1920, 1962), *The ABC of Communism* (Harmondsworth: Penguin).

Bures, A.L. and Tong, H.M. (1993), "Assessing Finance Faculty Evaluation Systems: A National Survey," *Financial Practice and Education* 3:2, 141–44.

Burrell, G. and Morgan, G. (1979), *Sociological Paradigms and Organizational Analysis* (Aldershot: Gower Publishing Company Limited).

Burt, R. (1983), *Corporate Profits and Cooperation* (New York: Academic Press).

Cahn, S.M. (ed.) (1996), *Classic and Contemporary Readings in the Philosophy of Education* (New York: McGraw-Hill College Division).

Carchedi, G. (1983), "Class Analysis and the Study of Social Forms," in Morgan (ed.).

Carnap, R. (1964), *The Logical Syntax of Language*, trans. Smeaton. (London: Routledge).

Carson, E. (1999), "Kant on the Method of Mathematics," *Journal of the History of Philosophy* 37:4, 629–52.

Cassidy, S.M. and Franklin, L. (1996), "Financial Education and Risk Perceptions," *Journal of Financial Education*, 22:1, 42–6.

Chambliss, J.J. (ed.) (1996), *Philosophy of Education: An Encyclopedia* (London: Garland Publishers).

Charlton, N. (1994), "In Defense of the Marxist Theory of Knowledge," *Nature, Society, and Thought* 9:4, 447–66.

Charreaux, G. (2004), "Corporate Governance Theories: From Micro Theories to National Systems Theories," Working Paper Number 1040101, Universite de Bourgogne – LEG/FARGO, January, <http://ssrn.com/abstract=486522>.

Cheng, L.T.W. and Davidson III, W.N. (1995), "The Characteristics of Job Applicants for Finance Faculty Positions: 1986–1992," *Financial Practice and Education* 5:2, 18–29.

Child, J. (1969), *The Business Enterprise in Modern Industrial Society* (London: Collier-Macmillan).

Chomsky, N. and Herman, E. (1988), *Manufacturing Consent: The Political Economy of the Mass Media* (New York: Pantheon).

Ciscel, D.H. and Heath, J.A. (2001), "To Market, to Market: Imperial Capitalism's Destruction of Social Capital and the Family," *Review of Radical Political Economics* 33:4, 401–411.

Coffee, J. (1999), "The Future as History: The Prospects for Global Convergence in Corporate Governance and its Implications," *Northwestern Law Review* 93, 641–707.

Constantinides, G., Harris, M., and Stulz, R. (eds) (2002), *North-Holland Handbooks of Economics* (Amsterdam, The Netherlands: Elsevier).

Cooley, P.L. and Heck, J.L. (1981), "Significant Contributions to Finance Literature," *Financial Management* 10:2, 23–33.

Cox, J. and Ross, S. (1976), "A Survey of Some New Results in Financial Option Pricing Theory," *Journal of Finance* 31:3, 383–402.

Crane, D. (1967), "The Gatekeepers of Science: Some Factors Affecting the Selection of Articles for Scientific Journals," *American Sociologist* 2:3, 195–201.

Cray, D. and Haines, G. (1992), "Do as I Say, Not as You Do: Prescriptive and Descriptive Models of Decision Making in Pension Fund Management," *Alternative Perspective on Finance Conference Proceedings*, 21–65.

Croce, B. (2000), *Historical Materialism and the Economics of Karl Marx,* translated by C.M. Meredith (Whitefish, MT: Kessinger Publishing).

Cromer, A.H. (1997), *Connected Knowledge: Science, Philosophy, and Education* (Oxford: Oxford University Press).

Cullenberg, S.E. (1994), *The Falling Rate of Profit: Recasting the Marxian Debate* (London: Pluto Press).

—— (1997, 1998), "Decentering the Marxian Debate over the Falling Rate of Profit: A New Approach," in Bellofiore (ed.).

Cutler, T. (2004), "The Wages of Capital: The Rise and Rise of 'Corporate Governance,'" *Competition and Change* 8:1, 65–83.

Dannhaeuser, N. and Werner, C. (2006), *Markets and Market Liberalization: Ethnographic Reflections* (New York and London: Elsevier Science and Technology Books).

Debreu, G. (1959), *The Theory of Value* (New York: John Wiley & Sons).

Denis, D.K. (2001), "Twenty-Five Years of Corporate Governance Research ... and Counting," *Review of Financial Economics* 10, 191–212.

Denis, D.K. and McConnell, J.J. (2003), "International Corporate Governance," European Corporate Governance Institute, Finance Working Paper Number 05/2003, January.

Diamond, C. (ed.) (1976), *Wittgenstein Lectures on the Foundations of Mathematics* (Brighton: Harvester Press).

Dickinson, J. and Russell, B. (eds) (1986), *Family, Economy and State* (London: Croom Helm).

DiMaggio, P. (1990), "Cultural Aspects of Economic Action and Organization," in Friedland, R. and Robertson, A.F. (eds).

Divers, J. (1999), "Arithmetical Platonism: Reliability and Judgment-Dependence," *Philosophical Studies: An International Journal for Philosophy in the Analytic Tradition* 95:3, 277–310.

Domar, E.D. (1946), "Capital Expansion, Rate of Growth and Employment," *Econometrica* 14, 137–47.

Donaldson, G. (1978), "Making Intellectual Waves," *Financial Management* 7:1, 7–10.

Douglas, M. and Isherwood, B. (1982), *The World of Goods* (New York: Norton).

Durand, D. (1968), "State of the Finance Field: Further Comments," *Journal of Finance* 23:3, 848–52.

Dworkin, G., Bermant, G., and Brown, P.G. (eds) (1977), *Markets and Morals* (Washington and London: Hemisphere Publishing Corporation).

Dyl, E.A. (1991), "Comment: The Teaching versus Research Conundrum," *Financial Practice and Education* 1:1, 11–2.

Ederington, L.H. (1979), "Aspects of the Production of Significant Financial Research," *Journal of Finance* 34:3, 777–86.

Ehrenberg, R.G. and Hurst, P.J. (1996), "A Hedonic Model," *Change* 28:3, 46–51.

Ellerman, D. (1999), "The Democratic Firm: An Argument Based on Ordinary Jurisprudence," *Journal of Business Ethics* 21, 111–24.

Ellis, A.K., Cogan, J.J., and Howey, K.R. (1991), *Introduction to the Foundations of Education* (New Jersey: Prentice Hall).

Engels, F. (1979), *On Historical Materialism* (New York: AMS Press).

Ewald, W. (ed.) (1996), *From Kant to Hilbert: A Source Book in the Foundations of Mathematics* (Oxford: Oxford University Press).

Ewen, E. (1985), *Immigrant Women in the Land of Dollars: Life and Culture on the Lower East Side, 1890–1925* (New York: Monthly Review Press).

Fama, E.F. (1970), "Efficient Capital Markets: A Review of Theory and Empirical Work," *Journal of Finance* 25:2, 383–417.

—— (1976), *Foundations of Finance* (New York: Basic Books).

—— (1978), "The Effect of a Firm's Investment and Financing Decisions on the Welfare of Its Security Holders," *American Economic Review* 68:3, 272–84.

—— (1991), "Efficient Capital Markets: II," *Journal of Finance* 46:5, 1575–617.

Farinha, Jorge (2003), "Corporate Governance: A Survey of the Literature," Discussion Paper Number 2003–06, Universidade do Porto Economia, Porto, Portugal, November.

Faulhaber, G.R. and Baumol, W.J. (1988), "Economists as Innovators: Practical Products of Theoretical Research," *Journal of Economic Literature* 26:2, 577–600.

Feenberg, A. (1991), *Critical Theory of Technology* (New York and Oxford: Oxford University Press).

Feenberg, A. (1999), *Questioning Technology* (Amsterdam).

Findlay III, M.C., Chapman, M., and Williams, E.E. (1985), "A Post Keynesian View of Modern Financial Economics: In Search of Alternative Paradigms," *Journal of Business Finance and Accounting* 12:1, 1–18.

Findlay III, M.C. and Williams, E.E. (1980), "A Positivist Evaluation of the New Finance," *Financial Management* 3:1, 7–17.

Fligstein, N. (1996), "Markets as Politics: A Political-Cultural Approach to Market Institutions," *American Sociological Review* 61, August, 656–73.

Fox, R. (ed.) (1996), *Technological Change: Methods and Themes in the History of Technology* (Canada: Harwood Academic Publishers).

Frank, R., Gilovich, T., and Regan, D. (1993), "Does Studying Economics Inhibit Cooperation?," *Journal of Economic Perspectives* 7:2, 159–71.

Frankfurter, G.M. (1995), "The Rise and Fall of the CAPM Empire: A Review and Some Philosophical Remarks," *Financial Markets, Institutions, and Instruments* 4:5, 608–28.

Frankfurter, G.M., Carleton, W., Gordon, M., Horrigan, J., McGoun, E., Philippatos, G. and Robinson, C. (1994), "The Methodology of Finance: A Round Table Discussion," *International Review of Financial Analysis* 3:3, 173–207.

Frankfurter, G.M. and Lane, W.R. (1992), "The Rationality or Dividends," *International Review of Financial Analysis* 1:2, 115–29.

Frankfurter, G.M. and McGoun, E.G. (1993), "The Event Study: An Industrial Strength Method," *International Review of Financial Analysis* 2:2, 121–41.

—— (1995), "The Event Study: Is It Either?," *Journal of Investing* 4:2, 8–16.

—— (1996a), "Toward Finance of Meaning: What Finance Is, and What It Could Be," *Journal of Investing* 5:1, 7–13.

—— (1996b), "But It Looked So Good On My Vita!," *Journal of Financial Education* 22:1, 14–25.

Frankfurter, G.M. and Philippatos, G.C. (1992), "Financial Theory and the Growth of Scientific Knowledge: From Modigliani and Miller to an Organizational Theory of Capital Structure," *International Review of Financial Analysis* 1:1, 1–15.

Frankfurter, G.M. and Phillips, H.E. (1994), "A Brief History of MPT: From a Normative Model to Event Studies," *Journal of Investing* 3:4, 15–22.

Frankfurter, G.M. and Wood Jr., B. (1995), "The Evolution of Corporate Dividend Policy," *Journal of Financial Education* 21:1, 31–51.

Freedman, J.O. (1996), *Idealism and Liberal Education* (Ann Harbor: University of Michigan Press).

Frege, G. (1959), *The Foundations of Arithmetic*, 2nd Edition, trans. Austin. (Oxford: Blackwell).

Friedland, R. and Robertson, A.F. (eds) (1990), *Beyond the Marketplace: Rethinking Economy and Society* (New York: Aldine de Gruyter).

Friedman, M. (1953), *Essays in Positive Economics* (Chicago: University of Chicago Press).

—— (1962), *Capitalism and Freedom* (Chicago: University of Chicago Press).

Friedman, M. and Schwartz, A.J. (1963), *A Monetary History of the United States: 1867–1960,* National Bureau of Economic Research, Studies in Business Cycles, No. 12, (Princeton: Princeton University Press).

Friend, I. (1973), "Mythology in Finance," *Journal of Finance* 28:2, 257–72.

Garrison, J. (1999), "John Dewey's Theory of Practical Reasoning," *Educational Philosophy and Theory* 31:3, 291–312.

Garvey, G.T. and Swan. P. (1994), "The Economics of Corporate Governance: Beyond the Marshallian Firm," *Journal of Corporate Finance* 1:2, 139–74.

Geertz, C. (1973a), "Deep Play: Notes on the Balinese Cockfight," in Geertz (ed.).

—— (ed.) (1973b), *The Interpretation of Cultures* (New York: Basic Books).

Ghilarducci, T., Hawley, J., and Williams, A. (1997), "Labor's Paradoxical Interests and the Evolution of Corporate Governance," *Journal of Law and Society* 24:1, 26–43.

Gibson-Graham, J.K., Resnick, S., and Wolff, R. (eds) (2001), *Re/presenting Class: Essays in Postmodern Political Economy* (Durham, NC: Duke University Press).

Gilbert, E. and Reichert, A. (1995), "The Practice of Financial Management among Large United States Corporations," *Financial Practice and Education* 5:1, 16–23.

Gill, S. (1999), "The Geopolitics of the Asian Crisis," *Monthly Review* 50:10, 1–9.

Gitman, L.J. (1992), "Why Can't Michael Jackson Do Heart Surgery?," *Financial Practice and Education* 2:1, 73–5.

Gordon, M.J. (1996), *Finance, Investment and Macroeconomics* (Brookfield, VT: Edward Elgar Publishing Company).

Gourevitch, P. (2003), "The Politics of Corporate Governance Regulation," *Yale Law Journal* 112:7, 1829–80.

Gragg, C.I. (1954), "Because Wisdom Can't Be Told," in McNair (ed.).

Granovetter, M. (1981), "Toward a Sociological Theory of Income Differences," in Berg, I. (ed.), pp. 11–47.

—— (1985), "Economic Action and Social Structure: The Problem of Embeddedness," *American Journal of Sociology* 91, 481–510.

Green, D. (2003), *Silent Revolution: The Rise and Crisis of Market Economics in Latin America* (New York: Monthly Review Press).

Gudeman, S. (1986), *Economics as Culture: Models and Metaphors of Livelihood* (Cambridge: Cambridge University Press).

Gutek, G.L. (1996), *Philosophical and Ideological Perspectives on Education* (New York: Allyn & Bacon).

Habermas, J. (1970a), "On Systematically Distorted Communication," *Inquiry* 13:1, 45–65.

—— (1970b), "Towards a Theory of Communicative Competence," *Inquiry* 13:3, 253–73.

—— (1970c), *Toward a Rational Society: Student Protest, Science, and Politics* (Boston: Beacon Press).

—— (1971), *Knowledge and Human Interests*, trans. Shapiro. (Boston: Beacon Press).

—— (1973), *Theory and Practice*, trans. Viertel. (Boston: Beacon Press).

—— (1979a), "What Is Universal Pragmatics?," in Habermas.

—— (1979b), *Communication and the Evolution of Society*, trans. McCarthy. (Boston: Beacon Press).

Hahn, F.H. (1965), "On Two-Sector Growth Models," *Review of Economic Studies* 32:4, 339–46.

Hahn, F.H. and Matthews, R.C.O. (1964), "The Theory of Economic Growth: A Survey," *Economic Journal* 74, 779–902.

Hale, B. (1999), "Frege's Philosophy of Mathematics," *Philosophical Quarterly* 49:1, 92–104.

Hancock, R.C. (ed.) (1999), *America, the West, and Liberal Education* (New York: Rowman & Littlefield).

Harrod, R.F. (1939), "An Essay in Dynamic Theory," *Economic Journal* 49, 14–33.

Hartmann, H.I. (1981), "The Family as the Locus of Gender, Class and Political Struggle: The Example of Housework," *Signs: Journal of Women in Culture and Society* 6:3, 366–94.

Harvey, D. (1982), *The Limits to Capital* (Oxford: Blackwell).

Haugen, R.A. (1995), *The New Finance: The Case against Efficient Markets* (New Jersey: Prentice Hall).

—— (1996), "Finance from a New Perspective," *Financial Management* 25:1, 86–97.

Hawley, J.P. and Williams, A.T. (1996), "Corporate Governance in the United States: The Rise of Fiduciary Capitalism – A Review of the Literature," Working Paper, Saint Mary's College of California, School of Economics and Business Administration, The first prize of Lens 1996 Corporate Governance Paper Competition, which is available online at the following address: <http://www.lens-library.com/info/competition.html>.

Hayek, F.A. (1960), *Constitution of Liberty* (Chicago: University of Chicago Press).

Heath, J.A. and Ciscel, D.H. (1988), "Patriarchy, Family Structure and the Exploitation of Women's Labor," *Journal of Economic Issues* 22, 781–794.

Heath, J.A., Ciscel, D.H., and Sharp, D.C. (1998), "The Work of Families: The Provision of Market and Household Labor and the Role of Public Policy," *Review of Social Economy* 56:4.

Heaton, H. (1992), "Comments on 'Chief Financial Officers' Views of Academicians' Views of Academicians versus Practitioners in the Field of Finance," *Financial Practice and Education* 2:1, 77–8.

Heck, J.L. (1989), *Finance Literature Index*, 2nd Edition. (New York: McGraw-Hill).

—— (1999), *Finance Literature Index*, 6th Edition. (New York: McGraw-Hill).

Heck, J.L. and Cooley, P.L. (1988), "Most Frequent Contributors to the Finance Literature," *Financial Management* 17:1, 100–108.

Heck, J.L., Cooley, P.L., and Hubbard, C.M. (1986), "Contributing authors and Institutions to the Journal of Finance: 1946–1985," *Journal of Finance* 41:5, 1129–40.

Heidegger, M. (1977), *The Question Concerning Technology* (New York: Harper Colophon Books).

Held, D. (1980), *Introduction to Critical Theory* (Berkeley and Los Angeles: University of California Press).

Hendricks, J.A. (1983), "Capital Budgeting Practices Including Inflation Adjustments: A Survey," *Managerial Planning* 31:4, 22–8.

Hickman, L. and Alexander, T.M. (eds) (1998), *The Essential Dewey: Pragmatism, Education, Democracy* (Bloomington, IN: Indiana University Press).

Hicks, J. (1965), *Capital and Growth* (Oxford: Oxford University Press).

Hirsch, F. (1976), *Social Limits to Growth* (Cambridge, MA and London: Harvard University Press).

Hollingsworth, J.R. and Boyer, R. (eds) (1997), *Contemporary Capitalism: The Embeddedness of Institutions* (Cambridge, England: Cambridge University Press).

Hollingsworth, J.R. and Lindberg, L.N. (1985), "The Governance of the American Economy: The Role of Markets, Clans, Hierarchies, and Associative Behavior," in Streek, W. and Schmitter, P.C. (eds), 221–67.

Hollingsworth, J.R., Schmitter, P.C., and Streek, W. (eds) (1994), *Governing Capitalist Economies* (New York: Oxford University Press).

—— (1994), "Capitalism, Sectors, Institutions, and Performance," in Hollingsworth, J.R., Schmitter, P.C., and Streek, W. (eds), 3–16.

Horkheimer, M. (1947 and 1974), *Eclipse of Reason* (New York: Oxford University Press and Seabury Press).

Horowitz, D. (1985), *The Morality of Spending* (Baltimore, MD: John Hopkins University Press).

Istvan, D.F. (1961), "The Economic Evaluation of Capital Expenditure," *Journal of Business* 34:1, 45–51.

Jasanoff, S., Markle, G.E., Petersen, J.C., and Pinch, T. (eds) (1995), *Handbook of Science and Technology Studies* (Thousand Oaks: Sage Publications).

Jensen, M.C. (1972), "Capital Markets: Theory and Evidence," *Bell Journal of Economics and Management Science* 3:2, 357–98.

—— (1978), "Some Anomalous Evidence Regarding Market Efficiency," *Journal of Financial Economics* 6:1, 95–101.

Jensen, M.C. and Ruback, R.S. (1983), "The Market for Corporate Control: The Scientific Evidence," *Journal of Financial Economics* 11:1, 5–50.

Jensen, M.C. and Smith, Jr., C.W. (1984a), "Introduction," in Jensen and Smith.

—— (1984b), *Modern Theory of Corporate Finance* (Toronto: McGraw-Hill).

—— (1985), "Stockholder, Manager, and Creditor Interests: Applications of Agency Theory," in Altman and Subrahmanyam (eds).

Joseph, M. (1998), "Mathematics, Mind, and Necessity in Wittgenstein's Later Philosophy," *Southern Journal of Philosophy* 36:2, 197–214.

Kaldor, N. (1956), "Alternative Theories of Distribution," *Review of Economic Studies* 23, 83–100.

Kavesh, R.A. (1970), "The American Finance Association: 1939–1969," *Journal of Finance* 25:1, 1–17.

Keasey, K., Thompson, S., and Wright, M. (eds) (1997), *Corporate Governance: Economic and Financial Issues* (Oxford: Oxford University Press).

—— (1997), "Introduction: The Corporate Governance Problem – Competing Diagnoses and Solutions," in Keasey, K., Thompson, S., and Wright, M. (eds), 10–15.

Kessler-Harris, A. (1981), *Women Have Always Worked* (Old Westbury, NY: The Feminist Press).

Kester, G.W., Chang, R.P., Echanis, E.S., Haikal, S., Isa, M.M., Skully, S.K., Tsui, K.C., and Wang, C.J. (1999), "Capital Budgeting Practices in the Asia-Pacific Region: Australia, Hong Kong, Indonesia, Malaysia, Philippines, and Singapore," *Financial Practice and Education* 9:1, 25–33.

Keynes, J.M. (1930), *A Treatise on Money*, 2 vols. (London: Macmillan).

—— (1936), *The General Theory of Employment, Interest and Money* (London: Macmillan).

Kim, S.H., Crick, T., and Kim, S.H. (1986), "Do Executives Practice What Academics Preach?," *Management Accounting* 68:5, 49–52.

Kimball, B.A. and Orrill, R. (eds) (1995), *The Condition of American Liberal Education: Pragmatism and a Changing Tradition* (New York, NY: College Entrance Examination Board).

Klammer, T.P. (1972), "Empirical Evidence on the Application of Sophisticated Capital Budgeting Techniques," *Journal of Business* 45:3, 387–97.

Klein, H.K. and Kleinman, D.L. (2002), "The Social Construction of Technology: Structural Considerations," *Science, Technology, & Human Values* 27:1, 28–52.

Klemkosky, R.C. and Tuttle, D.L. (1977a), "The Institutional Source and Concentration of Financial Research," *Journal of Finance* 32:3, 901–907.

—— (1977b), "A Ranking of Doctoral Programs by Financial Research Contributions of Graduates," *Journal of Financial and Quantitative Analysis* 12:3, 491–97.

Kopytoff, I. (1986), "The Cultural Biography of Things: Commoditization as Process," in Appadurai, A. (ed.), 64–91.

Kryzanowski, L. and Roberts, G. (1993), "Canadian Banking Solvency 1922–1940," *Journal of Money, Credit and Banking* 25:3, 361–76.

—— (1998), "Capital Forbearance: A Depression Era Case Study of Sun Life," *Canadian Journal of Administrative Sciences* 15:1, 1–16.

Kuhn, T.S. (1970), *The Structure of Scientific Revolutions* (Chicago: University of Chicago Press).

Larochelle, M., Bednarz, N., and Garrison, J. (eds) (1998), *Constructivism and Education* (Cambridge: Cambridge University Press).

Lea, S.E.G., Tarpy, R., and Webley, P. (1987), *The Individual in the Economy* (New York: Cambridge University Press).

Lee, S.H., Michie, J., and Oughton, C. (2003), "Comparative Corporate Governance: Beyond 'Shareholder Value,'" *Journal of Interdisciplinary Economics* 14, 81–111.

Lehrer, K. (1999), "Process of Self-Trust: A Study of Reason, Knowledge and Autonomy," *Philosophy and Phenomenological Research* 49:3, 1039–41.

Lenin, V.I. (1917a, 1966), *Imperialism: The Highest Stage of Capitalism* (Moscow: Progress Publishers).

—— (1917b, 1969), *The State and Revolution* (Moscow: Progress Publishers).

LeRoy, S.F. and Porter, R.D. (1981), "The Present Value Relation: Tests Based on Implied Variance Bounds," *Econometrica* 49:4, 555–74.

Letza, S., Kirkbride, J., and Sun, X. (2004), "Shareholding versus Stakeholding: A Critical Review of Corporate Governance," *Corporate Governance: An International Review* 12:3, 242–62.

Lintner, J. (1956), "Distribution of Income of Corporations among Dividends, Retained Earnings, and Taxes," *American Economic Review* 46:1, 97–113.

Lippmann, W. (2004), *The Good Society* (New York: Transaction Publishers).

Lukacs, G. (1971), *History and Class Consciousness: Studies in Marxist Dialectics* (London: Merlin Press) and (Cambridge, MA: MIT Press).

Luxemburg, R. (1951), *The Accumulation of Capital* (London: Routledge and Kegan Paul Ltd).

Magdoff, H. (2003), *Imperialism without Colonies* (New York: Monthly Review Press).

Magdoff, H. and Sweezy, P.M. (1987), *Stagnation and the Financial Explosion* (New York: Monthly Review Press).

Mantzavinos, Ch. (2001), *Individuals, Institutions, and Market* (Cambridge: Cambridge University Press).

Marcuse, H. (1964), *One-Dimensional Man: Studies in the Ideology of Advanced Industrial Society* (Boston: Beacon Press).

—— (1965), "Industrialization and Capitalism," *New Left Review*, March/April, No. 30, 3–17.

—— (1968a), "Industrialization and Capitalism in the Work of Max Weber," in Marcuse.

—— (1968b), *Negations: Essays in Critical Theory*, trans. Shapiro. (Boston: Beacon Press).

—— (1970a), "Freedom and Freud's Theory of the Instinct," in Marcuse.

—— (1970b), *Five Lectures*, trans. Shapiro and Weber (Boston: Beacon Press).

Markowitz, H. (1952), "Portfolio Selection," *Journal of Finance* 7:1, 77–91.

—— (1959), *Portfolio Selection* (New Haven, Conn.: Yale University Press).

Marples, R. (ed.) (1999), *The Aims of Education* (London: Routledge).

Marsh, J.I. (1995), *Critique, Action and Liberation* (Albany: State University of New York).

Marsh, R.C. (ed.) (1956), *Logic and Knowledge* (London: Allen and Unwin).

Maruyama, M. (1991), "Contracts in Cultures," *Human Systems Management* (Netherlands: IOS Press), Vol. 10, 33–46.

Marx, K. (1954), *Capital: A Critique of Political Economy,* Vol. I (London: Lawrence & Wishart).

—— (1959), *Capital: A Critique of Political Economy,* Vol. III, (London: Lawrence & Wishart).

—— (1969), "Preface to a Contribution to the Critique of Political Economy," in Marx, K. and Engels, F., *Selected Works: In Three Volumes*, Volume 1, 502–506.

—— (1970), *Economic and Philosophical Manuscripts of 1844,* in Struik (ed.) and (New York: International Publishers).

—— (1872 and 1932), *Das Kapital* (Wien-Berlin: Verlag fur Literatur und Politik).

Marx, K. and Engels, F. (1998), *The Communist Manifesto: A Modern Edition* (New York: Verso).

Matthaei, J.A. (1982), *An Economic History of Women in America: Women's Work, The Sexual Division of Labor, and the Development of Capitalism* (New York: Schocken Books).

McCall, J.J. (2001), "Employee Voice in Corporate Governance: A Defense of Strong Participation Rights," *Business Ethics Quarterly* 11:1, 195–215.

McGoun, E.G. (1992a), "The CAPM: A Nobel Failure," *Critical Perspective on Accounting* 3:2, 155–77.

—— (1992b), "On Knowledge of Finance," *International Review of Financial Analysis* 1:3, 161–77.

McIntyre, R. and Hillard, M. (1992), "Stressed Families, Impoverished Families: Crises in the Household and in the Reproduction of the Working Class," *Review of Radical Political Economics* 24:2, 17–25.

McLaren, P. (1998), "Revolutionary Pedagogy in Post-Revolutionary Times: Rethinking the Political Economy of Critical Education," *Educational Theory* 48:4, 431–62.

McNair, M.P. (ed.) (1954), *The Case Method at the Harvard Business School* (New York: McGraw-Hill Book Company, Inc.).

Menshikov, S. (1969), *Millionaires and Managers* (Moscow: Progress Publishers).

Merton, R.C. (1995), "Influence of Mathematical Models in Finance on Practice: Past, Present, and Future," *Financial Practice and Education* 5:1, 7–15.

Miliband, R. (1969), *The State in Capitalist Societies* (New York: Basic Books).

Miller, D. (1987), *Material Culture and Mass Consumption* (New York: Basil Blackwell).

Miller, M.H. (1986), "The Academic Field of Finance: Some Observations on its History and Prospects," *Tijdschrift voor Economie en Management* 31:4, 395–408.

—— (1994), "Is American Corporate Governance Fatally Flawed?," *Journal of Applied Corporate Finance* 6:4, 32–9.

Mises, L.V. and Greaves, B.B. (2005), *Liberalism: The Classical Tradition* (New York: Liberty Fund Incorporated).

Mitra, T. (1976), "On Efficient Capital Accumulation in a Multi-Sector Neoclassical Model," *Review of Economic Studies* 43, 423–429.

Modigliani, F. and Miller, M. (1958), "The Cost of Capital, Corporation Finance and the Theory of Investment," *American Economic Review* 2:2, 261–97.

Molbey, M.F. and Kuniansky, H. (1992a), "Chief Financial Officers' Views of Academicians versus Practitioners in the Field of Finance," *Financial Practice and Education* 2:1, 67–71.

—— (1992b), "A Reassessment of Academic Research Tradition: Is Balance Needed?," *Financial Practice and Education* 2:1, 79–81.

Monks, R.A.G. and Minow, N. (1995), *Corporate Governance* (Oxford: Basil Blackwell Publishers).

Moreland, P.W. (1995), "Corporate Ownership and Control Structures: An International Comparison," *Review of Industrial Organization* 10, 443–464.

Morgan, G. (1980), "Paradigm, Metaphors, and Puzzle Solving in Organization Theory," *Administrative Science Quarterly*, 605–22.

—— (1983), *Beyond Method: Strategies for Social Research* (Beverley Hills, California: Sage Publications).

—— (1984), "Opportunities Arising from Paradigm Diversity," *Administration and Society* 16:3, 306–27.

—— (1985), "Qualitative and Action Based Research," in Allaire, Landry, Mintzberg, and Morgan (eds.).

—— (1997), *Images of Organization*, 2nd edn, (California: Sage Publications).

Moy, R.L. and Lee, A. (1991), "A Bibliography of Stock Market Anomalies," *Journal of Financial Education* 20:1, 41–51.

Mukherjee, T.K. and Hingorani, V.L. (1999), "Capital-Rationing Decisions of Fortune 500 Firms: A Survey," *Financial Practice and Education* 9:1, 7–15.

Munshi and Abraham (eds) (2004), *Good Governance, Democratic Societies and Globalization* (Thousand Oaks: Sage Publications).

Naslund, B. (1986), "Some Views on the Current State of Finance Theory," *Liiketaloudellinen Aikak* 35:3, 26–74.

Niemi Jr., A.W. (1987), "Institutional Contributors to the Leading Finance Journals, 1975 through 1986: A Note," *Journal of Finance* 42:4, 1389–97.

Noddings, N. (1995), *Philosophy of Education* (New York, NY: Westview Press).

Norgaard, R.L. (1981), "The Evolution of Business Finance Textbooks," *Financial Management* 10:2, 34–45.

O'Barr, W. and Conley, J. (1992), *Fortune & Folly* (Homewood, IL: Richard D. Irwin).

Orrill, R. (ed.) (1999), *Education and Democracy: Re-Imaging Liberal Learning in America* (New York, NY: College Entrance Examination Board).

Ozmon, H.A. and Craver, S.M. (1998), *Philosophical Foundations of Education* (New Jersey: Prentice Hall).

Pagano, M. and Volpin, P. (2001a), "The Political Economy of Corporate Governance," Working Paper Number 29, Center for Studies in Economics and Finance, Universita Degli Studi Di Salerno, July.

—— (2001b), "The Political Economy of Finance," *Oxford Review of Economic Policy* 17:4, 502–519.

Parenti, M. (1995), *Democracy for the Few* (New York: St. Martin's Press).

Parry, J. and Bloch, M. (1989), *Money and the Morality of Exchange* (Cambridge: Cambridge University Press).

Pasinetti, L.L. (1981), *Structural Change and Economic Growth: A Theoretical Essay on the Dynamics of the Wealth of Nations* (Cambridge: Cambridge University Press).

Patinkin, D. (1956), *Money, Interest, and Prices: An Integration of Monetary and Value Theory,* 2nd Edition. (New York: Harper).

Payne, J.D., Heath, W.C., and Gale, L.R. (1999), "Comparative Financial Practices in the U.S. and Canada: Capital Budgeting and Risk Assessment Techniques," *Financial Practice and Education* 9:1, 16–24.

Peiss, K. (1986), *Cheap Amusements: Working Women and Leisure in Turn-of-the-Century* (New York and Philadelphia, PA: Temple University Press).

Percival, J. (1993), "Why Don't We Just Ask Them?," *Financial Practice and Education* 3:2, 110–17.

Perelman, M. (1987), *Marx's Crises Theory: Labor, Scarcity, Finance* (New York: Praeger).

—— (1993), "The Qualitative Side of Marx's Value Theory," *Rethinking Marxism* 6:1, 82–95.

—— (1999), "Marx, Devalorisation, and the Theory of Value," *Cambridge Journal of Economics* 23:6, 719–28.

—— (2006), *Railroading Economics: The Creation of the Free Market Mythology* (New York: Monthly Review Press).

Peressini, A. (1999), "Applying Pure Mathematics," *Philosophy of Science*, 66:3, 1–13.

Perlo, V. (1957), *The Empire of High Finance* (New York: International Publishers).

Petry, G.H. and Fuller, R.J. (1978), "The Geographic Distribution of Papers at the Seven Academic Finance Associations in the United States," *Journal of Financial and Quantitative Analysis* 13:4, 785–94.

Petry, G.H. and Sprow, J. (1993), "The Theory and Practice of Finance in the 1990s," *Quarterly Journal of Economics and Finance* 33:4, 359–81.

Pettijohn, J.B., Udell, G., and Parker, S. (1991), "The Quest for AACSB Accreditation: Must Finance Faculty Really Publish or Perish?," *Journal of Financial Education* 1:1, 52–5.

Pinch, T.J. (1996), "The Social Construction of Technology: A Review," in Fox, R. (ed.), 17–35.

Pinch, T.J. and Bijker, W.E. (1984), "The Social Construction of Facts and Artefacts: Or How the Sociology of Science and the Sociology Technology Might Benefit Each Other," *Social Studies of Science* 14:3, 399–441.

Plekhanov, G.V. (1969), *Fundamental Problems of Marxism* (New York: International Publishers).

Plumptre, T. and Graham, J. (1999), *Governance and Good Governance: International and Aboriginal Perspective* (Canberra: Institute of Governance).

Polanyi, K. (1944), *The Great Transformation* (New York: Farrar).

—— (1957), "The Economy as Instituted Process," in Polanyi, K., Arensberg, C.M., and Pearson, H.W. (eds).

Polanyi, K., Arensberg, C.M., and Pearson, H.W. (eds) (1957), *Trade and Market in the Early Empires: Economies in History and Theory* (Glencoe, Illinois: The Free Press and The Falcon's Wing Press).

Popkewitz, T.S. and Fendler, L. (eds.) (1999), *Critical Theories in Education: Changing Terrains of Knowledge and Politics* (London: Routledge).

Popper, K.R. (1979), *Truth, Rationality and the Growth of Scientific Knowledge* (Frankfurt and Maine: Klostermann).

Pound, J. (1993), "The Rise of the Political Model of Corporate Governance and Corporate Control," *New York University Law Review* 68:5, 1003–1023.

Powell, W.W. (1990), "Neither Market nor Hierarchy: Network Forms of Organization," *Research in Organizational Behavior* 12, 295–336.

Power, E.J. (1995), *Educational Philosophy: A History from the Ancient World to Modern America* (New York, NY: Garland Publishers).

Prahalad, C.K. (1994), "Corporate Governance or Corporate Value Added?: Rethinking the Primacy of Shareholder Value," *Journal of Applied Corporate Finance* 6:4, 40–50.

Radford, R.A. (1945), "The Economic Organization of a P.O.W. Camp," *Economica*, New Series, 12:2, 189–201.

Rajan, R. and Zingales, L. (2003), "The Great Reversals: The Politics of Financial Development in the 20th Century," *Journal of Financial Economics* 69:1, 5–50.

Reddy, W.M. (1984), *The Rise of Market Culture: The Textile Trade and French Society, 1750–1900* (Cambridge: Cambridge University Press).

Reed, D. (1999), "Stakeholder Management Theory: A Critical Theory Perspective," *Business Ethics Quarterly* 9:3, 453–484.

—— (2004), "Good Corporate Governance in the Global Economy: What is at Issue?," in Munshi and Abraham (eds).

Robbins, L. (1946), *An Essay on the Nature and Significance of Economic Science* (London: Macmillan).

Robinson, J. (1956), *The Accumulation of Capital* (London: Macmillan).

—— (1962), *Essays in the Theory of Economic Growth* (London: Macmillan).

Rochester, A. (1936), *Rulers of America* (New York: International Publishers).

Roe, M.J. (1990), "Political and Legal Restraints on Ownership and Control of Public Companies," *Journal of Financial Economics* 27, 7–41.

—— (1994), *Strong Managers, Weak Owners: The Political Roots of American Corporate Finance* (Princeton: Princeton University Press).

—— (1997), "The Political Roots of American Corporate Finance," *Journal of Applied Corporate Finance* 9, 8–22.

—— (2000), "Political Preconditions to Separating Owner from Corporate Control," *Stanford Law Review* 53:3, 539–606.

—— (2002), *Political Determinants of Corporate Governance: Political Context, Corporate Impact* (Oxford: Oxford University Press).

Roll, R. (1977), "A Critique of the Asset Pricing Theory's Tests, Part I: On Past and Potential Testability of the Theory," *Journal of Financial Economics* 4:2, 129–76.

—— (1994), "What every CFO Should Know about Scientific Progress in Financial Economics: What is Known and What Remains to be Resolved," *Financial Management* 23:2, 69–75.

Rorty, A.O. (ed.) (1998), *Philosophers on Education: Historical Perspectives* (London: Routledge).

Rosen, M. (1990), "Staying on the String: The Yo and the Market in Eighty-Nine," *Critical Perspectives on Accounting* 4:1, 337–65.

Ross, S.A. (1976), "The Arbitrage Theory of Capital Asset Pricing," *Journal of Economic Theory* 13:4, 343–62.

—— (1988), "Comment on the Modigliani-Miller Propositions," *Journal of Economic Perspectives* 2:1, 127–33.

Roy, W.G. (1997), *Socializing Capital* (Princeton: Princeton University Press).

Russell, B. (1990), *Introduction to Mathematical Philosophy* (London: Allen & Unwin).

—— (1914 and 1956), "On the Nature of Acquaintance," in Marsh (ed.).

—— (1918 and 1956), "The Philosophy of Logical Atomism," in Marsh (ed.).

—— (1926), *Our Knowledge of the External World as a Field for Scientific Method in Philosophy* (London: Allen and Unwin).

Sadovnik, A.R., Semel, S., and Cookson, P. (1994), *Exploring Education: An Introduction to the Foundations of Education* (London: Allyn & Bacon).

Sahlins, M. (1976), *Culture and Practical Reason* (Chicago: University of Chicago Press).

Sauvain, H. (1967), "The State of the Finance Field: Comment," *Journal of Finance* 22:4, 541–42.

Schlick, M. (1930 and 1959), "The Turning Point in Philosophy," in Ayer (ed.).

—— (1932 and 1959), "Positivism and Realism," in Ayer (ed.).

Schmitt, R. (1987), *Introduction to Marx and Engels: A Critical Reconstruction* (Boulder and London: Westview Press).

Schneider, L. and Bonjean, C. (eds) (1973), *The Idea of Culture in the Social Sciences* (Cambridge: Cambridge University Press).

Schrag, F. (1995), *Back to Basics: Fundamental Educational Questions Reexamined* (Sanfrancisco, CA: Jossey-Bass Education Series).

Schudson, M. (1984), *Advertising: The Uneasy Persuasion* (New York: Basic Books).

Schumpeter, J. (1942), *Capitalism, Socialism and Democracy* (New York: Harper).

Schwert, G.W. (1983), "Size and Stock Returns and Other Empirical Regularities," *Journal of Financial Economics* 12:1, 3–12.

Schweser, C. (1977), "The Doctoral Origins of Contributors to the Journal of Finance from 1964 through 1975," *Journal of Finance* 32:3, 908–10.

Scott, J. (1997), *Corporate Business and Capitalist Classes* (Oxford: Oxford University Press).

Sen, A. (1977), "Rational Fools: A Critique of the Behavioral Foundations of Economic Theory," *Philosophy and Public Affairs* 6, 317–344.

Sennet, R. (1998), *The Corrosion of Character: The Personal Consequences of Work in the New Capitalism* (New York: Norton).

Shleifer, A. and Vishny, R.W. (1997), "A Survey of Corporate Governance," *Journal of Finance* 52:2, 737–783.

Shanken, J. and Smith, C.W. (1996), "Implications of Capital Markets Research for Corporate Finance," *Financial Management* 25:1, 98–104.

Sherratt, Y. (1999), "Instrumental Reason's Unreason," *Philosophy and Social Criticism* 25:1, 23–42.

Shiller, R.J. (1981), "The Use of Volatility Measures in Assessing Market Efficiency," *Journal of Finance* 36:3, 291–304.

—— (1984), "Stock Prices and Social Dynamics," *Brookings Papers on Economic Activity* 2:4, 457–98.

Shin, T.S. and Hubbard, E.T. (1988), "Current Status of Doctoral Programs in Finance," *Journal of Financial Education* 14:1, 64–79.

Shipton, P. (1989), *Bitter Money* (Washington: American Anthropologist Association).

Simmel, G. (1978), *The Philosophy of Money*, trans. Bottomore and Frisby (London: Routlege & Kegan Paul).

Smith, A. (1776 and 1937), *The Wealth of Nations* (New York: Modern Library Edition).

Smith, B.H. and Plotnitsky, A. (eds) (1997), *Mathematics, Science, and Postclassical Theory* (Durham: Duke University Press).

Smith Jr., C.W. (1976), "Option Pricing: A Review," *Journal of Financial Economics* 3:1, 3–51.

—— (1979), "Applications of Option Pricing Analysis," in Bicksler (ed.).

—— (1990a), "Introduction," in Smith (ed.).

—— (ed.) (1990b), *The Modern Theory of Corporate Finance*, 2nd Edition (New York: McGraw-Hill Publishing Company).

Solow, R. (1956), "A Contribution to the Theory of Economic Growth," *Quarterly Journal of Economics* 70, 65–94.

Spencer, H. (2003), *The Social Statics* (New York: Continuum International Publishing Group).

Sraffa, P. (1960), *Production of Commodities by Means of Commodities: Prelude to a Critique of Economic Theory* (Cambridge: Cambridge University Press).

Stalin, J. (1940), *Dialectical and Historical Materialism* (New York: International Publishers).

Steger, M.B. (2002), *Globalism: The New Market Ideology* (New York, NY: Rowman & Littlefield Publishers, Inc.)

Stinchcombe, A.L. (1983), *Economic Sociology* (New York: Academic Press).

Stoney, C. and Winstanley, D. (2001), "Stakeholding: Confusion or Utopia? Mapping the Conceptual Terrain," *Journal of Management Studies* 38, 603–626.

Streek, W. and Schmitter, P.C. (eds) (1985), *Private Interest Government: Beyond Market and State* (London: Sage Publications).

—— (1985), "Community, Market, State – and Associations? The Prospective Contribution of Interest Governance to Social Order," in Streek, W. and Schmitter, P.C. (eds), 1–29.

Struik, D.J. (1948), "Marx and Mathematics," *Science and Society* 12:4, 360–80.

—— (ed.) (1970), *Economic and Philosophical Manuscripts of 1844* (London: Lawrence & Wishart).

—— (2002), *A Concise History of Mathematics*, 4th Edition (New York: Dover Publications, Inc.).

Sumner, W.G. (1968), *Financier and Finances of the American Revolution* (New York: Scholar's Bookshelf).

Sweetser, A.G. and Petry, G.H. (1981), "A History of the Seven Academic Finance Associations and their Contributions to Development of the Discipline," *Financial Management* 10:2, 46–65.

Sweezy, P.M. (1942, 1964), *The Theory of Capitalist Development: Principles of Marxian Political Economy* (New York: Monthly Review Press).

—— (1994), "The Triumph of Financial Capital," *Monthly Review* 46:2, 1–11.

—— (1997), "More (or Less) on Globalization," *Monthly Review* 49:4, 1–4.

Sweezy, P.M. and Magdoff, H. (1972), *The Dynamics of U.S. Capitalism: Corporate Structure, Inflation, Credit, Gold, and the Dollar* (New York: Monthly Review Press).

Taussig, M.T. (1986), *The Devil and Commodity Fetishism in South America* (Chapel Hill: University of North Carolina Press).

Taylor, S.J. and Bogdan, R. (1984), *Introduction to Qualitative Research Methods: The Search for Meanings*, 2nd Edition (New York: John Wiley & Sons).

Thaler, R.H. (ed.) (1993), *Advances in Behavioral Finance* (New York: Russell Sage Foundation).

Tilly, L.A. and Scott, J.W. (1987), *Women, Work, and Family*, 2nd Edition (New York: Routledge).

Tinker, A.M., Merino, B.D., and Neimark, M.D. (1982), "The Normative Origins of Positive Theories: Ideology and Accounting Thought," *Accounting, Organizations and Society* 7:2, 167–200.

Titmuss, R.M. (1971), *The Gift Relationship* (New York: Vintage Press).

Tompkins IV, J.G., Hermanson, H.M., and Hermanson, D.R. (1996), "Expectations and Resources Associated with New Finance Faculty Positions," *Financial Practice and Education* 6:1, 54–64.

Tompkins IV, J.G., Nathan, S., Hermanson, R.M., and Hermanson, D.R. (1997), "Coauthoring in Refereed Journals: Perceptions of Finance Faculty and Department Chairs," *Financial Practice and Education* 7:2, 47–57.

Trahan, E.A. and Gitman, L.J. (1995), "Bridging the Theory-Practice Gap in Corporate Finance: A Survey of Chief Financial Officers," *Quarterly Review of Economics and Finance* 35:1, 73–87.

Tripathy, N. and Ganesh, G.K. (1996), "Evaluation, Promotion, and Tenure of Finance Faculty: The Evaluators' Perspective," *Financial Practice and Education* 6:1, 46–53.

Turnbull, S. (1978), *Impact of Mining Royalties on Aboriginal Communities in the Northern Territory: First Report, October 1977* (Canberra, Australia: Parliament of the Commonwealth).

—— (1994a), "Beyond Markets and Hierarchies: Extending the theory of the firm," paper presented to the Twenty-Third Conference of Economists, Gold Coast International Hotel, 28 September, Queensland.

—— (1994b), "Stakeholder Democracy: Redesigning the Governance of Firms and Bureaucracies," *Journal of Socio-Economics* 23:3, 321–60.

—— (1997), "Corporate Governance: Its Scope, Concerns, and Theories," *Corporate Governance: An International Review* 5:4, 180–205.

Urquhart, A. (1999), "From Berkeley to Bourbaki," *Dialogue (Canada)* 38:4, 587–92.

Uzawa, H. (1961), "On a Two-Sector Model of Economic Growth," *Review of Economic Studies* 24, 40–47.

von Neumann, J. (1937), A Model of General Economic Equilibrium," *Review of Economic Studies* 13, 1–9.

von Wright, G., Rhees, R., and Anscombe, G. (eds) (1964), *Remarks on the Foundations of Mathematics*, trans. Anscombe (Oxford: Blackwell).

Walstad, W. (1997), "The Effect of Economic Knowledge on Public Opinion and Economic Issues," *Journal of Financial Education* 28:3, 195–205.

Walzer, M. (1983), *Spheres of Justice* (New York: Basic Books).

Weaver, S.C. (1993), "Why Don't We Just Ask Them?," *Financial Practice and Education* 3:2, 11–13.

Weber, M. (1978), *Economy and Society: An Outline of Interpretive Sociology* (Berkeley: University of California Press).

Weimer, J. and Pape, J.C. (1999), "A Taxonomy of Systems of Corporate Governance," *Corporate Governance: An International Review* 7, 152–66.

Weisskopf, W.A. (1973), *Alienation and Economics* (New York: Delta Books).

—— (1977), "The Moral Predicament of the Market Economy," in Dworkin, G. Bermant, G., and Brown, P.G. (eds), 33–41.

Weston, J.F. (1966), *The Scope and Methodology of Finance* (Englewood Cliffs, New Jersey: Prentice-Hall, Inc.).

—— (1967), "The State of the Finance Field," *Journal of Finance* 22:3, 539–40.

—— (1974), "New Themes in Finance," *Journal of Finance* 29:1, 237–43.

—— (1981), "Developments in Finance Theory," *Financial Management* 10:2, 5–22.

—— (1994), "A (Relatively) Brief History of Finance Ideas," *Financial Practice and Education* 4:1, 7–26.

Whaples, R. (1995), "Changes in Attitudes about the Fairness of the Market among College Economics Students," *Journal of Financial Education* 26:4, 410–19.

White, H.C. (1981), "Where Do Markets Come From?" *American Journal of Sociology* 87:3, 517–47.

Whitley, R. (1986), "The Transformation of Business Finance into Financial Economics: The Roles of Academic Expansion and Changes in U.S. Capital Markets," *Accounting, Organizations and Society*, 11:2, 171–92.

—— (1991), "The Social Construction of Business Systems in East Asia," *Organization Studies* 12, 1–28.

Whyte, W.F. and Whyte, K.K. (1988), *Making Mondragon: The Growth and Dynamics of the Worker Cooperative Complex* (Ithaca, New York: ILR Press).

Williams, C.C. (2006), "Beyond the Market: Representing Work in Advanced Economies," *International Journal of Social Economics* 33:4, 284–97.

Winch, C. and Gingell, J. (1999), *Key Concepts in the Philosophy of Education* (London: Routledge).

Wittgenstein, L. (1953 and 1968), *Philosophical Investigations*, trans. Anscombe. (New York: Macmillan).

—— (1964), "Remarks on the Foundations of Mathematics," in von Wright, Rhees and Anscombe (eds).

—— (1976), "Wittgenstein Lectures on the Foundations of Mathematics," in Diamond (ed.).

Wuthnow, R. (1987), *Meaning and Moral Order* (Berkeley: University of California Press).

Yoels, W.C. (1974), "The Structure of Scientific Fields and the Allocation of Editorships on Scientific Journals: Some Observations on the Politics of Knowledge," *Sociological Quarterly* 15:2, 264–76.

Zaretsky, E. (1976), *Capitalism, the Family and Personal Life* (New York: Harper & Row).

—— (1986), *Rethinking the Welfare State: Dependence, Economic Individualism and the Family,* in Dickinson, J. and Russell, B. (eds).

Zeitlin, M. (1974), "Corporate Ownership and Control: The Large Corporation and the Capitalist Class," *American Journal of Sociology* 79.

Zeitlin, M. and Norich, S. (1979), "Management Control, Exploitation, and Profit Maximization in the Large Corporation: An Empirical Confrontation of Managerialism and Class Theory," *Research in Political Economy* 2.

Zelizer, V.A. (1983), *Morals and Markets: The Development of Life Insurance in the United States* (New Brunswick, NJ: Transaction).

—— (1987), *Pricing the Priceless Child: The Changing Social Value of Children* (New York: Basic Books).

—— (1988), "Beyond the Polemic on the Market: Establishing a Theoretical and Empirical Agenda," *Sociological Forum* 3, 614–34.

—— (1994), *The Social Meaning of Money* (New York: Basic Books).

Zingales, L. (1998), "Corporate Governance," in Newman, P. (ed.), *The New Palgrave Dictionary of Economics and Law* (Oxford: Oxford University Press).

Zivney, T.L. and Bertin, W.J. (1992), "Publish or Perish: What the Competition is Really Doing," *Journal of Finance* 47:1, 295–329.

Zivney, T.L. and Reichenstein, W. (1994), "The Pecking Order in Finance Journals," *Financial Practice and Education* 4:1, 77–87.

Index